SWEET MAPLE

SWEET MAPLE

Life, lore and recipes from the sugarbush

❦

By James M. Lawrence & Rux Martin

Photography by Paul O. Boisvert

Vermont Life

6 BALDWIN STREET
MONTPELIER, VERMONT 05602

CHAPTERS PUBLISHING LTD.
SHELBURNE, VERMONT 05482

Co-published by

Chapters Publishing Ltd.
2031 Shelburne Road
Shelburne, Vermont 05482

Vermont Life Magazine
6 Baldwin Street
Montpelier, Vermont 05602

Excerpt on page 104 from *Amateur Sugar Maker* by Noel Perrin. Reprinted by permission of University Press of New England. Copyright ©1972 by Noel Perrin.

Excerpt on page 80 from *The Sugar Bush Connection* by Beatrice Ross Buszek. Reprinted by permission of Nimbus Publishing. Copyright ©1982 by Beatrice Ross Buszek.

Library of Congress Cataloging-in-Publication Data

Lawrence, James
    Sweet maple : life, lore and recipes from the sugarbush / by James M. Lawrence
& Rux Martin ; photography by Paul O. Boisvert.
    p.   cm.
    Includes bibliographical references and index.
    ISBN 1-881527-00-X   ISBN 1-881527-01-8 (pbk.)
    1. Cookery (Maple sugar and syrup). 2. Maple sugar. 3. Maple syrup.
    I. Martin, Rux. II. Boisvert, Paul. III. Vermont life. IV. Title.
    TX767.M3L38 1993
    664' .132' 097—dc20   93-24090

Trade distribution by
Firefly Books Ltd.
250 Sparks Avenue
Willowdale, Ontario
Canada M2H 2S4

Printed and bound in Canada by D.W. Friesen & Sons, Altona, Manitoba
Color separations by H. Horsman + Co., Burlington, Vermont

Book Design by Hans Teensma / Impress, Inc., Northampton, Massachusetts
Art Direction by Eugenie Seidenberg Delaney and Phyllis Bartling, Futura Design
Front Cover: "Gathering Sap at Misty Maples," W. Robert Howrigan Farm, Fairfield, Vermont / Paul O. Boisvert
Back Cover (Top): "Sugaring Off," Tomkins H. Matteson, 1845 / The Carnegie Museum of Art: Bequest of Rosalie Spang
Back Cover (Bottom): "Syrup in Glass" / Paul O. Boisvert

CONTENTS

ACKNOWLEDGMENTS

THIS BOOK would not have been possible without the genuine enthusiasm and unstinting support of a great many Americans and Canadians with a common bond of affection for the maple tree and the traditions of maple sugaring.

This is a subject with no accepted textbook, no definitive history, and a grand international tangle of contradictory ideas and beliefs. The authors accept the responsibility for all factual information presented and opinions expressed in these pages, except where attributed to a named individual. The errors are ours, not the work of those who helped guide us.

We would first like to thank the Proctor Maple Research Center, a facility unique in the tree world with people dedicated to understanding the still-mysterious maple and helping those whose livelihoods depend on it. From the beginning, Proctor's assistant director Sumner Williams lent his expertise, his library, and at several critical junctures, his good name. Sugarhouse doors opened everywhere in confidence that he was serving as a technical advisor for this project.

Other leaders in the maple field who most generously contributed their time and knowledge include Clarence Coons, Ontario Ministry of Agriculture; Sam Cutting, Sr., Dakin Farm; Nate Danforth, Danforth's Sugarhouse; Professor A.R.C. Jones, Macdonald College of McGill University and the Morgan Arboretum; Henry Marckres, agricultural products specialist, Vermont Department of Agriculture; David Marvin, Butternut Mountain Farm; Dr. Mariafranca Morselli, University of Vermont; Lynn Reynolds, president of the North American Maple Syrup Council and the International Maple Syrup Institute; and Dr. Fred Taylor, co-founder of the Proctor Maple Research Center. For assistance in tracking the biggest trees, we thank Professor Jeffrey V. Freeman, Castleton State College.

Months of legwork, library research, telephone interviews, tape transcribing and organizing of cartons of reference material were done by editorial assistants Candice Huber, Janice Heilmann and Melissa Cochran.

Many keepers of maple's sacred papers and art opened their vaults to us. The members of the University of Vermont's Special Committee on the History of Sugaring provided untold amounts of material and suggestions; Donald and Betty Ann Lockhart, Perceptions, Inc., generously gave us advice and access to their personal maple library; and Robert Coombs, Coombs Maple Sugar Products, shared his private collection of maple equipment, patent records and memorabilia.

Many of the wonderful historical photographs and art came from Tom and Dona Olson at The New England Maple Museum; the Vermont Historical Society; our fine neighbors, the Shelburne Museum; and through the cooperation of Connell Gallagher, assistant director for Special Collections at the University of Vermont Libraries. Dr. Bruce Parker of the University of Vermont Entomology Research Laboratory gave us access to their collection of scientific photographs.

Among the many others who played a role in the making of this book were: George L. Cook and Larry Myott of University of Vermont Extension; Dean Leary, the Rokeby Museum; Steve Selby, head of Small Brothers USA; John Record, general manager of G.H. Grimm; Tom Slayton, editor of *Vermont Life*; Wilson Clark and Bill Moore of the Vermont Maple Sugar Makers' Association; Michael Wilson and John Friauf of the Sagamore Institute; Mary Smallman, town historian in Hermon, New York; Christine Kulyk, historical researcher in Kingston, Ontario; Timothy Scherbatskoy, professor in the University of Vermont School of Natural Resources; Tom Hughes, editor of *Adirondack Life;* Jessica, Kerry and Bayley Lawrence, research irregulars; and the Abenaki storytellers Joseph Bruchac, author of *Keepers of the Earth*, and Wolfsong, of Vergennes, Vermont.

The University of Vermont Extension Service also generously shared their library of taped interviews with sugarmakers and researchers done for the state's bicentennial. These provided a number of enlightening quotations and insights available nowhere else.

Recipes and recipe inspirations came from Beau Benson, owner of Cobble House Inn, Gaysville, Vermont; Jim Dodge, author of *The American Baker*; Edith and Raymond Foulds, South Burlington, Vermont; Ken Haedrich, author of *The Maple Syrup Cookbook*; Brenda Larocque, Athelstan, Quebec; Chef Michel Le Borgne, New England Culinary Institute; and Sumner Williams.

Hundreds of recipes were scrupulously tested by Carolyn Gregson and Melissa McClelland using gallons of fine syrup contributed by Dakin Farm of Ferrisburgh, Vermont. Special thanks to Hans Teensma of Impress, Inc, whose design for the book reflects both the dignity of the tree itself and the honest character of sugarmaking. Art directors Eugenie Seidenberg Delaney and Phyllis Bartling of Futura Design deserve special credit for calm in the face of an intimidating task. Sincere thanks also to proofreader Wendy Ruopp, editorial assistant Cristen Brooks and indexer Andrea Chesman.

Paul Boisvert, who first conceived this project as a photographic record of the sugaring year, logged countless hundreds of miles on the back roads of sugar country photographing the sugarmakers and brought an enthusiasm to the project that proved infectious for all who volunteered to help over the past year and a half. His photographs brilliantly record the people and practices of sugarmaking today, but they also convey a strong sense of the timeless beauty of the sugar woods and the steamy mystique of the sugarhouse.

As the final gatekeeper of this project, Alice Lawrence deserves special recognition; behind almost every good book is an anonymous copy editor with an instinct for making text as readable and accurate as possible. It's mostly demanding, thankless work, but we want to make this an exception and extend our sincere gratitude.

FINALLY, TO THE UNKNOWN native man or woman who first discovered the sweetness of the maple and to the nameless people who planted the 200-year-old maples that shade our homes, enrich our everyday lives and, each spring, give us one of nature's most remarkable gifts, our humble thanks.

—*James M. Lawrence*
Rux Martin
Shelburne, Vermont
September 1993

PROLOGUE

"Although we are almost literally buried in books treating on almost every other subject," Vermont agriculturist A.M. Foster once complained, "there is an almost absolute lack on the subject of maple sugar-making."

The year was 1874, and when we waded into the subject of maple 118 years later, his words were still astonishingly current. As a backyard sugarmaker for the last 20 years, I had my own ragtag library of maple texts, some of them lovely books, but mostly slim volumes and none that aspired to capture more than a narrow facet of the story, usually hewing to the personal experiences and rewards of sugarmaking.

Many of us have shared, from comfortable armchairs, Noel Perrin's struggles and exhilarating moments in building his own sugarhouse and learning to make syrup, and most serious sugarmakers turn to Helen and Scott Nearing's classic 1950 text, *The Maple Sugar Book*, whenever historical questions arise.

Perhaps the most ambitious encyclopedic approach heretofore came in 1887, when a Michigan professor named A.J. Cook put aside his work with honeybees to write the first serious guide to the maple tree and maple sugaring. Without much in the way of scientific literature to consult, Cook relied on a lifetime of personal observation and his own experiences in a family sugarbush of 600 trees. It was a daunting task, considering the complexities of the tree and the accelerating evolution in harvesting methods he was witnessing.

"When a child," he wrote, "I saw an ax used to wound the tree . . . An iron gouge was driven into the tree under this ghastly ax-cut, and the curved cut thus made received the sharpened end of a basswood spout—we called it a spile—which was split from a block by the the use of the same gouge. Later, a two-inch auger drove the ax from the field of slaughter."

Amazingly, in Professor Cook we find a man whose life spanned the end of the Indian-style sugaring era and the blossoming of sugarmaking as it is still commonly practiced today. When his book appeared, many farm families were still making syrup under the stars, boiling in big, blackened kettles over open fires as it had been done for generations. Cook himself had just discovered one of the first of the multi-pan evaporators that presaged the typical syrupmaking units found in most sugarhouses today.

A little more than a century later, in assembling this book, we have found ourselves confronted with some of the very same quandaries that Cook faced: the maple tree itself is still a tower of unlocked secrets, and the business of making maple syrup continues to be a moving, elusive target.

While a great many tantalizing questions remain unanswered, it is not for lack of attention. If all the experts and authorities who shared their knowledge and ventured their best opinions to help make this book possible were gathered around the base of a single big maple, we would find a mind-boggling assemblage of talents, disciplines and one-of-a-kind characters.

They would include botanists, foresters and unschooled tree lovers; chemists, flavor experts and maple cooks; entomologists, plant physiologists and acid-rain activists; engineers, sheet-metal craftsmen and wild-eyed inventors; anthropologists, archaeologists and folk-tool collectors; ethnobotanists, historians and Native American storytellers; agricultural economists, farm marketing specialists and country kids with syrup stands; sugarmakers in frayed barn clothes, sugarmakers in the latest Patagonia parkas, grizzled sugarmakers from 97 years of age down to apple-cheeked youngsters trying to lug pails of sap.

These are, individually and as a group, some of the most remarkably nice, generous and intelligent people we've ever encountered; virtually every door we knocked upon was thrown open in welcome when we said we were gathering material for a book about maple sugaring and maple trees. Total strangers spent long sessions on the telephone sharing their thoughts; others gathered their precious collections of clippings, journal articles, recipes and photographs and passed them into our care. Many took hours out of their busy days to show their particular pieces of the puzzle and to talk about their favorite subject: maple. (For insiders, this is a magical, all-encompassing word, used as a shorthand way of including the many and varied facets of managing trees, making syrup and marketing the end products. "We've been in maple for five generations." "Once I start talking maple, I can't stop.")

In the end, I hope we haven't let these people down. Clearly, enough information was collected for a multi-volume set of books, and my office is awash with wonderful material and art that simply didn't fit. What started out as a book for the casual sugarhouse visitor or curious maple-syrup lover evolved into something more. The people of the maple community themselves made it abundantly clear that they, too, wanted a reference that brought as much knowledge and lore as possible into one accessible volume. (Preferably at a price less than a half-gallon of syrup.) This proved to be no mean feat.

T HEN THERE WAS THE UNEXPECTED but inescapable hurdle that other writers have found: for every question, maple people often have two or more equally believable—but contradictory—answers. Early on, one of the industry's leading spokesmen warned us: "If you want a second opinion about anything you hear, it will be as near as the next sugarhouse down the road." This subject proved to be an astonishing labyrinth of folk art and modern science, primitive craft and high-technology. True to the prediction, all of us doing research found conflicting opinions, divergent views and, in two noteworthy instances, unexpected darker sides to what is mostly a disarmingly innocent, down-to-earth business.

The first came when I started to ask the most elementary of questions: who were the first known sugarmakers? Whole academic careers, I quickly learned, have been built on debating this answer. School texts and most sugarmakers will tell you that it was the native tribes of the Eastern Woodlands of North America, the Algonquians and Iroquoians, whose survival depended on their intimate knowledge of every plant and animal in their realm. Not so, says a Wisconsin anthropologist named Carol Mason, who has repeatedly denied that there is any proof of North American Indians boiling maple sap before they were introduced to European cooking tools and methods. Many scholars consider her contention wrongheaded and flimsy, but the doubts she has cast over the origins of sugarmaking proved too pervasive for us to ignore.

To Native Americans, I found, Mason's assertion is patently hurtful and borders on racial arrogance. One Michigan anthropologist who has tried to counter Mason hopes that experienced sugarmakers will read this book and join the debate. Indeed, some join the fray for the first time in these pages.

"I'll give you my one-word opinion," says Lynn Reynolds, a noted Wisconsin sugarmaker and the current president of both the North American Maple Syrup Council and the International Maple Syrup Institute: "Nonsense. I've seen enough museum artifacts—birchbark sugar baskets, wooden boiling troughs and boiling stones—to know this wasn't something we taught the Indians."

The second contentious issue moves well beyond armchair anthropology and into the field of tree health, with clear and profound implications for hard-working family farms and all the others whose livelihoods are connected to the maple business. Here you will find earnest, intelligent, well-informed people bitterly split by one fundamental question: how healthy are the trees? Armed with results from a big, ongoing American-Canadian survey, one camp says the sugar maple is in fine shape and getting better. The other, pointing to sickly trees and questioning the validity of the official study, says there is no reason for such complacency. All rhetoric and diversionary issues aside, the maple world is divided between those who fear that acid rain and air pollution may be weakening the trees and those who say that absolutely no evidence exists to support such assertions.

Writing this book has been a transforming process. I now stand under the big maples in my yard and, looking west, face the high Adirondacks and ponder the fact that some 100 dead or dying bodies of water lie over there, shimmering in mute testimony to the invisible power of acid rain. About-face, my view includes the Green Mountains and Camel's Hump; this landmark crest is frequently bathed in acid clouds with a pH as low as 3.0—a drenching that approaches the acidity of mild salad dressing. Study after study has shown that the native spruce there are not weathering these storms well. How, I wonder, can we assume that our maples are immune?

We have tried to give both sides in this issue a fair say on the matter, but I find myself left with one particular memory from the past 18 months. It came on a blindingly clear summer morning atop a new 65-foot ozone-testing research tower at Vermont's world-renowned Proctor Maple Research Center in the foothills of Mount Mansfield. I was standing on the small platform with another sugarmaker I'd never met, both of us marvelling at the view above the canopy of what is one of the most intensely studied sugarbushes in the world. From this vantage point, one is struck by how a seeming wilderness stretches across Vermont in all directions. Millions of acres of green, with nary a smokestack or even a cloud as far as the eye can see. And yet, there are dismaying signs of trouble in the tree canopy just below us. My companion in the worn John Deere cap finally looked up and said, "Lot of these trees don't look so good." Judging by the number of crowns showing the skeletonized, defoliated branches that can be the first sign of the end for a maple, he was right.

We had come from the official acid-rain monitoring station not far from the base of the tower, and we had just heard that acid rain "events" are far from un-common at this seemingly remote site. Several weeks earlier, a rainstorm with a pH of 3.7 had been measured in this sugarbush—a 100-fold increase over the acidity of unpolluted rainwater. Measurements of all rainfall over the past decade in this area have an average pH of 4.4—more than 50 times worse than it should be and a serious, sustained insult to the trees and soil by any biological measurement.

THESE ARE SOBERING THOUGHTS, and I have found myself balancing them with a mental picture of an octogenarian named Dean Fausett, an artist who has never tapped a tree but who is clearly in league with all who cherish the maples. Fausett, an acclaimed portrait and landscape artist whose work includes several Presidential commissions, escaped to Vermont in 1940 to buy a farmhouse and got one of the country's oldest sugar maples in the bargain.

Fausett has spent the last 20 years in one of the longest, most acrimonious battles ever engaged over the life of a single tree. To condense an exasperatingly protracted tale, the town of Dorset, Vermont, and one of its lawyers were determined to move a public road closer to the tree, most likely speeding its doom by soil compaction and road-salt damage. Fausett, whose ancestors were feisty Vermonters who fought King George in 1773 over the ownership of native white pines, strenuously objected.

The tree itself, at least to eastern North American eyes, is an awesome specimen. Almost 20 feet around, its mammoth trunk dwarfed the 500 people who gathered around it for Fausett's 80th birthday. High overhead, a dogwood bush grows from the crotch of a massive branch; birds' nests and raspberry seedlings have found homes in various natural nooks and swirls in the ancient bark. Fausett's brother, a retired U.S. forest service big-tree expert, has estimated the tree at about 500 years of age. A nearby sugar maple, planted in 1791 to commemorate the statehood of Vermont, seems a mere stripling in comparison to Fausett's prize.

"The Spirit of America," one of the largest and oldest sugar maples in North America, standing by the historic Cephas Kent Dwelling in Dorset, Vermont. The smaller maple to the left was planted in 1791 to commemorate the state's independence.

Both trees stand in front of Fausett's home: the historic Cephas Kent Dwelling, which was a well-known meeting place for the Green Mountain boys during the time of the American Revolution. The formative meetings that led to Vermont's own statehood also started here. This rich history seems to have amounted to naught when the town elders decided to chance sacrificing the tree in order to straighten a curve in a sleepy back road.

Repeatedly threatened by town bureaucrats and vilified by the town's attorney, Fausett battled for years to save the tree, which he christened "The Spirit of America." Various environmental groups joined his cause, and in the end, Fausett triumphed in the Supreme Court of Vermont. Friends say he has spent a small fortune, both in legal expenses and tree-surgeon's fees, to protect the grand maple.

Dean Fausett still finds it incomprehensible that anyone would want to endanger the tree. "For all we know, the people who gave us an independent nation may have met under this tree. In many countries, this would be a historic shrine." Clearly ready to continue the fight, if necessary, Fausett is the living embodiment of the maple spirit and the sentiment about tree stewardship that runs deep in the maple community:

"I don't think of this tree as belonging to me," he says with finality, "It's been up to me to protect it, but it belongs to the country and to people who love these big, old trees."

To the spirit of Dean Fausett, to the conscientious sugarmakers, and to all who are working to understand and preserve the maples, we dedicate this book.

—*JML*

CHAPTER I

THE SWEET TREE

The long, colorful life of
Acer saccharum: Queen of the Forest

O N F I R S T M E E T I N G, Sam Cutting, Sr. can give the impression of a steely character, the guy that Central Casting might have sent over if you called for a professional boxing coach: the broken nose, close-cropped hair, the bearing of an ex-fighter pilot are all just right. The big toughened hands and rugged handshake do nothing to dispel the image. But initial reactions can be wrong, and as he lights up a pipe and starts talking about a grove of old trees on a hill overlooking the Champlain Valley, one's reckoning of the man softens, then deepens in appreciation. "These are some of the finest sugar maples I've ever seen. We don't tap them anymore," he says, almost sheepishly. "With trees like this, why take any chances?" Cutting, who is said to have syrup running in his veins, is dwarfed by the presence of the mammoth trees, their girths awesome, their crowns elegant and towering some eight or nine stories above the ground. Three adults with their hands joined would be hard-pressed to encircle the majestic trunks, with great ridges of bark as thick as a man's wrist flowing down like the deep folds in an ancient gray cloak.

Any one of these giants might provide

*Sugarmaker and sugar tree: Sam Cutting, Sr., **above**, and Acer saccharum with its full spectrum of autumn colors, **left**.*

Sam Cutting with one of his majestic old trees. A climax species in the eastern hardwood forest, the rugged sugar maple can live for centuries and is a premier source of both lumber and sweet sap.

land, and native maple sugar was being touted as the moral alternative to West Indian cane sugar. When these maples marked their 200th birthday, the great heyday of maple sugaring was over, but the owners of the land at that time, neighbors of Quaker Timothy Dakin and his family, doubtless were tapping the trees to meet the family's need for cake sugar and, perhaps, to market sugar and syrup as a cash crop.

"The sap from these big old trees out in the fields or along the roads is so much sweeter, it makes a sugarmaker's job a lot easier. This is the kind of tree they used to put eight or ten buckets to," Cutting says.

The founder of one of Vermont's premier retail and mail-order maple companies, Sam Cutting is no man's fool when it comes to business. With thousands of cob-smoked hams, maple-glazed turkey breasts, tons of aged Cheddar cheese and some 50,000 containers of maple syrup flying out the door each year, his once-modest Dakin Farm roadside maple stand is now a bustling seven-figure operation and a model of a family enterprise that competes in a world of corporate food conglomerates.

Despite the complexities and pressures, it is clear that Cutting's feelings for the maple trees have not been lost in the twentieth-century forest of unsentimental commerce. In truth, throughout the maple industry, there is a decidedly nonindustrial sense of respect—at times bordering on awe—for the living tree that has made it all possible.

HARD ROCK HARPS

To many observers, the sugar maple is the Queen of the Forest, a species of majestic scale in its own range and with a constellation of unique qualities that even the behemoths of the rain forest are hard-pressed to match. Its ability to give up prodigious quantities of sap, year in and year out, is virtually unmatched in the known plant king-

enough firewood to heat a home for the winter, and they are the kind of trees North America's early settlers felled mercilessly for fuel, timber and to make potash for the woolen factories of England. The crown of one of these ancient maples, with 300,000 to half a million leaves, is a giant solar collector—some 5,000 square feet of photosynthesizing green that is the true engine for this huge, noble plant.

These maples in Ferrisburgh, Vermont, were just unfurling their first leaves around 1700—well before the first white settlers ranged this far north into New England. By the time the trees were just hitting their stride at 100 years of age, John Adams was President of the United States, George IV was King of Eng-

dom. And within that watery sap—the sugar at this stage is a barely discernible, elusive trace—is a sweetness and flavor that is unforgettably rich, inimitably complex and beloved by millions who have grown up in the maple belt of North America.

This is a tree that commands the knowing respect of people who plant, cut and spend their working days in the forest, mills or woodworking shops. Its wood is dense, often perfectly grained and unbelievably tough—not for nothing is the sugar maple also known as the hard or rock maple. At the beginning of the nineteenth century, maple was prized for steamship interiors, railway cars, butcher blocks, carriage spokes and all manner of homestead tools—from rolling pins and butter molds to spinning wheels and gunstocks. Curly, bird's-eye or fiddleback sugar maple was a woodworker's favorite for cabinetry, marquetry and for custom-finishing the interiors of urban mansions. A proper dance floor was almost always made of maple. Woolen mills depended on the indestructibility of maple spools, shuttles and bobbins. Printers, in the era of hand-carved letters, counted on maple for its ability to take a flawless polish, and violinmakers cherished its resonating qualities. It is still the lumber of choice for bowling lanes and pins, standing up to years of murderous abuse that would make kindling of lesser woods. On a more delicate note, maple is called for in one of the most crucial components of a fine piano, the pin plank, which anchors the pins that hold the strings taut. Save for the spruce sounding board, an entire concert harp might be crafted in maple.

Living upwards of 400 years, the sugar maple can tolerate decades of crowding and deep shade as a young tree, patiently waiting for a chance to catch its share of the sun and become one of the giants of the Eastern

Woodland canopy. Its resilience is remarkable: it handily resists tornado-force winds and bitter cold, shrugs off most insects, disease and even minor fires. Repeated browsing by white-tailed deer will not necessarily set a maple sapling back, while cut stumps eagerly regenerate with vigorous sprouts. A century or

The largest living sugar maple, its trunk more than 23 feet around, grows in Norwich, Connecticut, and is shown with the late William Linke, who nominated it for the National Register of Big Trees.

more of sap harvesting by humans hardly fazes a productive, growing tree, which promptly heals over tap-holes as if they were mere pinpricks.

The natural range of the sugar maple extends as far north as Newfoundland, west to Kansas and Manitoba, south to Georgia and Texas. In the great Adirondack virgin forest, it was a key species, and in upstate New York today, the maple is estimated to comprise 16 percent of the tree cover on commercial forestlands. Almost one out of every four wild trees in Vermont is a sugar maple. Of the various species of maples on this continent, the sugar maple is not only the most common, but the longest-lived and most elegantly shaped. It is a stubbornly North American tree: extensive, repeated attempts to establish it in Europe and elsewhere have failed or met with only marginal success.

Its leaf is the national icon of Canada, flying proudly in red and white over the Houses of Parliament in Ottawa, symbolically sitting on the most prominent dividing line between English and French Canada and speaking eloquently to Canadians in both directions and in both official languages. Emblazoned on hockey jerseys, outlined in neon on motel signs, cast in molten gold by the Royal Canadian Mint, the maple leaf is the universal symbol of Canada and the Canadian spirit. Immediately south, the sugar maple is claimed as the Official Tree of no fewer than four states—New York, Vermont, West Virginia and Wisconsin, which was the first to declare it, in 1947.

Most telling, however, are the countless mailboxes and farm signs throughout maple country that proclaim the affection our settler forebears—and the native people before them—felt for the great landmark trees and sugarbushes: Maple Ridge, Maple Lane, Maple Corners, Sugar Hollow, Maple Brook, Sugarloaf and on through a geographic hill-and-dale of names that is both amusing and significant. From Maple, Ontario, to Maple Corners, Vermont, to Maple, Texas, this was a tree that bespoke honesty, dignity, beauty and permanence.

For many of the early homesteaders, the maples also meant economic survival—a fact that has relevance for North America's countryside even today. Stately giants, such as Sam Cutting's, have traditionally been hung with four buckets or more each, giving upwards of 100 gallons of extra-sweet sap a year, or perhaps three gallons of finished maple syrup. At today's prices, this tree could yield its owners tens of thousands of dollars in syrup alone over two centuries of productive life. This, of course, would be an exceptional tree, but a grove of healthy sugar maples numbering in the hundreds or thousands can clearly be a family resource that spans the generations—a living, arboreal heirloom. Fortunately, the outspoken environmentalists of centuries past foresaw the maples' true worth. Early texts of practical information for settlers in the new colonies of North America are filled with advice on acquiring, preserving and planting maples on the homestead.

A LEGACY OF LEAVES

A BRANCH OF RURAL economy and comfort peculiar to North America," noted one British guide published in 1833, "is the manufacture of maple sugar. The settler should examine his farm, and where he can get from 200 to 500 or more maple trees together, and most convenient, that should be reserved for a *sugary*."

In 1854, Josiah Marshall gave this advice: "All good citizens, who are desirous of doing good deeds, and of being remembered by posterity hereafter, we would recommend to transplant a goodly number of sugar maples round their dwellings."

By 1935, writer Julia Rogers was able to look back and observe: "Wise men were they who set hard maples along the boundary lines of their farms in earlier days. They now have avenues to be proud of. And they have also a source of revenue, for these low-branched, isolated trees give abundant flow of sap in the early spring."

Those of us with a grand old maple in the yard,

Gloriously unpredictable in its autumn coloration, the sugar maple can turn yellow, red, orange or any combination of these hues. The phenomenon is clearly visible from space, and fall's finest colors emerge in years with crisp, dry weather conditions.

and others who just marvel at the annual display of fall-foliage colors, can thank forebears like Ethan Greenwood, who wrote to *The New England Farmer* in 1832 to say:

"While ever ready to depart, the lover of beautiful trees should act as if he expected to live a thousand years. I have set within the last three years, on both sides of the road which passes the distance of a mile through my farm, upwards of 400 sugar maples.

"Though I shall never see them grown very large, yet someone else will; and I hope that whoever may successively occupy the same place hereafter, will not only see them of large size, but have taste and feeling to enjoy their beauty and preserve them for their usefulness."

The legacy of Ethan Greenwood and other forgotten tree planters and protectors of the past two centuries comes brilliantly to life each fall in a display of foliage that is one of North America's unmistakable hallmarks. As the most widespread and common of the maples, the sugar maples' characteristic brilliant yellow, red and orange autumn colors draw millions to view the three-week spectacle that is plainly visible from space, a tide of gold surging south at a rate of 40 miles a day as the height of the fall season progresses from Canada down through the Carolinas.

In truth, this annual foliage fandango is the sugar maple's primary economic asset, helping to draw hundreds of millions of tourist dollars into those states and provinces blessed with an annual influx of leaf peepers. On the surface, this is a boon for tour operators and innkeepers, but for the rural economy in many of these regions, it is also an annual harvest of vital importance. For the sugarmakers, fall foliage season means glorious direct sales, getting full retail value by selling directly to the eager consumer—and along the way having the satisfaction of explaining that, no, maple sugar is not made when the leaves turn color.

As with everything else associated with this tree, the fall turning of the leaves is wondrously complex and not entirely predictable. A sugar maple leaf in the height of autumn's colors may be yellow, it may be orange, it may be red—or a combination of all three, with a brilliant palette of in-between hues.

The yellows, in fact, have been there all summer, masked by the presence of chlorophyll, the green pigment that is essential for photosynthesis. As dropping daytime temperatures and frosty nights cause chlorophyll production to stop and the green to fade, the yellow pigments are revealed: carotenoids, carotenes and xanthophylls—the same agents that give B-vitamin-rich carrots and squash their coloration.

The anthocyanins that produce red leaves develop best in dry, cold—but not frigid—fall weather. These pigments are dissolved in the leaf sap, and are created by reactions between the cell sugar and organic compounds known as anthocyanidins. The strength of the red coloration is directly related to the acidity of the cell sap in the leaves. (In other species with alkaline sap, these same pigments produce purple and bluish fall colors.) Dazzling sunshine further enhances the development of red in maple leaves.

Autumn leaves are made for reveling in—and for blanketing tree-root systems and fallen seeds from winter weather.

In the northern range of the sugar maple in Quebec and Ontario and on the higher elevations in New England, the great color shifts start. To the hypothetical observer from space, it might appear to be a brilliant swan song, with the Earth's mantle of lush green bursting into an unbelievable display of crimson and gold fireworks that rapidly fade to lifeless browns and grays.

Fall foliage involves such a compression of emotions—from the heights of a perfect Indian Summer day, perhaps North American weather at its finest, to the depths of colorless, leafless, foreboding November—that it never fails to be a time for rejuvenation and personal reflection.

"Vermont? You from Vermont? I grew up in Vermont!" a cabdriver in southern California recently told me. "I haven't been back to Vermont in 17 years. I don't even get homesick for the old white Christmas any more. But fall . . . fall I miss. In the fall, I know I'm missing something."

MEADOW MAJESTIES

THE TREE that is called the sugar maple, hard maple, rock maple and sugar tree is botanically known as *Acer saccharum*. The worldwide genus of maples known as *Acer* numbers some 148 species, with the majority found in Asia. Many are shrublike, and only two have the ability to produce unusually sweet, fine-quality sap in prodigious quantities. These are the sugar maple and the black maple (*Acer nigrum*), which some botanists argue are really just variations of one species.

Most botany references list the black maple separately, while for loggers and sugarmakers, the qualities of their wood and syrup are virtually identical. The black maple ranges from southern Ontario south to Tennessee, and from a few isolated groves in New England to western Iowa and northwest Missouri. Many sugarmakers, and even foresters, are blissfully unaware of the black maple. "I never noticed the difference," says one Midwestern extensionist, "until a

Needing 30 to 40 years to reach tapping size, the sugar maple grows slowly and deliberately, but is among the most resilient of North American trees, commonly surviving extreme temperatures, high winds and periodic attacks by insect defoliators.

few producers pointed it out to me." The black maple is abundant only in Indiana and Iowa, and for the purposes of this book will be considered a sugar maple.

Other tappable maples include the red, silver and Manitoba maples, which all have a sap flow and yield syrup with essentially the same maple flavor. At least one Ohio sugarmaker taps only red maples, and Prof. A.R.C. Jones of Canada's Macdonald College says that the red maple is commonly tapped in the Gaspé Peninsula region of Quebec. Throughout the maple belt, some sugarmakers tap the red and silver maples along with their sugar maples, while others have rigorously culled them from the sugar woods. Compared to the sugar maple, these species have a thinner sap—requiring up to twice the boiling time—and the resulting syrup tends to be darker and "slightly peculiar" to the educated tastes of sugar maple purists. (See *Poor Man's Maples,* page 42.)

Sugar maples have reportedly grown to be 135 feet tall and 7 feet in diameter, although current living specimens on the big tree list (see page 45) fall short of this. The current North American record holder is almost as wide as it is tall, at 93 feet in height with a crown 80 feet across. In most settings, mature maples usually top the forest canopy at 80 to 100 feet in height with trunk diameters of 2 to 3 feet. They are slow growing, but exceptionally tolerant of shade. In a deep woods, the sugar maples rise tall and straight, stretching for the sky and producing a clear, perfect bole without side branches for a considerable height—the perfect trunk for loggers and sawyers.

The freezing nights and warm days of autumn cause the maples' sap to run, but prewinter tapping is considered financially impractical and potentially harmful to the trees.

The crown in a dense woods is a reduced affair, a burst of branches and foliage high overhead where it vies for precious solar radiation.

With room to stretch out in a field, pasture, roadside or yard, however, the maple takes on an entirely different form, spreading into a majestic tree with a large, full crown and branches low enough to climb. It is the perfectly shaped deciduous tree that school children love to draw.

Sap-Flow Mysteries

BUT OF ALL THE TREES in the surrounding forest, indeed, of all the trees studied by man, the sugar maple is unique. To a beaming child tucking into a stack of syrup-drenched hotcakes or to the octogenarian savoring an impossibly rich slice of maple-cream pie whose recipe has been in the family for five generations, the taste is like nothing else. To the flavor chemists, it is a tree that combines a little-understood brew of amino acids, phenols and organic acids that defies imitation in the laboratory.

To the botanist, as well, it is a delicious mystery, a species that has evolved a method of storing and moving sap that seems unlike anything else in the plant kingdom. Known as the "sap-flow mechanism," the sugar maple's biological pump gets a four-to-six-week jump on the neighboring birches and oaks and butternuts—all of which will have a sap run, but one that will start later, when the forest floor begins to warm and the roots signal the start of a new spring.

A sugar maple, however, works differently. Its trunk and branches have been likened to a tremendous bundle of microscopic straws that direct the flow of water and nutrients up and down the tree. This is an oversimplification, but the analogy is still useful.

The basic botany lesson most of us learned says that water and stored nutrients move up the tree from the roots, through the xylem or sapwood, while the carbohydrates produced by photosynthesis in the leaves move down the tree through the phloem layer just under the bark. Conventional wisdom says that a sugar maple's roots are forcing sap up through the tree to feed the branches with water and sugars stored below for the winter. Although it is generally true that "sap rises," the story is much more complex in the early spring.

Reacting to a combination of thawing temperatures and sun on the twigs, the sugar maple starts to become a bundle of positive and negative pressure points while other nearby species remain dormant. Current thinking, supported by research in Canada, Scotland and Vermont, is that maple sap pouring into sugarmakers' buckets is *not* simply being carried up from the roots, as is widely believed.

When botanist James Marvin, in a classic bit of experimentation at the University of Vermont, injected red dye into a maple tree three feet below a taphole during the spring run, reddened sap appeared in about 30 minutes, to no one's surprise. It had moved upward, as everyone expected. However, when he injected dye above a taphole, the telltale red also appeared in the taphole below at about the same speed. Injections to the sides failed to show themselves, and Marvin had clearly demonstrated that sap will flow both up and down the maple—simultaneously. (Subsequently, it was found that pigments or other injected substances will also migrate slowly from one side of the tree to the other, proving the flaw in the bundle-of-straws analogy.)

Perhaps triggered by a warm day that breaks the frozen lock of winter, the fine uppermost and outermost twigs of the sugar maple first thaw, then begin to freeze as night falls. Because the spaces in the sapwood fibers in a maple are filled with gas, rather than with water as in other tree species, frost forms within the tree. Exactly what happens next is the subject of ongoing debate, investigation and experimentation. Plant physiologist Dr. Melvin Tyree, the current director of the Proctor Maple Research Center, likens the powerful accumulation of fluid in the sapwood to the build-up of frost in fields that forces large stones to the surface or that heaves pavement in the spring. Suffice it to say that whatever mechanisms are at work in the maple are exquisitely complex, even for plant physiologists. All agree, however, that tremendous sucking forces are created in the sap-transporting vessels, and that significant amounts of fluid are moved as the temperature plummets.

With the freezing process continuing, ever larger branches and then the trunk experience the same phenomenon, freezing from the outside bark inward, pulling sap upward from the relatively inactive areas of the tree below. (The cumulative effect of these countless invisible vessels drawing fluid upward is the truly staggering ability of a maple to lift water 80

or 100 feet into the air.) Apparently, as water is dragged up from the roots, sugar and amino acids stored in the sapwood enter the solution in the xylem storage cells; this creates an osmotic pressure imbalance, which in turn draws more water into the cells.

And so, with this sugary solution of maple proteins filling the upper reaches and trunk of the tree, where it tends to freeze, things are as they should be when the sun rises the next morning. As the day progresses, the sap thaws, while, at the same time, carbon dioxide gas is being generated in the sapwood. The storage cells, reversing the action of the previous night, now want to expel fluid. Thus, the warming sap vessels are not unlike bottles of carbonated beverage that have been shaken—the gas wants to escape, and will immediately take advantage of any leak or weak point it can find.

After a night of filling with fluid and a morning of generating internal gas, the sapwood of the maple is engorged with sap, and a measurement of the pressure at this point is typically 20 pounds per square inch—about two-thirds the pressure in an automobile tire.

A single taphole is commonly counted upon to yield 10 gallons of sap per spring, which, with an average sugar content, will condense into one quart of syrup.

MAPLE COUNTRY

Autumn in Waitsfield, Vermont: One in every four trees in northern New England is a sugar maple, and, as everywhere in its range, Acer saccharum defines the look, the character and the spirit of the countryside it graces.

Along comes a sugarmaker who drills a pinkie-finger-sized hole in the lower trunk of the tree. Things start to happen immediately. Sap from above and below the taphole, under the forces of gravity and hydrostatic pressure, takes the path of least resistance and begins to seep through the walls of the cavity that has just appeared. The sugarmaker gently taps a metal spout into the hole, hangs a bucket, and within seconds the realization of all these unseen forces appears: *plink! plink! plink!* Clear, watery maple sap begins a steady drip into the bucket. A good tree, the old-timers will tell you, runs at a steady "two drops per heartbeat." The vigor of this flow—up to 200 drops of sap per minute from a hole less than a half-inch in diameter—startles sugarbush visitors and hardly ever fails to bring a smile to the face of a sugarmaker as the first run starts.

This is a simplified explanation of some complex, and still debated, actions and reactions in the tree. Whole careers have been spent pondering the sap flow of maples, and conundrums remain. There is no doubt, however, that sap moves to the taphole from above *and* below and is not simply pushed up from the roots (which show no increased pressure to suggest that they are the heart of any kind of biological pump). Experimenters who have cut down maples during the night in the midst of the sap-flow season have seen further evidence: virtually no sap is forced up from the fresh stump, while the cut trunk bleeds sap downward exactly as if it is being pulled by gravity.

To be sure, water is generally moving upward in the tree. Sugarmakers know that tremendous sap flows can occur after a rain, when the roots of the trees are bathed in easily available water. Typically, the tree is recharged with water drawn up from the roots by capillary action during the night.

It appears that the previous night's cold snap is the primary conditioning factor in driving a sap run, with the amount of sap positioned to flow determined by the extent of the temperature drop. Following an extremely cold night, a big run lasting 24 hours or more may follow. In a typical sugaring day, however, the sap

From tightly packed, sharply pointed buds to full leaf within about three weeks, the sugar maple displays explosive growth in early spring. It is among the earliest-blooming plants of the north, and the drooping, yellowish flowers, which appear within a week of budding, are an important—if inconspicuous—source of nectar for honeybees.

may start running at 9 or 10 A.M. and reach its peak flow shortly after noon. By late afternoon or early evening, the day's run is normally over. While the sap may run like clockwork for days on end, more typically the tapping season progresses in fits and starts, often shutting down for days as cold temperatures bring all these reactions to an abrupt halt. "If only the weather would cooperate," says sugarmaker Robert Adams of Wilmington, Vermont, with a resigned laugh, "we'd all be rich."

The sap-flow mechanism remains an enigma, but for the sugarmaker, the net result is an awesome display of nature's power and generosity: a tree that, for a fleeting few weeks in pre-spring, literally pushes its

which emerge from long, sharply pointed buds. The tiny seeds that form hide among the swaying leaves in papery, winged casings called maple samaras, or keys. From each pair of samaras, only one seed will germinate; the other key is sterile and never destined to sprout. (The samara is the feature that visually links the 148 species of maples around the world into one family.)

Good seed seasons come at two-to-five-year intervals, but the heavy years more than make up for the bad, with almost unbelievable numbers of keys spinning dizzily to earth. Despite the fat-looking seeds, the winged keys are featherweights, and it takes some 6,100 of them to make a pound. In studies of a virgin maple stand in northern Michigan, U.S. Forest Service researchers trapped falling seeds and estimated more than 8.5 million samaras per acre—90 to 95 percent of which would actually germinate. (The number of seeds in a selectively cut area was still in the range of 4.3 million per acre.) Even in the off years, seed counts were shown to be approximately 125,000 per acre.

Seeds that come showering down in or near the protective shade of the forest or sugarbush tend to do best, spending the first winter buried under a blanket of leaves. Then, early in the spring and several weeks before the danger of frost has passed, the fertile seed cracks open, sending an anchoring root into the soil and throwing two narrow, straplike cotyledons, or first leaves, upward. On the forest floor, this new crop of sugar maples can form an unbroken expanse of lush green, but seeds that fall in open areas are typically choked out by the rampant growth of grasses and weeds. Although winds can carry airborne maple samaras several hundred feet from the parent tree (children call the spinning wings helicopters for good reason), the survival rate beyond the protective canopy of mature trees is low.

An inconsequential percentage of the fallen seeds will be eaten by squirrels and game birds, but once sprouted, the young maples become prime, tender browse for white-tailed deer. "Where deer population

sap out through any convenient exit, filling buckets and bulk storage containers with a watery lode of sugar and the amino acids that provide the flavor we know as maple. Then, if the sugarmaker has not been overly greedy, the tree will continue to grow and thrive and repeat the gift for season after season, decade after decade, even century after century.

SEEDY BUSINESS

THE FINALE of the tapping season is just the start of things for the sugar maple, which is able to transmit its sap movements into a display of budding and leaf growth that is virtually explosive.

As beekeepers know, the maple is among the first nectar sources of the spring, blossoming up high and unnoticed by all but hungry bees, tree lovers and allergy sufferers. Sometime in April or May, the tree may be covered with a haze of yellowish flowers,

ameter expanding to an inch or inch and a half in the first decade, depending on the amount of light and the soil conditions. The height increases at a rate of about a foot per year for the first 30 to 40 years, at which time it may have reached a foot or so in diameter and be ready to receive a sugarmaker's tap. (Growth rates are tremendously dependent on the extent of competition from other trees.)

The tree will cease to grow taller after about a century and half, but will continue to thicken—inexorably adding a fresh ring of wood just under the bark each year—as long as it remains alive. The fact that upward growth occurs at the tips of the branches, not in the trunk, means a nail or fence wire stapled to a maple will always remain the same height from the ground. As the diameter expands, it will eventually envelop the nail or wire—and heal over any tapholes or other wounds the tree may have suffered.

UNDER THE MICROSCOPE

FOR A FASCINATING LOOK at the natural history of the sugar maple under the microscope lens and through the eyes of the people who study this species for a living, a drive up the base of Vermont's highest peak is in order. Here on the heavily wooded lower slopes of Mt. Mansfield near the town of Underhill is the Proctor Maple Research Center, where many of the knottiest questions about the sugar maple have been unraveled.

This is the headquarters for Sumner Williams, 46, assistant director of the lab and the public persona of the University of Vermont's maple program, a wiry triathlete who travels easily in the ranks of rural sugarmakers, camouflaging his academic credentials under well-worn field clothes and an old baseball cap. Walking through the new, airy 6,000-square-foot center, he gives a capsule his-

A healthy maple crown, **top,** *and a tree severely defoliated by insects. Some observers believe that acid rain and air pollution may be lowering the trees' natural defense barriers against such attacks.*

is high," one government forester has noted, "as in northeast Wisconsin and the Adirondack region of New York, deer browsing has been so severe in places that if the maple didn't reproduce in such abundance, it would be questionable if it could survive."

And so the tree grows steady and true, with the ditory of maple research and the landmark findings that have come from this unusual hillside station.

"When the Proctor Center was started by Dr. James W. Marvin and Dr. Fred H. Taylor in 1947, they were both botanists, and the main thrust of all their research was toward the resource itself, the tree. They were interested in how the maple worked and why one tree or stand was sweeter than another.

"One of the first and most significant things they did was to go out and number every mature tree that was 10 inches in diameter or greater, and they started recording diameter growth and sugar sweetness on a lot of those trees. Today, we have a great deal of history on these trees."

Set within 200 acres of mixed forest, the 40 acres of monitored sugarbush are unique in the world, and Vermont's researchers have led the way on many of the major issues and developments in the maple industry since the beginning of the twentieth century. While the U.S. Department of Agriculture did maple research prior to 1970, and while Cornell University has a maple-demonstration site near Lake Placid, New York, the Vermonters have clearly been at the center of some of the most heated research and development issues, including sap flow, maple genetics, evaporator efficiency, reverse osmosis, plastic pipeline usage, forest fertilization and ongoing work on maple diseases, pests and the effects of air pollution.

"Some people jokingly asked us what we were doing in maple research," chuckles Dr. Fred Taylor, who retired in 1975. "And there were times when we asked ourselves, 'Why didn't we pick something like beets or carrots that you can grow to maturity in a single season and keep under controlled conditions?'

"Here is this tree sitting out there in nature, and you don't know too well what is going on in the soil around it, and there are all kinds of influences on that tree that we can't control. To get at these influences is a long-term process. There are no easy answers."

Still, there have been some highly satisfying moments for the researchers, and one of the landmark practical discoveries at the Proctor Center was made by Marvin when he was attempting to track down a phenomenon in which sugarbushes converted to plastic tubing seemed to drop in sap production. Marvin discovered that, in the early morning and late afternoon, the shaded side of a maple might have negative pressure (in effect, wanting to draw fluid in), while the sunny side of the same tree was merrily pouring sap out. This might seem nothing more than a bit of botanical trivia, but Marvin identified it as the hidden production drain in pipeline systems. He showed that, at certain times of the day, one tree could be madly pushing sap as the next tree down the pipeline—or even the backside of the same tree— was hungrily drawing it back in. In response, Marvin and his colleague Fred Laing devised a dropline and redesigned the standard spout to prevent sap from being pulled back into the trees.

The guiding spirit for Marvin, Laing, Taylor and those who have followed was a gruff, practical-joking chemist named Charles Howland Jones, who came to Vermont in 1896 from Massachusetts and virtually single-handedly yanked the maple tree out of the sixteenth century.

PROBING THE PROVERBS

BEFORE JONES, man's understanding of the maple was a mare's nest of folklore, conflicting anecdotes and the collected wisdom of stubborn farmers who thrived on contrariness. Consider these well-entrenched Yankee proverbs:

"The lower you tap, the sweeter the sap."
"The higher you tap, the sweeter the sap."
"Shallow boring yields better quality, less quantity."
"Deeper borings yield darker sugar, greater quantity."
"A tree will run the most sap on the side with the coarsest bark."
"Sap is sweeter from trees that have been previously tapped."
"The older the tree, the sweeter the sap."

Jones—known to colleagues and students as C.H.—a tall figure with wire-rimmed glasses and a

Cross-section of a sugar maple approximately 150 years old, showing dark, sealed-in tapholes. A healthy maple will encap-sulate tapping wounds within a year or two, burying them under layer after layer of new wood as the tree expands outward.

Mark Twain mustache, attacked the controversies and mysteries of sap flow head-on. He located an available sugarbush in Jeffersonville, about 20 miles from the University of Vermont campus in Burlington, and convinced a reluctant dean to allow him to lease the trees. C.H. dubbed the place Melody Hill and, for the next few sugaring seasons, took his assistants and gear to the country, traveling by train and spending weeks on end bivouacked in a local hotel. By day, they collected sap samples and recorded weather and soil conditions and the internal temperatures and sap pressures of the trees. By night, they analyzed the perishable sap in their crowded rooms.

"A hotel room makes a very poor laboratory," says Mary G. Lighthall, a Charlotte, Vermont, resident who knew Jones while working as a research associate and who has written a short biography of the chemist. "Those of us who have had difficulties in well-equipped chemistry labs can imagine the problems C.H. had to put up with.

"He started at the beginning, measuring and recording how much and how fast the sap ran, from what part of the tree and from which side. To get this information, he had devised a fairly simple gadget, a sort of blind sap spout made from a section of galvanized pipe with one end plugged. The sap was forced out through a slot cut in the pipe, and by rotating different spouts, Jones was able to determine the direction of the sap flow within the tree."

Tantalized by the apparent pressure forcing the sap from the spouts, Jones began attaching brass gauges to his spouts, and with his assistants, he slogged through the sugarbush at regular intervals to record the readings. "They measured the sap pressure up, down and sideways," says Lighthall. "The conditions and equipment could not have been more rudimentary, yet out of this came a little-known masterpiece of scientific research. It was one man's attempt to measure, understand and explain a small piece of his natural world."

Jones published "The Maple Sap Flow" as a hefty paper in 1903, and according to Lighthall, many of his findings are as relevant today as the day they were released. Perhaps under pressure from Dean J.L. Hills, C.H was diverted from his maple work into animal-feeding studies, but later became determined to pick up where he left off. "Having studied the maple tree during sap season," Lighthall recalls, "he began to study it year-round. He set up a series of experiments that would have overwhelmed a man of lesser perseverance. Every month for 27 months, he had a full-grown maple tree cut down, rushed to the lab and sectioned. He analyzed the sections for water, sucrose, hexose, starch, ash and hemicellulose content."

Jones's paper, "The Carbohydrate Contents of the Maple Tree," was a scientific tour de force, but Jones would be remembered most for a curious calculation he devised as a result of this work. His various talents came together in a clever statement of the relationship of sugar content in maple sap to the amount of syrup a given amount of sap will produce. Jones explained to sugarmakers that if the percent of sugar is known and used to divide into the constant 86, the number of gallons of sap needed to produce one gallon of finished syrup would be known. Thus sap with a concentration of 2 percent would dictate a total of 43 gallons of sap to produce one gallon of syrup.

"Eighty-six is really a factor to use as a shortcut for some pretty involved chemical calculations," says Lighthall. "It is based on some very precise measures of the density of weak sugar solutions." Jones, however, made it all seem rollickingly simple by spinning out the rule in doggerel that is still tacked up on beams in sugarhouses throughout New England.

Sumner Williams, whose mustache is an almost perfect match for that sported by C.H. Jones 90 years ago, says the Rule of 86 is one of the benchmarks for all who are involved with the sugar maple: "Jones's Rule is very accurate. In fact, it is one of the only hard-and-fast rules of sugaring. Talk to almost anyone about some aspect of sugaring and you can go down the road to the next sugarhouse and they will tell you something almost totally different. But Jones's Rule of 86 has stood the test of time. It is sort of the Newton's First Law of Sugarmaking. It is actually a universal law, because it works even in metric and liters." (For Imperial gallons in Canada, it becomes Jones's Rule of 105.)

According to Williams, Jones's Rule set out new challenges for the maple world that are still unmet: "With it, you can test a sugarbush and thin it to make it sweeter. We know that a tree produces the same concentration of sap year after year, so if all our trees could be 10 percent sweet, that would only take 8.6 gallons of sap to produce a gallon of syrup. It would eliminate reverse osmosis and back pans on evaporators and make the sugarmaker's life a heck of a lot easier."

THE 10% TREE

IF THERE IS A HOLY GRAIL in the world of maple researchers, it is a big sugar maple standing out in front of a weathered farmhouse in north central Vermont. As one of the oldsters in the neighborhood might put it, "You can't always tell by the looks of a toad how far he can jump." This tree has seen healthier days, and from all external appearances is just another old sugar maple. But over decades of testing, it has consistently given sap with a sugar con-

"You can't always tell by the looks of a toad how far he'll jump," says an old farm proverb, and maples within a single sugarbush such as this have been discovered to vary dramatically in the amount and sweetness of the sap they yield. Sugar content ranges from about 1.5 percent up to 10 percent in very rare instances. Maple cloning research is underway in Ohio.

centration of about 10 percent—at times as high as 10.5 percent. This is the sugar-maple equivalent of a runner doing a one-minute mile or a full-sized car getting 150 miles per gallon.

An average maple yields about 2.2 percent sap, of which 40 gallons are needed to make a single gallon of syrup. Sap from the 10 percent tree makes syrup at a rate of one gallon for every 8.6 gallons of sap.

According to Dr. Mariafranca Morselli, research professor emerita of the University of Vermont's Botany Department, this tree may have been discovered by C.H. Jones in the early part of the century and has fueled the dreams of maple researchers ever since.

Morselli says that it was botanist Fred Taylor who first confirmed that "there are trees that are always sweeter than others" and that in her own research she

was able to take his monitoring of supersweet trees a step further: "I decided that if there were high-sugar-concentration trees, these trees probably were also producing a higher volume of sap.

"We looked at the records of 29 trees over 25 years, measured continuously during the tapping season. I was able to find out that the trees that are high in sugar-sap concentration are also the ones that produce a double volume of sap."

According to Morselli's research, the high-volume and high-sugar trees have a doubled area of sugar storage in the sapwood compared to trees that are low in sugar and volume. "This indicated to me, at least from three parameters, that there must be a gene for sap sweetness."

Her hunch led to years of research into maple genetics and many attempts in Vermont to clone the 10 percent tree. "I tried all possible tissue-culture recipes to get cambial cells to differentiate [in simplified terms, to develop leaf and root systems] and we got some very beautiful shoots growing in test tubes. They grew to this size," she says, indicating a height of an inch and half or so, "but they never developed roots. They just grew this high and then the little leaves turned red and they died. "

"Ohio Supersweets"

WHILE MORSELLI and her colleagues failed to produce tissue clones of superior maples, research into genetics and cloning done at the former George D. Aiken-U.S. Forest Service lab in Vermont by William Gabriel, Robert A. Gregory, Harry W. Yawney and Clayton M. Carl in the 1970s and 1980s helped spur attempts to propagate the sugar maple vegetatively. One promising experimental sugarbush now growing in Ohio is based on the simpler technique of taking cuttings from supersweet trees. Standing at the Wooster Agriculture Experiment Station, the 18 trees date back to the 1950s when maple geneticist Howard Kriebel went on a collecting expedition through Massachusetts, New Hampshire, Vermont, Ohio and New York, bringing back cuttings from the upper crowns of trees with higher-than-average sugar-sap levels. These cuttings were grafted onto maple rootstocks and planted in a relatively isolated area—well away from other sugar maples.

According to Dr. Robert P. Long, research plant pathologist for the U.S. Forest Service, the original trees planted by Kriebel are showing an average sugar concentration of 4.2 percent—almost double that of the average maple.

Daniel Houston, a forest geneticist at Ohio State University, has been pushing the research forward, planting cuttings from the Kriebel trees and obtaining highly encouraging results, with average sugar concentrations in the 4 percent range. The biggest stum-bling block, according to the researchers, is the low early-survival rate of cuttings and the amount of labor involved.

"The sugar maple isn't the hardest tree to root successfully," says Long, "but it still poses a lot of problems and the success rate is low." Half of the cuttings, which are treated with gibberellin (a growth stimulator extracted from certain mold fungi) to encourage rooting, do not make it through the first winter. According to Long, the gibberellin causes "bizarre things to happen" with some cuttings, and further mortality is common before the trees can even be set outdoors.

Geneticist Houston has high hopes for the propagation of seed collected from the genetically superior trees. In the Ohio Supersweet Program, seeds are collected from the Kriebel sugarbush, and the resulting seedlings sold to interested landowners. Unfortunately, as of this writing no data have been released on the actual sap-sweetness of these trees. (A 30-year test plot of a similar nature in Vermont has given disappointing results. Because each seed naturally produced by a maple may have two parent trees, there is no guarantee that the resulting progeny will have pure "sweet-tree" genetics.) Houston is confident that the Ohio breeding program is working and says that the original 18 trees planted by Howard Kriebel have the potential of casting enough seed to start millions of maples in a good seed year, and that large-scale propagation is being planned in the Ohio tree-nursery system, either at Marietta or Zanesville. Other observers say the jury will remain out on these seed-propagated trees until sap-sweetness tests confirm that the genetic superiority has been passed along.

While maple breeding hasn't yet broken out of the laboratory, other advances from the researchers were quickly put to work in the sugarbushes and sugarhouses of the United States and Canada. It was Fred Laing, as Proctor's director during the height of technological change in the '70s and early '80s, who carried on the research work of retired botanists Marvin and Taylor at the Underhill lab, and while he continued to monitor the trees, the Center took off in new directions.

According to Sumner Williams, "Fred Laing's area of expertise was more in the applied research—looking at gathering sap with tubing, using vacuum pumps, various types of evaporators, looking at the efficiency of evaporators, addressing basic questions about how to make the industry more efficient." Under Laing's pragmatic direction, the lab played a key role in helping the maple industry out of an apparently worrisome downhill slide, giving farmers new methods of production that, beginning in the early 1970s, reversed the declines in syrup sales. Canadian production, similarly, took a jump a decade later when the technological advances began to be adopted wholeheartedly in the big sugar regions of Quebec. With strong government encouragement and funding, in fact, Quebec is considered by some to be the home of some of the most innovative forces in maple technology today.

WHITHER THE MAPLE?

IN VERMONT, following Laing's retirement in 1986, Dr. Melvin Tyree assumed the directorship of the laboratory and has moved things back in the direction of studying questions about tree physiology and the maple itself.

Tyree's personal interests have been directed toward the study of tropical trees under stress, research which he says may eventually benefit the maple. Test plots in Vermont are now being watched for the effects of various forms of pollution, and experiments using fertilizers to revitalize unhealthy maples are under way.

Unfortunately for those who fear that there may be a cloud over the future of the American hardwood forest, and the sugar maple in particular, funding for rain-forest studies is more easily come by than research money for trees closer to home. Everywhere in the maple community, quiet worries can be heard about the number of unhealthy trees for all to see.

Following the alarming deaths of several sugarbushes in the province of Quebec beginning around 1982, and with other reports of apparently sick or dying trees gaining public attention, a major study was undertaken. Beginning in 1988, The North American Maple Project (NAMP) set out to measure the health of maples—both in the forest and in working sugarbushes—in four Canadian provinces and nine states. The results to date have actually been encouraging to some observers.

"Things look pretty darn good," says Dr. David Houston, a plant pathologist at the U.S. Forest Research Station in Hamden, Connecticut, and brother of Ohio State's Daniel Houston.

David Houston says that a single culprit for the maple's woes has not been identified, and that fears of a Dutch-elm-like disease being responsible for sugar tree deaths seem to be unfounded. "We expected to find more decline in tapped trees," says Houston, "but, in fact, the sugarbushes are generally looking quite healthy."

Houston says that the decline and dieback of maples can be attributed to a number of direct causes, including:

1. **Road salt.** Maples on the downhill side of heavily salted roads frequently appear stunted and less vigorous than their uphill counterparts. Houston says that the decline of highly visible roadside maples has led some people to assume that the whole maple population is in worse shape than is actually the case.

2. **Localized insect defoliation.** Gypsy moths, pear thrips, saddled prominent caterpillars and other leaf-eating plagues have threatened maples in various regions. Countermeasures are often warranted.

3. **Damage to trees during logging and thinning operations in sugarbushes.** Fungus attacks on sugarbush trees can be fatal and are often traceable to

---

Fearing a plague like those that decimated the American elms and chestnuts, scientists have initiated a major study to track maple health in Canada and the United States.

Pear-thrip damage, far and near. Brownish areas and bare treetops show heavy defoliation in Vermont in 1993, **top.** *Surviving leaves, shown close-up, can be undersized, deformed and tinged with yellow.*

4. **Severe weather in some regions.** According to some sources, the devastated sugarbushes in Quebec may have been the victims of consecutive winters with severe cold and no protective snow cover, leading to root death.

5. **A combination of factors.** These include instances of maple stands stressed by two or more factors, such as drought followed by insect attack, and also the most controversial factors of all: acid rain and other forms of air pollution.

Acid rain has been implicated in the decline of other tree species, especially the spruce in higher New England elevations, and there is no shortage of suspicion that it is also taking its toll on hardwoods, including the maples.

While most government-affiliated foresters are loath to comment on acid rain's possible role in maple decline, many professional foresters and botanists have privately voiced concerns about the health of maples—and other hardwoods in the eastern woodland mix.

"They're scared to death to say anything," says David Marvin, a University of Vermont forestry graduate and outspoken sugarmaker. Marvin uses the case of a well-known eastern researcher who linked acid rain with the decline of red spruce stands and was hauled before a Congressional committee and came out "shell-shocked" by the ferocity of the attack by coal-burning interests.

"Take a look at how much acid-rain research is being funded by the utilities that create acid rain, and you'll start to see why we have a problem," Marvin says. "My dad [noted maple botanist James W. Marvin] used to say we were really lucky that we have a species that is not so susceptible to disease. Today, when we see exotic pests

injuries received by the trees—often years earlier—that created entry points for fungal spores. Houston says that the advent of pipeline systems has reduced traffic and wear-and-tear on the sugarbush, with positive long-term effects for sugarbushes.

like gypsy moths and pear thrips attacking maples, you have to wonder whether we still should feel as safe as we used to. You can't help but think about what happened to the elm and chestnut." (The American elm and the American chestnut were both virtually wiped out by blights during this century.)

"I am really worried about the health of the resource," continues Marvin, who believes that maples in decline may be symptomatic of bigger problems than we want to admit—or that we can presently understand. "A lot of what we think we see [in unhealthy maples] could very well be evidence of what we can't see."

Marvin ranks the potential threats to maple health as follows:

1. **Acid rain, heavy metals deposited by air pollution and global warming.** Mature maples are sensitive to abnormal levels of sunlight, and holes in the ozone layer are a real concern to some tree observers.

2. **The possible synergy between these stress factors and various pests and diseases.** A tree weakened by changing soil conditions is less able to fend off attacking insects and pathogens.

3. **Land-use trends, in which maple woods are being taken out of production by development.** "Who can afford to buy a sugarbush to make syrup today?" he asks.

Marvin fears that there may not be enough incentive to keep sugarbushes producing when the immediate financial gain in letting a developer carve the land into subdivisions is so great: "It's hard for government policymakers to think in terms of centuries—or even decades, and compared to the life of a sugarbush, a decade is just a sneeze in time."

He would turn the tables on the corporations and utilities producing acid rain, airborne pollutants and threats to the ozone layer. "Why should *we* have to prove that what they are putting into the environment is harmful? Why shouldn't they be told to stop until *they* can prove that it's *safe*?"

Marvin, who shared the Tree Farmer of the Year Award with his wife, Lucy, in 1983 (having been chosen out of a field of more than 50,000), is an eloquent defender of the maple. He was named one of the most influential young Americans under the age of 40 by *Esquire* magazine in 1984, and his sense of urgency about airborne pollutants rankles those who prefer a go-slow approach to acid rain.

SCIENCE OR SMOKESCREEN?

ONE SCIENTIST with impeccable credentials who is not afraid to speak out is A.R.C. ("Arch") Jones, retired forestry professor and director of the renowned Morgan Arboretum at Macdonald College of McGill University, west of Montreal. Respected as one of the great gentlemen of twentieth-century maple research and held in high regard on both sides of the Canadian-American border, Jones fears that acid raid is a much greater threat to tree health than is widely believed.

"I'm worried," says Jones, one of the "core scientific review group" consulted at the beginning of the North American Maple Project. "Everywhere you look, there are trees—and not just maples—in terrible shape. I'm a bit disquieted by the tendency to sweep this situation under a rug."

Jones says he is "not convinced by the NAMP" surveys and pronouncements such as Houston's that seem to give maples a clean bill of health. "In the first place, we [Jones and other scientists consulted] argued against the way the study was constructed . . . the way they eliminated plots with too many dead or dying trees."

The failure to count dead trees and the very limited scope of the study—only two measurements are being taken in each test plot—are frustrating to Jones, who says that some provincial foresters in both Quebec and Ontario are seeing more problems than the NAMP data suggest. "In Quebec, at least, we have seen that wetter sites and mountaintops are being hammered, and the incidence of maple defoliation in 256 monitored plots [in Quebec] is growing steadily."

Canadian forestry expert A.R.C. (Arch) Jones inspects branches covered with fungus—a possible symptom of acid rain lowering the resistance of trees to disease and predators. "I'm worried," says Jones, who fears that government scientists are trying to "sweep this situation under a rug."

most heavily affected sugarbushes in the Beauce region south of Quebec City, where large numbers of maples started dying in 1979. A number of whole sugarbushes were leveled in the early 1980s, and the cause today is commonly ascribed to several hard winters or drought.

A more rigorous study of the situation, says Jones, reveals significant soil problems in the areas with the worst decline—low potassium, for example. "Potassium combines readily with nitric acid and sulfuric acid, two of the more common components of acid rain, and leaches out of the soil.

"We still haven't proved that acid rain is killing trees, but the reality is that acid rain may never be shown as the immediate cause of tree death. What kills the trees, once they are in a weakened, stressed condition, is *armilleria* [shoestring fungus], insects or bad weather."

Jones has received threatening letters from the Canadian federal government for uttering such statements, and he says he was told by one high official, "We don't want the public worrying about acid rain. They might stop planting trees."

It will take better studies than the current NAMP survey, Jones feels, before political minds can be made aware of the urgency of the problem. He would like to see NAMP reevaluate its study design and start to include soil sampling and crown sampling—conducting annual tests of leaf samples to get a better measure of tree health and possible deficiencies. He says the policy of eliminating dead trees from the study ought to be changed or clarified if any sort of credible results are to be obtained. [The most recent published report from NAMP quietly notes that a number of the test plots in the study have been lum-

Jones cites the Quebec government's FIDS (Forest Insect and Disease Survey) data to show that 91 percent of the test plots are now showing some signs of decline. He says he has visited and studied the

(density)

Bad weather *

*

insects

fungus

* Shooting

but
well seen tells
Still learnt piano

bered or otherwise taken out of the survey and replaced with new ones. It is this kind of unorthodox manipulation of statistics that has critics such as Arch Jones wondering if the survey is more political smokescreen than rigorous science.]

Douglas Allen, a forest entomologist at Syracuse University who is tabulating the NAMP data, strenuously argues that "there is no conspiracy" in the way the study was designed. He says that no tree-mortality figures are available, but reiterates Houston's statement that maple health "by and large looks better today than it did in 1988."

Allen confirms that the areas suffering the worst maple dieback were kept out of the study. "We set out to see what might be happening to healthy trees, and so I guess you can say that our data is biased and we cannot make a blanket statement about the health of the resource in general."

What Jones and Marvin and others fear is that dying maples excluded from the study may be a clear warning signal of bad things to come in prime maple country.

Looking up from a cross-section of a 150-year-old maple and staring off into the sun-dappled sugarbush that surrounds his laboratory sugarhouse, Sumner Williams says there are enough villains in the wind and puzzles left in the sugar maple to keep researchers challenged well into the next century.

"We have come back again to looking at the tree itself, and we can't forget that the maple is still the most important thing," he notes. Having given the industry a quantum boost with the technological advances of the last 20 years, Vermont's maple-research specialists have largely moved out of the sugarhouse and back into the woods. "The maple tree itself is why this lab got started," says Williams, "and when you think about what it would be like if we were to lose this resource, all the other research doesn't shine as brightly."

Bare upper branches and a thinning crown are the characteristic signs of a declining and possibly dying maple, here seen on a Montreal street.

SAM CUTTING STANDS next to the stump of a fallen maple that had been an old favorite on a Vermont hilltop. "You look at these trees and some of them are fine, but others seem like they're on their way out. The crowns just aren't filled in the way they should be, some of the leaves have a yellowish cast—they must be lacking something—and, you know, there's hardly any maple regeneration in this stand." Cutting has been persistent. He has been to Washington twice to seek answers about maple decline. "They say its not acid rain, but you have to wonder about trees that ought to be in the prime of life dying with no apparent reason. You have to suspect that something's wrong."

Arch Jones is even more direct: "All of the wonderful improvements in maple production could be nullified if we persist in assuming that the biosphere will continue to absorb growing quantities of pollutants by uncontrolled emissions from every conceivable source.

"We must then face the fact that the business of maple is a 'sunset industry' with little long-term future, and the sweet taste of maple will become just a memory." 🍁

Just Call Her Dr. Maple

"I was a shock to a lot of people . . ."

WHEN SHE TRAVELS to Italy, a coveted box in the house at LaScala is reserved, and one seriously doubts that the glittering opera crowds suspect that the sophisticated older woman sitting just above the stage is an award-winning maple sugarmaker.

When the Vermont Sugar Makers' Association chose Dr. Mariafranca Morselli as its Maple Producer of the Year in 1984, a century of unspoken precedents were broken, but there was no arguing the fact that her sugarmaking—all done in a laboratory—was worthy of the highest honors.

Her continental manners, Milanese accent and aristocratic Italian upbringing are worlds away from the rutted backroads of Vermont's sugar country, but Dr. Morselli will long be remembered as a feisty, brilliant friend of sugarmaking who loved her native opera but also found a home in the heart of maple country. With a doctorate in natural science from the University of Milan, Morselli joined University of Vermont botanist James Marvin's team of researchers in 1964, assigned to study maple anatomy, the bio-

chemistry of sap, sap microbiology and the chemistry of syrup in ways that harked back to C.H. Jones's methods in 1900.

Morselli says that, while the USDA laboratory in Philadelphia was "working on sap from a chemist's point of view," she and the Vermont team chose to come at the subject "from a plant physiologist's point of view."

"It is very difficult to explain the difference," she explains, "but as a plant physiologist I tried to look at the sap as a natural product that is composed of the nutrients that allow the growth of the maple, and therefore, my approach was very different.

"Just to give you an example of the Philadelphia laboratory's methods, they were working on the chemistry of sap by diluting canned syrup back to the concentration of sap. This meant they were forgetting what was the contribution of the tree cells to the biochemistry of the sap," she says, her eyes flashing. "It seemed far-fetched to me, really, to start like this if you wanted a real understanding of the scientific facts behind sap and syrup.

"When I started working on the biochemistry of the sap and chemistry of the syrup in 1971, after the Philadelphia lab closed, we began by obtaining sap samples directly from individual trees, using aseptic ways of tapping trees, and boiling them to syrup in the laboratory. In Philadelphia, I think, they had sap samples from a few trees outside the laboratory. We had a full-fledged maple bush up at the Proctor Center, 1,400 taps and individual trees to work with, trees that were being monitored for all different variables, from sap-flow volume to sap concentration to sap-flow rate, to the air temperatures in the woods, the temperatures in the soil, the temperatures in the roots of the trees, temperatures of the twig . . . and sap pressures in the trees at different levels. We really had an integrated system of research."

Still an active voice in maple affairs, Morselli is known for speaking her mind, and has made a life-long career of not being deterred by set-in-their-ways male sugarmakers and academics. "I was a shock to a lot of people," she says, with more than a trace of a smile. She says that Marvin and Fred Laing, who succeeded him as director of the university's Maple Research Center, were "never bashful" about giving her credit, but both the university and the maple industry were male dominions.

She helped change that, and the 35 scientific papers—many with popularized versions for the maple industry—she authored or co-authored, many with Lynn Whalen, constitute an achievement that will not soon be equaled in mapledom. To Morselli's credit are many significant findings about maple sap and syrup quality as it was being affected by major changes in gathering and evaporating methods. She conducted studies into plastic tubing, vacuum pumping, reverse osmosis and ultraviolet sap sterilization—all of the significant advances that have helped many sugarmakers survive and thrive in difficult times.

The essence of these studies is an arsenal of facts about the perishability of sap, a delicate substance that must be kept clean and cold; to do otherwise is to roll out a red-carpeted invitation for microorganisms to attack. While these bacteria and yeasts are killed in boiling and pose no threat to human health, they are deadly enemies in the syrupmaker's battle to produce Fancy or high-grade syrup. Morselli helped prove why cleanliness and ice-cold sap make for the finest syrup, and that the real maple flavor is preserved by the sugarmaker's quality standards—not absorbed from the smokiness of the sugarhouse.

FANTASTIC SYRUP

THE ENERGY CRISIS brought another challenge: how to reduce the amount of fuel required to boil sap down to syrup? One answer the researchers put to the test was reverse osmosis, and it worked. In reverse osmosis, a single stream of sap enters a high-pressure chamber, and ultra-pure water seeps through a high-tech membrane. Out of the unit come two lines: one with water, the other with now-enriched sap.

"Concentrating sap with RO (reverse osmosis) is the equivalent of desalinization of water," says Morselli, "except that we were bringing the sugar to a higher concentration so that there would be less water to boil in the evaporator."

Morselli, the consummate scientist, nevertheless has tremendous respect for old-fashioned, high-quality syrup. "We had to come to grips with the energy crisis, to find ways of producing maple syrup from sap that were energy-saving, but that were still making the same beautiful and delicious product that was done with the traditional systems.

"Maple producers have great common sense and naturally great experience in producing maple syrup. In some cases, when we pointed out an obvious change that sugarmakers could make to improve things, they would say that they always knew that.

"We found that there were things that maple producers did intuitively well, that they had been doing for years, and in some cases we simply proved that their way was the way to do it. There are some people out there making some fantastic syrup." ✺

A BOTANICAL SNAPSHOT

Acer saccharum through scientific eyes

Common Names: Hard maple, rock maple, sugar maple (wood also known as curly maple, bird's eye maple).

Family: Maple or Aceraceae. Consists of two genera, *Acer* and *Diptoneria*, the latter including two small species in Central China.

Genus: *Acer*. Made up of about 148 wild or cultivated species of trees and shrubs that are widely scattered throughout North America, Europe and Asia, with the greatest abundance of species in the eastern Himalayas and central China. (Some older references state that there may be 200 species.) Old World maples range south to North Africa and Java; New World species are found from eastern Canada to Alaska south to the mountains of Guatemala.

Range: Eastern Canada and the United States. In Canada: from the mouth of the St. Lawrence River west to southeastern Manitoba. In the U.S.: Maine south to northern Georgia, west to western Minnesota, south to central Iowa, eastern Kansas and Missouri. Scattered as far south as Texas and Louisiana.

In its northern range, it is found at elevations up to 2,500 feet; in the Lake States, up to 1,600 feet; in the southern Appalachians, it occurs in a zone from 3,000 to 5,500 feet.

In lower elevations, the sugar maple grows most commonly on cooler north slopes; in the Southern

Forest region, it commonly occurs in moist flats and ravines and along streams at elevations of 2,000 to 4,000 feet.

Soil: Prefers fertile, well-drained loams and sandy loams, occasionally silt loams. In the Adirondacks, New England and Canada, it thrives on rock-strewn hillsides and slopes, but some of the biggest old trees are found in rich, well-drained agricultural lands. In the Midwest, it occurs in level, old pastures. Nowhere does it tolerate swampy conditions, which are more favorable to the red and silver maples.

Associated trees: Balsam fir, basswood, beech, black cherry, Fraser fir, hemlock, hickory, paper birch, persimmon, red oak, red spruce, sassafras, white pine, white ash, white oak, white spruce, yellow birch.

Associated shrubs: American elder, blackberries, Canada yew, dwarf bush honeysuckle, pagoda dogwood, red raspberry, scarlet elder.

DESCRIPTION

Leaves: Not serrate (smooth edges, not toothed), as in the red and silver maples. Opposite (leaf pairs emerging opposite each other from stem); leaves 3 to 5 inches across; 5-lobed (rarely 3-lobed); bright green above, lighter below. In autumn, colors turn to yellow, orange, red and various combinations.

Flowers: Begin in early spring as inconspicuous clusters with the emerging leaves and appear from a distance as a yellowish haze. Some trees bloom annually, others only every two to five years. Most trees have both unisexual and bisexual flowers, the latter with only one sex active. Male flowers typically outnumber female by 10 to 1 and up to 50 to 1 on some parts of the tree. (Some trees bear only male or female flowers.) Pollinated by bees (important first nectar source for bee colonies in some regions).

Seeds/Fruit: Ripened and dropped in autumn; paired 1-inch samaras, keys or wings (one is fertile). Eight million seeds per acre have been counted in old stands in good seed years, which occur every 2 to 5 years. Perhaps 500,000 to 1.5 million seeds from a large, mature tree. Sugar maple has a relatively large seed, at approximately 6,100 per pound. Seeds need at least 90 days cold dormancy before sprouting.

Bark: Gray; smooth on young trees, becoming deeply furrowed with long, irregular, thick ridges in older specimens; sometimes scaly, highly variable.

Size: Maximum known: 135 feet tall with 7-foot diameter (no longer living). Average at maturity: 60 to 80 feet, 2-to-3-foot diameter.

Shape: In woods or dense stand: clear, straight bole, small crown high in the canopy. In the open: branches near the ground, with large, dense rounded or oval crown. Unusually windfirm, enduring up to tornado-force winds.

Age: Lives 300 to 400 or more years.

Uses: Timber, ornamental, important source of browse, maple syrup and sugar. Tourist attraction.

Varieties: Botanists recognize at least three races or ecotypes, with varying levels of drought endurance and resistance to strong sunlight. Hybrids have been reported between sugar, black and red maples. Geneticists are working on a "supersweet" strain.

Growth: Grows at a rate of about one foot in height per year for first 30 to 40 years, depending on the amount of shading and soil conditions. Under average conditions, the trunk diameter reaches tapping size—10 to 12 inches—in about 35 years. After 140 to 150 years, the height does not increase, but the diameter spreads slowly as long as the tree lives.

With scarlet fall foliage and distinctly toothed leaf edges, the red maple is a respectable sap producer.

POOR MAN'S MAPLES

A short guide for the resourceful tapper

A DAIRY FARMER I once knew raised big black and white Holsteins—purebreds—and he liked to chide his neighbor, who kept Jerseys, saying that the little brown beasts were for "the man who's too poor to own a cow, too proud to own a goat."

Those with sugar maples to spare won't give other trees a second thought while tapping, but this shouldn't stop anyone with a taste for homemade syrup from tapping the other species of *Acer*.

Even serious sugarmakers in fringe areas will gladly tap silver maples or red maples to augment the sap harvest, and one successful sugarbush in Ohio is comprised completely of red maples. According to Professor Arch Jones, retired woodlot management advisor for Quebec, the red maple is also heavily tapped in the Gaspé region of that province.

As for the Manitoba maple or boxelder, an old New England saying applies: "Milk the cow which is near." About the only similarity of this tree to the other common North American maples is the classic seed form: samaras, or keys. Still, many backyard sugarmakers say the Manitoba maple gives sap in good quantity, and the flavor is distinctly maplelike.

The white birch also produces sap, although it is so low in sugar concentration that it takes about 90 gallons of sap to yield a single gallon of syrup. Birch syrup is currently being produced commercially in Finland, where it is regarded as a health tonic, but the high-tech process being used calls for intense use of reverse osmosis and boiling in a vacuum to achieve a palatable product. A more traditional birch-syrup operation is also underway in Alaska, where homemade birch syrup has been made for many years. (Birch is probably the billy goat of the tapping world, somehow suitable for the Alaskan spirit.)

Occasionally the weather conditions for a good sap flow—freezing nights and warm spring days—extend into regions that have maples but no commercial syrup production. Amateurs with the desire to try their hands at making syrup may try a bold experiment—and they will at least be rewarded with great stories to tell. Sumner Williams, a Vermont maple expert, recalls just such a fluke spell of weather on the West Coast, where he and some friends took advantage of the unusual conditions to tap a few bigleaf maples. The experience, he says, was far more memorable than the flavor of the syrup. (Various attempts to develop a sugaring industry in Oregon have met with little success.)

Intrepid tappers will be encouraged by the words of a fellow underdog sugarmaker: "I've tasted a lot of homemade syrup, and—unless it's been burned—the worst stuff was still wonderful." The following guide is offered for newcomers who don't want to be remembered like one poor soul who is still laughed about at sugarmaker's gatherings, who placed all his taps in basswood trees and wondered why the rest of the world was tasting syrup when his buckets were still bone dry.

RED MAPLE
(Swamp Maple)
Acer rubrum

Known for its brilliant scarlet foliage in autumn and for the year-round reddish tinge to its twigs. A medium-sized forest tree able to tolerate wet—even swampy—soil. Ranges from Newfoundland west to Minnesota, south to Florida and Texas. Wood not as dense and hard as the sugar maple.

Leaves: Toothed or serrated edges; 2 to 6 inches across; 3 to 5 lobes (usually 3): acute sinuses; light green above, pale and waxy-white below (glaucous). Usually solid, bright red in fall, sometimes yellow. (Buds are noticeably reddish, rounder and fatter than those of the sugar maple.)

Bark: Young trees have smooth, grayish bark as on sugar maples. Turning dark brown and scaly or shaggy at maturity.

Size: 50 to 70 feet tall, 12 to 24 inches diameter; record tree: 179 feet tall, 6 feet in diameter.

Seeds: Red before they dry; shed in early summer rather than in fall; germinate immediately, unlike sugar maple.

Age: 70 to 80 years maturity, can live to 150 years. Crown shape more irregular than sugar maple and branches more brittle and prone to storm damage. The state tree of Rhode Island.

Tapping Remarks: Typical maple flavor, but considerably more boiling necessary, as sap has less than half the sugar density of sugar maple, with a shorter run. Syrup tends to be darker.

SILVER MAPLE
(White Maple, Soft Maple)
Acer saccharinum

A popular yard and shade tree from colonial times, owing to its rapid growth—especially in comparison to the sugar maple. Unfortunately prone to storm damage and major limb and trunk problems after about 100 years of age. Short-lived compared to *Acer saccharum*.

Leaves: Toothed or serrated edges; 5 to 7 inches across; 5 lobes, with deep divisions on either side of central lobe; pale green above, silvery below. Yellow in fall.

Bark: Young trees have smooth, grayish bark similar to beech. Forms long, thin scales or vertical plates that curve away from trunk at the ends.

Size: Commonly 60 to 80 feet tall, 24 to 36 inches in diameter. Maximum recorded: 125 feet tall, 7 feet in diameter. (Trunk characteristically divides into several upright branches.)

Seeds: Large, 2-inch keys, with approximate 90-degree angle between. Borne in spring and germinate immediately.

Age: Matures at 125 years, can live to 150 years.

Tapping Remarks: Typical maple flavor, but considerably more boiling necessary, as sap has less than half the sugar density of sugar maple. Botanist André Michaux believed that the silver maple made a lighter, "more tasty" sugar, although in lesser quantity.

BOXELDER / MANITOBA MAPLE
(Ash-Leaved Maple)
Acer negundo

This is the oddball of North American maples, with atypical leaves (composed of 5 to 7 leaflets on a single stem) and rampant growth habits. Because of its hardiness and ability to create shade quickly—even aggressively—it was a popular street tree in some towns and on midwestern and prairie homesteads.

Leaves: Compound (not a single leaf, but rather 5 to 7 leaflets on each stem). Quite variable (3 or 9 leaflets; deeply lobed or not). Yellow in autumn.

Bark: Light brown, thin-skinned when young. Narrow ridges in older trees.

Size: Small or medium-sized tree, 30 to 40 feet high and 18 inches in diameter. Maximum recorded, 75 feet tall by 4 feet in diameter. Has an irregular bole, shallow root system and a bushy, spreading crown.

Seeds: Typical maple keys or samaras, but with thin, pointed bulbs and a clear V-shape between the two wings.

Age: Considered short-lived but self-rejuvenating; new sprouts usually appear when the trunk is cut or broken.

Tapping Remarks: Typical maple flavor and voluminous flow of thin sap. The last tree a professional sugarmaker would tap but beloved by many backyard tappers. This is the true underdog maple, but the syrup "fits just right over a stack of hotcakes."

BLACK MAPLE
Acer nigrum

So similar to sugar maple as to be considered a sub-species by some. Quality of wood and sap is identical. Largest stands found in Midwest in rich, flat, loamy lands.

Leaves: Dark green, drooping, velvety on bottom side and on stem. Usually 3-lobed.

Bark: Darker than sugar maple and more finely corrugated, rather than coarsely ridged.

Seeds: Similar to sugar maple, but slightly larger bulb.

EXOTIC POSSIBILITIES

NORWAY MAPLE
Acer platanoides

Introduced as a nursery favorite from Europe, this is a suburban lawn favorite that is now reaching tapping size in many areas. Shape of leaves similar to sugar maple; often reddish-purple. Fast-growing, with maximum height of about 75 feet. Because of its ornamental value, not usually tapped, but sap quality is reported to be good .

SYCAMORE MAPLE
Acer pseudoplatanus

This is a large species much loved in England, where it is valued as a shade tree and source of lumber. Introduced as a landscaping tree in North America and not recommended for tapping because of its ornamental value. Sap quality unknown.

WESTERN MAPLES

These maples, have been the object of a number of sugaring trials in western areas. Little success has resulted, largely because of the lack of a predictable sugaring season—at least 4 weeks of freezing nights and warm days. Backyard sugarmakers may wish to try tapping such trees on an experimental scale if a period of appropriate weather occurs.

CANYON MAPLE
(Big-Tooth Maple)
Acer grandidentatum

Found in Utah canyons and referred to optimistically as sugar maples by the first Mormon settlers. Sap quality unknown.

BIGLEAF MAPLE
Acer macrophyllum

One of the few commercially harvested hardwood species in the Pacific Northwest. Its nicely grained lumber is in strong demand. Weather conditions do not usually favor tapping, but it can be done.

Sources: *Silvics of Forest Trees of the United States*, Agriculture Handbook Number 271. Published by U.S. Forest Service and U.S. Department of Agriculture (1965). *Textbook of Dendrology*, by William M. Harlow, Ellwood S. Harrar and Fred M. White. McGraw-Hill, Sixth Edition (1979).

LARGEST LIVING MAPLES

Species & Year of Most Recent Measurement	Circumference	Height	Crown Spread	Location
Bigleaf Maple, 1977	419"	101'	90'	Jewell, OR
Black Maple, 1987	198"	118'	127'	Allegan Co., MI
Canyon Maple, 1989	80"	68'	44'	Lost Maple State Natural Area, TX
Douglas Maple, 1989	53"	80'	33'	Sandpoint, ID
Florida Maple, 1989	139"	100'	64'	Jasper Co., GA
Norway Maple, 1991	235"	137'	116'	New Paltz, NY
Red Maple, 1984	222"	179'	120'	St. Clair Co., MI
Silver Maple, 1989	293"	115'	110'	Columbia Co., WI
Silver Maple, 1972	276"	125'	134'	Rochester, MI
Striped Maple, 1991	50"	77'	28'	Bailey Arboretum Nassau Co., NY
Sugar Maple, 1984*	**269"**	**93'**	**80'**	**Norwich, CT**
Sugar Maple**	240"	98'	82'	Bedford, PQ
Sugar Maple	240"	82'	NA	N. Pelham, ON

Notes: Circumference measured in inches at 4.5 feet above ground. Height and crown spread measured in feet.
(*U.S. Sugar Maple Champion.) (**Canadian Sugar Maple Champion.)
Sources: 1992 National Register of Big Trees. Ontario and Quebec Ministries of Agriculture.

Young Sugar Makers, Vermont.

THE SUGARBUSH STEWARD

A short course in keeping maples healthy and productive

ONE OF THE GREAT JOYS we found on moving to an old farm in Ontario in the early 1970s was a neighbor's ancient sugarbush tucked well back from the nearest dirt road and framed with tumbledown stone fences. Here, delighting in the lack of brush and the almost complete absence of face-slapping saplings and tripping undergrowth, we picked trilliums, which grew in multitudes of both white and red, and wild honey mushrooms. It seemed like a well-tended park, yet we never saw any traces of the owners, who had given us permission to wander and "take all the toadstools you find."

What we didn't know at the time was that this pristine maple bush was dying, the huge old trees a monument to misguided woodlot management. The smoking gun, in fact, could be seen grazing in a nearby meadow: the farmer's yearling Holstein heifers, whose pasture rotation included these quiet woods.

Cattle, as many sugarmakers now know, should be kept out of the sugarbush. This is, in fact, relatively new advice by maple standards, and Everett Willard, a retired maple inspector for the Vermont Department of Agriculture, says he learned the lesson by accident on his family's home farm in northern Vermont. When his father was sugaring in the 1940s, there were about 900 tappable trees. "It wasn't big, but it was one of the best sugar places in Vermont," says Willard. "Like other farms in the area, we let the cows run in the woods, and they would eat the little maples. Well, there were wild leeks in half of that woods, and we had a fence running through that part to keep the cows out because the leek flavor would spoil the milk."

Willard says that when the longer-term effects of letting cows graze half the sugarbush became apparent, the demonstration was painfully clear: "When you stood 1,000 feet back from that bush, you could see the difference in the two halves: on one side there were lots of healthy young trees, and on the other there was nothing but old maples." The leeks had inadvertently protected the next generation of sugar trees in half the bush, and today the number of tappable sugar maples has more than doubled, to 1,900. Willard says the sugaring operation has continued to do well, even as the dairy cows faded in importance.

"Probably the biggest part of my father's income came from that sugar place, both because of the trees and because he made an excellent quality of syrup. The money didn't come from those cows, 'cause he was a darn poor dairyman, I can tell you that."

Grazing animals can ravage the young trees in a sugarbush and also damage the root systems of the maples through soil compaction and hoof damage, opening them to attacks by fungus (including the delicious honey mushrooms that we sought in the old Ontario bush). But the hand of man can be of great benefit to a stand of maples.

LESS IS MORE

Left to its own devices, a maple bush will tend to become crowded and not nearly as healthy and profitable as it might be with judicious thinning. As sugarbush-management specialist for the province of Ontario and a well-known figure in North American maple circles, Clarence Coons says that the well-managed sugarbush can produce more syrup and do it with less work on the part of the sugarmaker. "It's hard to think of anything else on the farm with a productive life anywhere near as long as that of a properly cared for maple tree," he says. "About the only thing that might run longer is the farmer's well."

Speaking to a group of sugarmakers, Coons runs through an eye-opening slide show, using as a case history a sugarbush in his province that produced 283 Imperial gallons of syrup from 1,700 taps in 1950. Through intelligent management of the trees alone—selecting the best crop trees and thinning the competition—the same bush was producing 485 Imperial gallons of syrup from the same number of taps in 1970.

Thus productivity jumped more than 70 percent with the modest investment in time to select and thin on a regular basis. "If you're paying attention to your trees, you may get a sore neck from looking up all the time," says Coons. "But the owners of this sugarbush obviously think it's been well worth it."

Coons says there are three main components to good sugarbush stewardship:

1. Thinning

"You've got to rogue out the defective stems, the maples producing sap with a low-sugar content and the other species," says Coons. "You've got to thin to release the best trees from competition." He advises selecting for single-trunk seed-grown trees (avoiding multiple stems and/or saplings that have sprung up from cut stumps). Look for the dominant trees, those that are naturally beating the competition and, usually, the trees with the widest, deepest crowns. "A good tree will be 50 to 85 percent crown," says Coons, "and the goal is 50 to 70 percent live crown to bole [trunk] for the whole stand. The dominant trees will respond best to thinning [around them], and they are the trees that typically produce more and sweeter sap."

Coons, who works out of the Kemptville Agricultural College in eastern Ontario, says that good trees can easily produce twice the syrup of average trees.

Coons suggests "getting the conifers out—they just shade your taps and tubing and reduce production."

SUGARBUSH PRODUCTIVITY	
Productivity Class	Taps Needed per Gallon of Syrup
Excellent	Less than 3
Good	3 to 4
Average	5 to 6
Poor	7 to 10
Bad	More than 10

Red and silver maples may be left in the stand, as long as they are not competing with sugar maples, but he feels that they, too, should be eliminated if there are sugar maples coming along to replace them.

Contrary opinion and advice on thinning is not hard to find, and a number of other experts are strongly urging that maple monocultures not be created. "A complex system is always better if you want to minimize insect and disease damage," says Dr. Bruce Parker, University of Vermont extension entomologist. "We know, for example, that sugar-maple-borer infestations are much worse when you open up the stand and leave only maples. Farmers aren't happy to hear this, because until five years ago, they were being told to clear out their sugarbushes, but it's pretty clear that a mixed stand will be healthier in the long run."

Coons is not swayed by such arguments. "If there is any evidence that pure maple stands are faring less well than mixed, unmanaged forests, I don't know of it. If the average maple bush is 40 or 50 acres, are you really talking about monoculture? We aren't telling people to go out and create thousands of continuous acres of pure maple. I don't think of a well-managed sugarbush surrounded by woods and farmland as a real case of monoculture."

Coons says that leaving maples in a crowded state—whether with other species or their own kind—means dramatically slower growth. "If you have a stand with a number of 5-inch diameter trees, you can decide if you want them to reach a tappable size within your lifetime or not."

2. Protection

"Keep the livestock out of your woods," says Coons. "They browse on the young maples, they compact the soil, they leave undesirable species like prickly ash to grow, and the sugarbush will eventually show

increased decay and mortality because of injuries caused to the trunks and roots."

Likewise, skidding logs out can wreak havoc where traffic moves over the exposed roots of maples. The appearance of decay several years later is a likely consequence. "Minimizing felling and skidding damage to remaining trees when thinning is a must to avoid tree-health problems a few years down the road," says Coons.

Coons and others say that the heaviest thinning should not be left too late, and that by selecting the future tapping trees when they are 3 to 5 inches in diameter, there is less potential damage to the bush and less chance of serious fungal attack.

3. Tap by the Book

"There are people out there who think, 'If this tree will hold a bucket without falling over, I can tap it,' but there are going to be serious consequences for this maple, over time. You cannot tap a tree under 10 inches in diameter without serious ramifications.

"The Ontario Tapping Rule has proved reliable in ensuring the continued health of sugar trees in sugarbushes where it has been in use for over 30 years. It is meant for commercial operations in healthy sugarbushes where the owner wants to maximize production without significantly risking the health of the trees."

Coons says that Ontario is sticking with these guidelines, despite a move to lighter tapping recommendations in some parts of the United States. "Tapping in accordance with these well-established guidelines has not been shown to reduce the lifespan of a healthy sugarbush. Naturally, landowners with severely stressed, unhealthy trees should tap more conservatively.

"People have to have realistic income expectations to keep sugaring, and I'm not sure how that works

ONTARIO TAPPING RULE

Tree Diameter	Number of Taps
10 - 14 inches	1
15 - 19 inches	2
20 - 24 inches	3
25 + inches	4

when someone recommends putting only one tap in a tree that is 14 to 18 inches in diameter and at one of the strongest and most effective production stages of its life."

STAND DEVELOPMENT

IN A WELL-MANAGED sugarbush, young trees are selected to become "crop trees" at least by visual criteria: in a group of trees of the same age, choose the tree that is tallest, has the widest and deepest crown, the most vigorous and with the fewest injuries or deformities of trunk or crown. In trees 12 inches in diameter, the stocking rate for crop trees will be about 64 maples per acre, with a distance of 25 to 30 feet between trees.

In addition, progressive sugarbush managers are also testing for sap sweetness when deciding which trees to save and which to thin. David Marvin, head of Butternut Mountain Farm in Johnson Vermont and a University of Vermont forestry graduate, begins the testing process early. He and his assistants get out in the young sugarbush during the tapping season and drill tiny sapholes (perhaps ⅛ inch in diameter). They withdraw a small amount of sap with a syringe and do an on-the-spot sweetness test with a hand-held refractometer. Trees with notably high- or low-sugar content are color-coded with Magic Markers for later thinning decisions.

Marvin says that a single acre of naturally seeded sugarbush may start out with 4,000 to 6,000 maple seedlings and, through a series of thinnings over a period of years, end up at 25 to 50 "crop" or permanent trees. Marvin is a staunch believer in selecting for the sweeter trees, and his dream is a sugar orchard full

of specimens like the tree he affectionately calls "Champion," his best maple, with a sap-sugar concentration in excess of 9 percent. "If I had 500 trees like this," he laughs, "I guess I'd be set for life."

Individual trees selected as crop trees are "released," if necessary, from shading competition. The chosen tree is generally encouraged to develop a large crown by cutting any competing trees whose branches touch its crown. (Such thinning must be done with care, however, and over a period of years. A severe thinning can be very stressful to a sugarbush, leading to bark damage from "sunscald" in the heat of the summer or during alternating freezing and thawing spells in late winter. It may also create large, sunny openings that invite weed growth, soil drying and "windthrow" or the toppling of trees exposed to high wind.)

As the trees mature, the selective thinning continues, always working to keep crown competition under control. Most sugarbushes are managed as virtual monoculture plots—that is, all non-sugar maples are thinned out. This practice is questioned by some, who feel that other tree species will help mitigate severe pest outbreaks (of both insects and fungi) that can be more serious when only a single crop is present to attack.

Coons doesn't share fears about creating a maple-only stand. "Sugar maple is a climax tree species, a long-lived tolerant tree that has, over the years, demonstrated its ability to survive as a monoculture. Problems can be managed when necessary, and greater production and efficiency of a pure maple stand far outweigh the risk."

There is good evidence that coniferous windbreaks can be highly beneficial to a sugarbush, creating a sheltered environment that fosters more rapid growth

TREE DIAMETER CLASSIFICATIONS

🍁

Term	Trunk Diameter
Seedling	Less than 1-inch
Sapling	1 to 4 inches
Pole	5 to 9 inches
Small Sawlog	10-14 inches
Medium Sawlog	15-19 inches
Large Sawlog	20 inches and over

Note: Diameter of stem or trunk at breast height (4.5 feet above ground).

How many buckets or taps per tree? The experts are at odds, with the most cautious now suggesting a maximum of two per tree, as practiced by some sugarmakers 50 or more years ago. Others, including Ontario's Clarence Coons, argue that a big, healthy maple such as this should be able to handle four buckets without overstressing or threatening the health of the tree.

and faster warming during the tapping season. One current recommendation is to leave (or plant) a 25-foot-wide windbreak of cedar, spruce or balsam fir along the sides exposed to prevailing winds. (An opposing view comes from those trying to minimize rodent damage to tubing systems. Some are removing any cone- or nut-bearing trees in or near the sugarbush to discourage squirrels from settling in.)

Old sugarbushes or those with large open areas can be rehabilitated, and a professional forester's advice is highly recommended.

Similarly, expert advice may be needed if insect or fungal attacks appear serious. Insect species that feed on sugar maples are legion, and each year there are

problem outbreaks somewhere in the tree's range.

Among the foes are forest tent caterpillars, fall cankerworms, Bruce spanworms, greenstriped mapleworms, maple leafcutters, gypsy moths, pear thrips (which only recently targeted sugar maples as a food source) and saddled prominent caterpillars. For the most part, the sugar maple is a hardy tree that survives without human intervention.

In some cases, however, severe defoliation can threaten large acreages of trees, and spraying will be recommended. Two or three years of successive defoliation can seriously weaken or kill a maple. In 1981, a large number of maples in Delaware County, Pennsylvania, were killed in a single season by tent caterpillars that ate the terminal buds of the trees' branches. Fortunately, for those who choose to spray, there are now effective biological pesticides for most of these defoliators.

FERTILIZERS

ONGOING TESTS on liming and fertilizing sugarbushes may or may not result in recommendations to correct soil deficiencies and imbalances. Dr. Robert Long of the U.S. Forest Service in Ohio says that there are now some reasonably encouraging results emerging from 10-year tests in which lime was applied to sugarbushes with stressed or declining maples. Lime works to bring acidity in the soil down, among other things, and where soils are low in buffering capacity and calcium, liming may have the potential to reverse maple decline. However, at this writing, liming has yet to be recommended for widespread use, and most sugarmakers have adopted a wait-and-see attitude on the questions of sugarbush liming and fertilization.

Arch Jones of Macdonald College in Quebec says that positive results have been obtained by fertilizing declining maples in some areas of that province. "The problem is that we can't give blanket guidelines the way we can advise farmers on fertilizing a crop of trefoil. In some areas calcium is deficient, in others, potassium or manganese. Testing the soil in a woodlot is very tricky, and if you take four samples around the same tree, you may get four very different results."

Jones says the best method of determining if mineral imbalances exist is to take foliage samples in midsummer for lab analysis. Deficiencies that show up in the leaves can then be remedied by fertilizer applications. "Down in Franklin County (a southwestern Quebec area bordering northern New York State and long famous for making high-quality syrup), some of the producers have taken things in their own hands and started fertilizing individual trees with manures—particularly chicken, which is high in potassium—and wood ashes from their evaporators. They are convinced it's having a positive effect."

Jones is quick to caution that commercial fertilizer should only be applied on a case-by-case basis, with the treatment tailored to the site. He and others note that feeding trees the wrong supplement can backfire and harm the trees. For trees under his own care at the Morgan Arboretum in St. Anne de Bellevue, Quebec, Jones prescribed an ongoing fertilization program and believes it has helped preserve the health of the collection, which includes prize specimens of every native tree species found in Canada.

Sumner Williams of Vermont's Proctor Maple Research Center suggests that any landowner with evidence of maple decline in a sugarbush contact his or her local county forester. If the trees were his own, he says he would try to get soil and foliar tests done to help chart a course of action and would reduce tapping on stressed trees.

Diseases and attacks by fungi that cause root rot and cankers, among other things, may need expert attention. The most common remedies are preventive: removing afflicted trees and generally keeping the sugarbush thinned and vigorous, with trees of various ages present at all times.

MARAUDERS

GRAZING ANIMALS, as well as rampaging all-terrain vehicles, four-wheel-drive cowboys and snowmobile joyriders, should be kept out of the sugarbush—or at least confined to the main through trails.

Deer, mice and porcupines have all done considerable damage in sugarbushes from time to time, but the need for control measures is usually judged on a case-by-case basis. Mice and porcupines can girdle maples, leading to sure death. In some sugarbushes, mouseproof mesh must be wrapped around the base of young trees, and a den of porcupines with a taste for maple may have to be eliminated. ❧

CHAPTER 2

GLOOSKAP'S LEGACY

The origins & history of sugarmaking

"I F YOU WOULD NOT BE FORGOTTEN," Benjamin Franklin once opined, "either write things worth the reading . . . or do things worth the writing." Sadly, the discoverer of the maple tree's sweet potential, while richly deserving to be remembered, lived in a time and place when greatness was recorded not on paper or stone but rather in evanescent oral remembrances. Even the deeds most worthy of being remembered eventually faded with the passing of time and of the gray-haired storytellers who tried to keep them alive, vanishing up into the smoke of campfires that illuminated their telling centuries or millennia ago.

So it is that maple sugar is one of the curious and controversial legacies of a culture without a written record, a culture that may well have included the American Indian equivalent of a Ben Franklin, an inventive genius known throughout the land for his or her wonderful knowledge of the botanical world and the ability to extract delicious foods from it. Without written documents to guide us, however, we are left to speculate about the unknown discoverer of maple syrup and sugar. Was the first sugarmaker a hero who turned the desperate, hungry end of winter into a month of extraordinary sweetness and reawakened

Native sugaring in the early 1600s, as imagined by an engraver in Europe, **left,** *and re-created by Penobscot sugarmakers at a Vermont maple theme park in the 1920s.*

hope for the coming spring? Or, as many have speculated, was it a hungry child, an accident-prone cook or a curious hunter who, accidentally and anonymously, gave us the wonderful legacy of maple?

MYTHOLOGY

WHAT WE DO KNOW is that the origins of sugaring on the North American continent go so far back into prehistory that, by the time the first Europeans arrived with quill pens and foolscap, oil paints and canvas, to begin the written and illustrated history of this land, the natives could only say that maple sugar came from a time so long past that its origins had been lost in the misty beginnings of the ancient tribes.

In place of fact, however, a myth about maple had crystallized with astonishing universality among the Indian tribes of the Eastern Woodlands, in which the Creator had at first made life altogether too easy for his People, filling the maple trees with a thick syrup that flowed year-round. (Much, in fact, as the denizens of urban America still believe it runs today.)

According to the legend, one day the mischief-making young Glooskap (variously known, from tribe to tribe, as Gluscabi, Kulóscap, Manabozho, Odzihózo or Djokábesh) happens along and finds a village of his People strangely silent. The cooking fires are dead. The gardens are overgrown with weeds. The dogs don't bark and no children run out to greet him. Glooskap finally discovers the villagers in their maple grove, and there they lie—men, women, children and dogs—eyes closed, letting the delectable syrup drip from the trees into their contented mouths.

Having special powers, which he is occasionally known to misuse, Glooskap brings fresh water from the lake in a birchbark bucket and, rising above the trees, fills them until the syrup runs thin and fast.

"Rise up, People," Glooskap calls out. "The trees are no longer filled with the maple syrup the Creator gave to you. Now there is only this watery sap and it will soon run dry. You will have to hunt and fish and

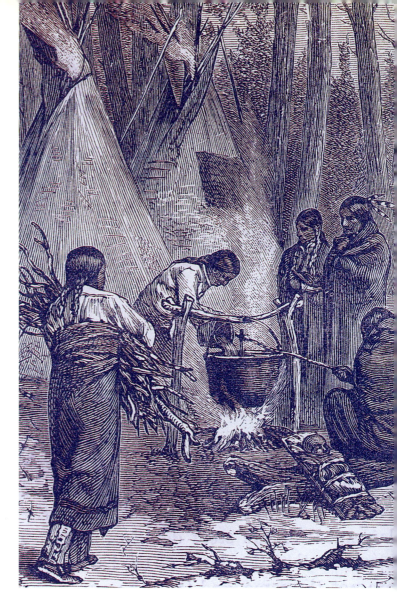

After contact with white traders, native sugarmakers, as in this scene from the Canadian backwoods in the late 1800s, quickly adopted iron and copper kettles, but continued to tap and catch sap with the traditional method shown.

go back to growing your corn and beans and squash.

"The sap will run again, but only at the end of winter when game is scarce and the lake is still frozen and no crops grow. Then you can gather the sap in birchbark vessels like mine. You will have to gather firewood and heat round stones from the river and drop them into the sap to make it boil. It will turn to syrup, but not for a long time.

"You will no longer be fat and lazy. You will once again appreciate this maple syrup that the Creator gave to you. This is how it is going to be," says Glooskap. And that, as the native storytellers still say, is how it is for all of us to this very day.

Unfortunately, for those who would like less fanciful evidence of maple sugaring before the arrival of the first European explorers and missionaries, very little exists. Historians trying to make sense of the earliest records of maple sugaring have long been frustrated by a scarcity of archeological findings—the moist, acidic soils of the Eastern Woodlands tend to consume rather than preserve artifacts. Once-great Iroquoian communities, with huge longhouses and moated, castlelike wooden palisades, are now mere mold stains buried in the earth, requiring exquisite care and patience to unearth and interpret. Add to this the complete lack of written records before the arrival of the first white observers and we have a situation in which almost anyone can put forward a theory about how sugaring got its start.

A number of Canadians, especially, are partial to the notion that the first sugarmaker was *Tamiasciurus*

hudsonicus, the common red squirrel, which is known to seek out tender, thin-skinned maple branches in late winter. With a sharp-toothed nip, the squirrel can create deep bite wounds that, with the right weather conditions, freely ooze sap. Those who have observed this curious behavior say that the squirrels range from tree to tree, creating a tapline of wounded maples. They return after their tapholes have had a chance to exude sap, which dries quickly on the outer bark, leaving a crust of sugar that the animals eat with obvious relish. From watching the squirrel, the theory goes, some unknown native hunter or gatherer, hungry after a long winter, was inspired to adapt the sugary harvest to a human scale.

REALITY?

A TINY BUT VOCAL group of academics currently led by Carol I. Mason, a University of Wisconsin (Fox Valley) anthropology professor, argues that the first sugarmakers were neither animals nor native peoples, but rather French explorers or missionaries who, spotting the sweet potential of maple sap, taught the Indians to boil it in iron and copper kettles to make syrup and sugar. Mason and others who have advanced this controversial scenario say that the native Micmacs, Iroquoians, Hurons, Ojibway, Abenaki and others in the heart of maple country drank maple sap but did not have the technology (metal pots) or the motivation (an appetite or market for syrup or sugar) to make maple products until the Europeans, with their fondness for sucrose, arrived.

"Bunk," says sugarmaker Don Harlow of Putney, Vermont, whose sugarhouse sits just above a tremendous fertile plain in the Connecticut River Valley where eighteenth-century historians say the Abenaki fished, hunted, planted their crops and gathered each spring to tap the maples.

"Anyone who's spent time in these woods in sugaring season knows that icicles form where winter storms have broken branches in the maples," says

For Eastern Woodland native families, spring meant a return to the ancestral sugar camps where bark sap buckets, stirring paddles and other sugarmaking tools were stored year-round in birchbark shelters. Kettles were often buried for safekeeping.

Harlow. "Ask any kid who's tasted one of these and you have your answer: they taste wonderful, especially if you haven't been getting a lot of sweets." He, along with the vast majority of maple historians, believes that the natives who foraged in these forests would have known very well that the maples provided a toothsome harvest each spring and that they would have made the most of this special gift.

Harlow, who is as famous for his syrup as for his Yankee yarns, believes a giant old maple on his property is 450 years old and bears scars that prove it was tapped by the farm's first settlers—and the native people before them.

"There was a Capt. John Kathen down in Massachusetts around 1750 who heard about this thing called 'sugar from a tree' that the Abenaki Indians were making," Harlow relates. "So he sent his son

Alexander Kathen up the Connecticut River by boat to see it being made—and there's a hint, if he came by boat and the ice was out of the river, it was too late for sugaring. Well, he found the Indians all right, and the next year he came back overland when there was still snow and ice and he was there for the sugaring. When he got back home, he told of them getting 10 pounds of sugar from one tree. My son says this proves at least one thing: sugarmakers exaggerated back then just like we do today.

"Well, this happened right here at Kathen Meadows. You can see where they chopped at the trees to get the sap flowing." The Harlows' farm is just up from the great bottomlands and near the land where the Kathen family supposedly established Vermont's first "sugar orchard" around 1764.

Now gnarled and having lost much of its crown, the

huge, misshapen old maple tree seems to offer testimony to Harlow's homespun history: it bears massive amounts of scar tissue from about waist height to about 10 feet up the trunk, suggestive of the tomahawk and axe tapping the Eastern Woodland Indians and the earliest settlers were known to practice. "We're kind of proud of this tree," he says. "We like to think that it was right here that sugaring was discovered. If only that tree could talk."

For as long as mankind has sugared, storytellers and fireside historians have tried to reconstruct the discovery of maple's sweetness, and perhaps the most widely known account appeared in the April 1896 issue of *The Atlantic Monthly*.

The author was a country intellectual from Vermont named Rowland E. Robinson, who had a reputation among a highly critical citizenry for the accuracy of his accounts of natural history, the folk arts of the early settlers and the ways of the Algonquins who had only recently retreated from their lands. Robinson reported that the Indians gathered sap from gashes in the maples or from broken branches, collecting it in boxy birchbark pails and boiling it in earthenware "kokhs, or pots, some of which had a capacity of several gallons."

In *The Atlantic* article he elaborated on a discovery myth, crediting an Indian woman named Moqua, who was more interested in her porcupine-quill embroidery than the prime cut of moose she was simmering in water for her spouse, the "mighty hunter Woksis."

According to Robinson's detailed and imaginative account, it was not the best of days for Moqua, who boiled her pot dry not once but twice, the second time after hurriedly deciding that she had no time to melt snow and instead refilled the kokh with maple sap she had been collecting—for use as a beverage—from the giant tree behind their wigwam.

Rather than flying into a rage when he found his dinner sitting in a pool of dark, thick goo in the bottom of an apparently burned pot, Woksis tasted the meat and syrup and was instantly transfixed. "His face shone with an expression of supreme content-

ment and enjoyment," Robinson wrote. "With wonder she watched him devour the last morsel, but her wonder was greater when she saw him deliberately break the earthenware pot and lick the last vestige of spoiled cookery from the shards. . . .

" 'Let me embrace thee!' he cried, and upon his lips she tasted the first maple sugar.

"The discovery was made public, and kokhs of sap were presently boiling in every wigwam. All were so anxious to get every atom of the precious sweet that they broke the kokhs and scraped the pieces, just as Woksis, the first sugar-eater, had done. And that is why there are so many fragments of broken pottery, and so few whole vessels to be found."

A CURIOUS CASE

JACQUES CARTIER is credited by some historians for the first recorded sighting of maples in the account of his third voyage to Canada in 1540. As early as 1557, André Thevet, the "Royal Cosmographer of France," was probably referring to earlier expeditions of Cartier when he wrote:

"For a long time it was thought that these trees were fit for nothing. . . . One day, however, someone cut down one of them and found that the sap which poured forth from it possessed a fine taste resembling that of one of the good wines of Orleans or Beaune. A number of our party, including the Captain and other gentlemen of this company, once they had the experience pronounced it delicious, so much so that in an hour they filled four or five large pots with sap. I leave it to you to imagine how zealously the Canadians, much liking the drink I have described, now care for these trees in order to make it, inasmuch as it is of surpassing excellence."

This reference is perplexing in the extreme. Who is the "someone" who cut down the tree? Why does he exaggerate the taste of maple sap, which, before boiling or freezing, is virtually flavorless with only a vague hint of sweetness? Thevet's own editors have suggested that he often embellished stories told to

him by Cartier and possibly fabricated others. Most scholars accept Thevet's "someone" as a native and credit the Indians with showing the French their native wealth. Anthropologist Carol Mason takes an opposing stance and says that this and other accounts "do not specifically refer to Indians at all.

"In the earliest accounts of the sixteenth century,

the French, like the Indians, used maple sap as a drink," she has written. "By the mid to late seventeenth century, maple sugar was being described, and Europeans were beginning to hear about it as a new and curious phenomenon." Mason cites two travelers, Pierre Esprit Radisson and Nicholas Perrot, who moved among the native tribes in the Midwest in the

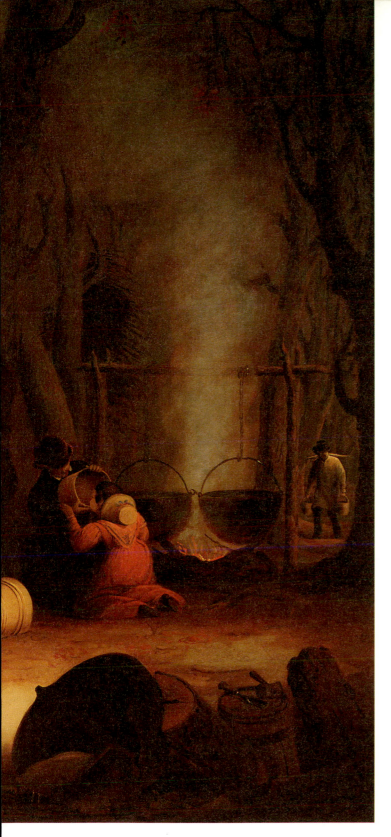

"The dog did nothing in the night-time."

"That was the curious incident," remarked Sherlock Holmes.

Mason says: "It is difficult to understand how Perrot could have missed sugaring had it been present; he is one of those dogs that did nothing in the night, and he has to be answered before anything can be said about the aboriginality of maple sugaring." Mason theorizes that the Europeans were probably guilty "of pushing an addictive, consumable resource" on the hapless natives.

Anthropologist James F. Pendergast of the National Museums of Canada has strenuously argued the case for the native origin of maple sugar, in part using a letter that Sherlock Holmes would have found most appropriate, as it was written in London for delivery to botanist John Ray, eminent author of *Historia Plantarum*, at his country house in Black Notley:

London
March 10, 1684

Dear Sir,

I have enclosed you some sugar of the first boiling got from the juice of the wounded maple: Mr. Aston, Secretary of the Royal Society, presented it to me. 'Twas sent from Canada, where the natives prepare it from the said juice; eight pints commonly yielding a pound of sugar. The Indians have practiced it time out of mind; the French began to refine it; and to turn it to advantage. If you have any of these trees by you, could you not make the trial proceeding as with the sugar cane?

—Dr. Robinson

Without Holmes and Watson to rush off to Black Notley to question Ray, Pendergast and others offer numerous timely accounts to refute Mason. In 1606,

seventeenth century and who, apparently, did not mention maple sugar being eaten. Mason then recites several lines from a Sherlock Holmes mystery by Sir Arthur Conan Doyle:

"Is there any point to which you would draw my attention?"

"To the curious incident of the dog in the night."

Marc Lescarbot's *Histoire de la Nouvelle France* noted: "If they [the Indians] are pressed by thirst, they draw juice from trees and distil a sweet and very agreeable liquid, which I have tasted several times." This flies in the face of Mason's contention that only sap was consumed; "distil" clearly implies a manufacturing process, usually involving heat and boiling.

Various other references are variations on this British Royal Society paper from 1685: "The Savages of Canada, in the time that the sap rises, in the Maple, make an incision in the Tree, by which it runs out; and after they have evaporated eight pounds of the liquor, there remains one pound as sweet . . . . The Savages have practiced this Art longer than any now living among them can remember."

While archeologists have interpreted sites in Michigan as Late Woodland prehistoric sugaring camps, Mason says there is no physical proof that sugarmaking was done there. She ignores the fact that maple sugar could have meant life or death to societies having had 10,000 years, since the end of the Ice Age, to learn the virtues of every root, bark, berry and living thing in the Eastern Woodlands. Indeed,

their pharmacopoeia astonished some early European visitors, who carried a number of herbal remedies home with them. These tribes were accomplished at cooking with hot rocks, boiling liquids in vessels made of bark, pottery and hollowed logs. Various reports also describe the natives allowing the sugar to concentrate by evaporation and by removing ice from collected sap each morning, the ice being mostly water. (To show that maple syrup could be made with prehistoric methods, Margaret Holman and Kathryn Egan of the Michigan State University Museum performed a series of experiments in 1985. Using a variety of techniques, including freezing and boiling, they succeeded, finding that birchbark trays and heated rocks made an effective combination that produced syrup almost as quickly as did metal pots on a kitchen range. Narrow-mouthed ceramic pots did not work well, and the researchers say that looking for pottery boiling pots as proof of sugaring may be a mistake.)

One early settler named James Smith, who was taken prisoner by the Caughnawagas, wrote in 1756 of their sugaring practices in what is now Ohio. Starting in February, the small band made more than 100 elm-bark vessels that would hold about two gallons each. In addition, they constructed, near the boiling fires, 100-gallon bark tanks. "In the sugar tree they cut a notch, sloping down, and at the end of the notch stuck a tomahawk. In the place where they had stuck the tomahawk, they drove a long chip, in order to carry the sap out of the tree. Under this they set their vessels to receive it."

Closer to the major French trade routes down the St. Lawrence, a Jesuit Father named Sebastien Rasles spent time among the Abenaki in the 1690s and made this observation: "It is curious to know that the

Early settlers at first made few changes in the rustic techniques of native sugarmakers, and the syrup and sugar they produced was dark and strongly flavored.

Entitled "An American Forest Scene," this Currier & Ives print catches the quintessential spirit of traditional sugarmaking: the entire family gets involved and the sweet clouds of steam invariably attract friends, neighbors and curious passersby.

method of extracting the bayberry wax and making maple sugar, articles of considerable importance to us, has been learned of the aborigines." Rasles said the sugar was mixed with cornmeal broth to make it more palatable and noted: "There is no lack of sugar in these woods."

Further to the south, Robert Beverley's 1722 account of the early history of Virginia notes that the English, like the French, learned sugarmaking from the natives. "The Sugar-Tree yields a kind of Sap or Juice, which by boiling is made into Sugar. This juice is drawn out, by wounding the Trunk of the Tree, and placing a Receiver under the Wound. It is said, that the Indians made on[e] Pound of Sugar, out of eight Pounds of the Liquor. Some of this sugar I examined very carefully. It was bright and moist, with a large full Grain; the Sweetness of it being like that

of good Muscovada. Though this discovery has not been made by the English above 28 or 30 years; yet it has been known among the Indians before the English settled there."

Other sojourners through Indian country came away with an appreciation for the taste of maple and its myriad uses, which they likened to the European reliance on salt to improve the flavor of many foods. They also reported the consumption of prodigious amounts of maple sugar, especially in the food-scarce months of early spring. "We hunted and fished," wrote Alexander Henry of his time in Canada from 1760 to 1776, "yet sugar was our principal food during the whole month of April. On the mountain, we ate nothing but our sugar . . . each man consumed a pound a day, desired no other food, and was visibly nourished by it." Another observer reported a band of

1,500 Menominee Indians who made "almost 90 tons of sugar" virtually all it for their own use, or 120 pounds per person. (The current North American consumption of cane, beet and corn sugars and sweeteners is estimated at 137 pounds per capita.)

Further evidence of the antiquity of native sugarmaking is found in the language and rituals of the various tribes from the mouth of the St. Lawrence to the headwaters of the Great Lakes. The time of sugaring was widely known as the Maple Moon or the Sugar Moon (the Iroquois called it Sopomakwin)—the first full moon of the sap-running season in March or April—and the Maple Dance is still practiced by some members of the old Iroquois Confederation.

"Other evidence is linguistic," writes Virgil J. Vogel, author of *The Blackout of Native American Cultural Achievements*. The Algonquins called maple sugar Sinzibuckwud (meaning "drawn from wood"), while the Cree used the variant Sisibaskwat.

"Generally the Northeast Woodland tribes had separate terms for maple sugar and the white man's cane sugar," says Vogel, who cites entirely different terms for the two in Montagnais, Menominee, Cree, Winnebago and Ojibwa. In 1634, Jesuit missionary Paul Le Jeune reported that the natives had coined their own term for white sugar: "French snow."

Vogel draws attention to two predecessors of Carol Mason—Felix Keesing and Reginal Flannery—who wrote separate papers in 1939 arguing that there was no evidence for native sugarmaking.

Vogel says the art of downplaying native contributions to modern North American culture is not restricted to maple, but has notorious counterparts in the development of herbal medicine, the cultivation of corn and the use of crop fertilizers.

"Not only are Indian achievements overlooked, they are specifically denied even in the face of overwhelming evidence of their reality," says Vogel. "So pervasive is this practice that it is difficult to avoid suspicion that it is often motivated, consciously or not, by ethnocentric arrogance. It is not necessary to exaggerate Indian achievements. Their demonstra-

ble attainments are enough to place their intelligence and adaptability beyond doubt. If their technology in some ways was behind Europe's, we can say that Europe's was, in turn, only a few centuries before the invasion of America, similar to what they later encountered in America. A few centuries is but a moment in the time span of human development."

Vogel also offers the ultimate challenge to Mason and others: produce a single record of any native conceding the discovery of maple sugar to the white newcomers. Given the explorers' penchant for braggadocio, one would also expect Mason to produce many and detailed accounts of the French teaching the natives to make sugar. The early European explorers of North America, fiercely determined to find wonders and riches worthy of their patrons' investments, would surely have sung their own praises vigorously and frequently.

We give the last word on the subject to a Kickapoo chief who was confronted on the same issue in 1823: "Can it be that thou art so simple as to ask me such a question, seeing that the Master of Life has imported to us an instinct which enables us to substitute stone hatchets and knives for those made of steel by the whites? Wherefore should we not have known as well how to manufacture sugar?"

LES HABITANTS

Speaking of the conquest and colonization of the New World, historian Francis Parkman once wrote: "The Spanish slaughtered the Indians, the English pushed them away, and the French embraced them." While France's colonies in Quebec were small and slow-growing compared to those of the English further south, the early, close contact with the natives may have given the French settlers, known as *habitants,* an advance start in sugarmaking.

While many of early French visitors came either to trade for furs or to convert souls, those who attempted to live off the land rather quickly found themselves mimicking native ways. The soils and climate forced them to grow the same crops and hunt the same game the Indians had come to depend upon. Baron Louis de La Hontan, who visited Quebec in the spring of 1684, reported that the food of the French-Canadian settlers was bountiful and varied, but nothing like the table fare common in France: Moose, porcupine, rabbit and beaver were the mainstay meats; pigeon, partridge and waterfowl were their poultry; corn, oats, beans, peas and barley served as staple starches; maple sugar was their sweet.

Another observer noted that the average land concession was 80 acres, of which two-thirds was commonly left as woodlot with maple trees carefully spared the axe to provide "*sirop*" and "*sucre de érable.*" In preserving the sugar trees, the French were a century ahead of the British colonists who would settle to the south.

In a historical tract published in 1912 by the Vermont Maple Sugar Makers' Association, both Indians and French Canadians were credited with passing on the secrets of sugarmaking: "Along with maize and tobacco, maple sugar had its origin among the Indians. The various tribes of Canada, Vermont, New Hampshire, Massachusetts, Connecticut, New York, Pennsylvania, Ohio and Michigan all knew of this art. Where ever the white people came in contact with the Indians in a region where the maple tree grew, they found them making this delicious sweet, and it was from them the white man learned the process."

The same book makes a rather dramatic assertion, given the pride Vermonters take in their own sugarmaking history: "The first white people to make maple sugar were the Canadians. For a hundred years

Open-air sugarmaking as practiced by American and Canadian colonists until late in the nineteenth century, with even the family dog begging a taste.

or more the methods of production remained without material change, save the substitution of iron or copper kettles for vessels of clay or bark, and the use of better utensils."

"Indian melasses" and "Indian sugar" were frequently mentioned in the diaries of the early settlers in various regions, and maple became the household sweetener throughout the Canadian and American colonies. White sugar, when available, was extremely expensive. Maple was free for the making, and sugaring season came at a time of year when other agricultural pursuits were at a standstill. Several weeks of concerted effort could fill the pantry with hard, easily stored sugar cakes for the year ahead, to be chunked down as needed or broken loose with an augerlike forged tool called a sugar devil. This trove of sweetness came entirely from the family's own toil and teamwork—an unusually quick and satisfying harvest compared to the growing of most crops and the husbanding of sheep and other domestic livestock. If maple sugar proved a salvation in lean years and the only easily obtained sweet in the wilderness, it was a natural gift almost squandered in the Yankee colonies.

MAN VS. MAPLE

FOR SEA-WEARY SETTLERS arriving in the early American colonies, there was little time to quibble over the origins of sugar or anything else; survival was the first matter at hand, and the view from the boats as they landed was terrifying. Trees came right down to the water, trees covered the land as far as the eye could see—trees bigger and more intimidating than any they had ever seen. In Europe, the forests had been cleared and tamed and claimed by private landowners for centuries. This was a jungle—a jungle filled with mosquitoes, snakes, carnivorous bears, panthers and savage men with bows and arrows. Clearings were few and far between, and the first order of business was to move back the trees.

Felling the virgin forests, in fact, give the settlers in the American colonies an instant economic base, selling timber for shipbuilding and construction in Britain and getting ready cash for burning the giant hardwoods and turning their ashes into potash. In 1751, the British Parliament passed an "Act for encouraging the making of Pott Ashes and Pearl Ashes in the British Plantations in America" and coincidentally gave maple sugaring its first big boost. The potash was urgently needed to make soap for a burgeoning wool industry, as well as for making gunpowder, glass, fertilizer and bleach. The big iron

A hand-tinted photograph shows sugarmaking "Ye Ancient Way"—and also records the scorched-earth look of the denuded New England countryside in the late 1800s.

kettles that became essential equipment for potash making on every piece of settled land also served perfectly for boiling maple sap.

"Carry with you wherever you go a large kettle, in which you may make maple sugar in summer and potash in winter," urged one written flyer aimed at new settlers in 1789. "The Process [of making potash] is easy; the Expence Small; the Profit certain," touted another.

Potash became known as black gold, and the trees believed to be the best sources were maple, hickory, elm, black ash, basswood and beech. Using water to leach lye out of ashes, the settlers then concentrated caustic black potash in the big kettles.

"Most all the money they had around here from the 1760s to 1812 came from potash," an old Vermonter is quoted as telling author Ruth Rasey Simpson in *Hand-Hewn in Old Vermont*. "After the War (of

1812), they had two or three spells of making potash again, but it didn't last."

If the potash trade gave sugaring a boost, it also threatened to end any possibility of a maple industry enduring in New England. A tremendous influx of British colonists had begun with the signing of the Treaty of Paris in 1763, which ended the French and Indian War and unleashed a wave of settlement and tree-cutting that denuded much of the eastern United States in a matter of decades. Seeing that clearing was taking a toll unimagined when the first axes began nibbling at the edges of the massive forest, far-sighted farmers began to urge their fellow landowners to spare the maples and even to start replanting to repair the devastation done. Consider that a state like Vermont had gone from an unsullied wilderness in 1760 to three-quarters denuded by 1850, and the worst environmental records of Third World rainforest countries come to mind.

Fortunately, urgent warnings to "save your maples" gained attention, and many woodlots and sugar-bushes were spared. Early spring everywhere in the colonies saw pillars of maple steam rising from the big black kettles. Even today, octogenarians still carry fond memories of being able to see dozens of "steams" from the vantage point of their own sugarhouses.

The earliest settlers almost exactly mimicked the Indian method of tapping. The trees were slashed, or "boxed," with a diagonal or "V" cut made to create a heavy flow of sap. Then a stiff piece of birchbark, a quill or a thin splint of wood was inserted at the bottom of the wound to carry the sap out and away from the tree. From there, it dripped into a hollowed-out length of log set at the base of the maple.

The gathered sap was carried to a big kettle suspended over an open fire, where boiling was done in big batches, with cold sap, ashes, bits of bark, lichen, sap moths and rainwater all freely entering the thickening mass. The molten sugar was pronounced done when a looped twig dipped into the syrup and blown upon yielded a long, sticky bubble. As is done today, the other test involved drizzling the hot syrup on snow to see if it formed taffy, or jack wax.

At this stage, of course, syrup turns to sugar when it cools, and this was exactly the intent of the boilers. Syrup was devilishly tricky to keep, so except for what was eaten during the sugaring season and immediately after, the entire crop was made into caked sugar, which was easily stored in the pioneer pantry. (Some granulated or "grain sugar" was also made, according to Indian custom, by diligently stirring the hot syrup as it cooled and crystallized.)

With virtually no market for the product, most homesteads at first were producing sugar almost exclusively for their own needs and for bartering. (Mother England and Mother France never showed much interest in maple sugar, having a newly created abundance of white cane sugar flowing in from the Caribbean.)

Yankee ingenuity may be a cliché, but during the formative years of the sugaring industry, it was in its unfettered glory. Almost immediately, the inventive sugarmakers began to devise new tools and methods. Wooden buckets replaced the heavy sap-catching troughs. The Shakers, renowned for their woodworking skills, turned out beautifully crafted white pine buckets by the thousands, and many remained in annual use well into the twentieth century.

Round and half-round spiles, or spouts, began to appear (gashing the trees was termed "barbarous" around 1800) and tapholes drilled with simple augers made the old methods obsolete. The first augers were huge by today's standards, often 1¼ inches or more in diameter. As sugarmakers experimented, the holes got smaller and smaller, allowing the maples to heal faster. Sugarmaking gradually gained in sophistication, and a sense of stewardship began to develop in the maple bush; the settlers could see how slowly the sugar maple grew, and began to appreciate that this was a resource that would not be replaced overnight.

The wooden sap yoke came in sizes for men, women and children and preceded gathering tubs, sleds and wagons.

Boiling innovations came at a slower pace, mainly with the use of kettles in graduated sizes. By about 1790, progressive sugarmakers used three kettles. The cold sap always started in the largest kettle for the initial boiling, was moved to the medium-sized vessel for further thickening and then finished in the smallest kettle. Wool blankets served as filters for the hot syrup.

These were the heady days following the American Revolution, and in hopes of cutting all dependence on Mother England, a number of visionaries saw maple sugar as the perfect homegrown replacement for white cane sugar from the British sugar islands.

A confidante of Thomas Jefferson and fellow signer of the Declaration of Independence was Dr. Benjamin Rush, a controversial Philadelphia physician who wrote as his own epitaph: "He aimed well." Although cast as a black sheep among the American Revolutionaries for his verbal attacks on George Washington, Rush was a humanitarian and ardent foe of slavery. Deploring the conditions of African slaves on the Caribbean sugar plantations, he urged the young United States to declare its independence of this tainted sugar that a French traveler in 1788 had branded "a product washed with the tears and blood of slaves."

"No more knowledge is necessary for making this sugar than is required to make soap, cyder, beer, sour crout, etc., and yet one or all of these are in most of the farm houses of the United States," said Rush in 1892. "The kettles and other utensils of a farmer's kitchen will serve most of the purposes of making sugar, and the time required for the labor (if it deserve that name) is at a season when it is impossible for the farmer to employ himself in any species of agriculture."

Thomas Jefferson, who visited Bennington, Vermont, in 1791 to greet the country's newest state, was so impressed with the prospects of a serious maple industry that he ordered 60 saplings to start his own sugarbush at Monticello. Writing to George Washington, he waxed enthusiastic about the maples and about a quantity of olive-tree seedlings he was also about to have planted. He believed the country might become self-sufficient in sugar and oil by encouraging these crops. Unfortunately, while Jefferson and Washington both tried to establish sugar orchards on their Virginia plantations, the trees failed to flourish, and the short-lived belief that maple could become a major national industry became known as the "maple sugar bubble." (According to Monticello's horticulturist Peter Hatch, the last of Jefferson's sugar maples, probably from a planting that he had done in 1798, died in July 1992, having reached a diameter of 5 feet.)

Graphically contrasting former slaves and free maple producers, a sugar license from the early 1890s represents the U.S. government's failed attempt to manage production.

Jefferson, Rush and others misjudged two factors at the time of their enthusiasm for sugar independence: The sugar maple needs the seasonal freezing and thawing conditions of a northern spring to produce well. Although maple sugar has been made in at least 30 states, its production in warmer latitudes is unpredictable at best. The idealists also underestimated the mass-production capacities of the tropical sugar producers, whose giant cane presses and ruthless use of black laborers would have made the most serious of maple operations seem a Sunday picnic by comparison. Cane sugar, even after slavery was abolished in most of the Caribbean in the 1830s, was a commodity whose price would prove all too competitive for the maple producers.

Still, passions ran high in the States, and maple sugar was clearly the moral choice for many in the late eighteenth and early nineteenth century.

In a letter written in 1790, a Pennsylvania sugar-maker named William Cooper spoke of the good income his maple trees provided, then elaborated on the relative purity, both ethical and practical, of maple sugar:

"It has moreover other things in its favor to recommend it in preference to the sugar which is imported from the West-India Islands. It is made by the hands of freemen, and at a season of the year when not a single insect exists to mix with and pollute it; whereas the West-India sugar is the product of the unwilling labour of negro slaves, and made in a climate and in a season of the year, in which insects of all kinds abound, all of whom feed upon and mix with the sugar, so that the best India sugar may be looked upon as a composition consisting of the juice of the cane—and of the juices or excretions of ants, pismires, cockroaches, borers, fleas, mosquitoes, spiders, bugs, grasshoppers, flies, lizards; and twenty other West-India insects. To these ingredients is added the sweat of the negroes, and when they are angry, nobody knows what else."

SWORDS TO EVAPORATORS

JEFFERSON IS REPORTED to have served maple sugar at his influential tables at Monticello and the White House, and remained a maple booster, using it in his own coffee and urging others to plant trees: "I have never seen a reason why every farmer should not have a sugar orchard, as well as an apple orchard. The supply of sugar for his family would require as little ground, and the process of making it as easy as that of cider."

The production of this homespun sweet continued to grow, and the heightening of emotions before the American Civil War once again boosted demands for sugar produced by free men. The year 1860 marked the historical peak of maple production in North America. Curiously, it was the invention of the tin can during the Civil War that gave maple sugaring its second major technological boost, its first being the arrival of iron kettles more than two centuries before. According to John Record, today's general manager of the G.H. Grimm Company, the sudden availability of sheet metal, produced by the same rollers developed to make cans, marked the dawning of the maple-equipment industry.

The first metal sap spout was patented by Eli Mosher of Flushing, Michigan, in 1860, touching off a race to create the perfect spout that continues even today. Metal sap pails and lids would follow, but it was the evaporator that blossomed most impressively at the hands of tinsmiths and sheet-metal craftsmen. Realizing that sap could be evaporated much more quickly from a shallow, open pan than from a deep kettle, various tinkerers began fabricating flat pans and placing them over stone or brick fireboxes. Between 1858 and 1863, D.M. Cook of Ohio received four patents for evaporating pans.

Examples of these primitive evaporators can still be seen in various maple museums, and some of the ear-

Replacing the cumbersome outdoor kettles, evaporators meant faster boiling, cleaner sugar and a roof overhead.

lier models were little more than wooden-sided boxes with sheet-metal bottoms. In 1864, *The Canada Farmer* from Toronto offered plans for a simple 3-foot-by-6-foot pan that, it estimated, could be made by any blacksmith for $3.22 in materials.

The same paper later reported that a Norwich, Ontario, maple producer came back from visiting some State Fairs in the States with the notion of using design ideas from the makers of sorghum syrup evaporators. As a major improvement over the simple flat pan, the inventor used a concept of channeling the boiling sap around a series of baffles, making it flow in a back-and-forth ribbon pattern as it made its way through the pan. Some sugarmakers adopted a system using one very long channeled pan—20-footers can

Boiling sap in improved evaporator. Making Maple sugar.

evaporator pan and shaped it over a length of railway track to form deep crimps or ridges. The increased surface area speeded the boiling significantly, and Ingalls patented the idea. Two enterprising sugarmakers, Stephen and Reid Small, bought Ingalls's patent and incorporated it into their first evaporator—the progenitor of today's Small Brothers' Lightning models. The evaporator was coming of age, promising to make sugaring cleaner, faster and, it was hoped, better able to meet the demands of the market.

Unfortunately, population growth began to outpace sugar production, tariffs protecting maple disappeared, and hopes of it being able to withstand the influx of the cheaper West Indian product slipped away. Cane sugar, no longer tainted by the slavery issue (although working conditions on the former slave islands were not greatly improved) became both morally acceptable and ever more competitive in price. With the population moving to the cities and losing its affection for country things, demand for maple sugar began to sink, and it soon had neither popular righteousness nor lower cost on its side.

OUT OF THE WOODS

IF MAPLE SUGAR'S great marketing opportunity had been lost, excitement and enthusiasm at the farm level nevertheless continued to grow as new equipment brought the primitive era of sugarmaking to a close. By the turn of the century, the leading sugarmakers were producing maple sugar and syrup much as it is still done today. They had left the kettles in the dust, adopting strict standards of cleanliness, using strainers and filters and treating sap as the perishable commodity it is. They had learned that shallow, fast evaporating made the fanciest-tasting light syrup, and they were beginning to foresee a day when demand for maple syrup might outpace that of maple sugar.

still be found at the back of old equipment sheds in maple country—while others opted for a series of three or four pans placed over a brick firebox, or arch.

In 1872, a Vermonter named H. Allen Soule developed one of the first of the modern-era "patent" evaporators, which featured two connected pans, a metal arch and significantly increased speed. This would become the vaunted King evaporator, still in production today by the Leader Evaporator Company of St. Albans, Vermont, which itself was founded in 1888 by Wm. E. Burt. This period, in fact, would be the genesis of many of today's maple-equipment manufacturers. The Vermont Farm Machine Company of Bellows Falls, the G.H. Grimm Mfg. Company of Hudson, Ohio, and Rutland, Vermont, were early competitors. Around 1889, an inventor in East Dunham, Quebec, named David Ingalls took a piece of tin that was about to become the bottom of an

While some of the early native sugar camps had had snug birchbark shelters that were used each spring, the settlers for the most part boiled their sap in the open, enduring the elements or having a small evergreen lean-to near the fire to allow the boiler to escape rain or snow. With the advent of evaporators after the Civil War, sugarhouses sprang up to protect them, and gradually the old boiling sites in the woods were abandoned for spots located closer to roads or laneways, often near the bottom of maple-covered slopes to make gathering the increasing numbers of buckets easier.

In his 1896 article in *The Atlantic*, Rowland Robinson bemoaned the end of open-air, rustic sugaring, fearing that maple would never taste the same again:

"One unreckoned item of cookery, the bit of fat salt pork suspended from the kettle bail, that kept the sap from boiling over was never eaten, except in the infinitesimal contribution to a sea of sap. A suspicion of its savor, lapped wafts of smoke, the subtle aroma of woods' breath, wind-blown leaves, and bits of bark gave the old-time maple sugar a wild, woodsy flavor that has been tamed out by the neater modern processes, just as modern culture has taken the tang out of our dialect—refinements, no doubt, yet one likes to know a Yankee by the flavor of his speech, and maple sugar by its taste."

Robinson may have been partially right about the changing taste of maple, but flavor experts would later prove that the perceived taste of "woods" and "wood smoke" are very much present in syrup produced in a sterile laboratory. They come from the sap, not the boiling environment. Discriminating buyers seemed to understand this, for while maple sugar consumption dropped, maple syrup sales held steady, and in the early twentieth century, the lightest, fanciest product was appreciated, as it is today, for having the most complex, sought-after maple "bouquet."

In 1893, the Vermont Maple Sugar Makers' Association was formed with a few hundred members and a dedication to making sure the public knew good syrup from bad. At the time, various cheap table syrups made from corn or sugar cane were being sold under the "Vermont" name, implying that they contained real maple syrup. Adulteration with cane or beet sugar was considered a serious problem, and it was often said that "10 times as much Vermont maple syrup is being made in Chicago as in Vermont." The group would eventually fail in stopping what they perceived as an abuse of the good name of Vermont (the "Vermont Maid" brand, made in New Jersey with only 2 percent maple syrup, continues to be sold, and has successfully repelled several legal challenges). The Association did, however, aggressively raise the standards of sugarmaking within their own ranks and throughout Vermont, establishing the strictest grading rules of any state or province and convincing the state to enforce them with year-round random inspections. (Occasionally, the long arm of Vermont's maple laws reach outside the state. In 1988, Bruce Martell of the state Agriculture Department flew to California to expose a syrup counterfeiting operation selling 98 per-

A Vermont Maple Sugar Camp.

A typical maple sugarhouse, circa 1900; the tinsmithing boom of the late nineteenth century brought metal spouts, sap buckets and well-sheltered evaporators.

cent corn syrup as pure maple. Fake products from the "Sleepy Hollow Packing Company" or the "Nathan Pilgrim Syrup Farm" were found in 10 states, from Maryland to Oregon. Federal officials charged Pilgrim with 12 felony offenses in 1989.)

MAPLE TYCOONS

ONE OF THE FIRST to envision a legitimate empire in the maple business was Abbot Augustus ("A.A.") Low of Brooklyn, New York, who carved a bustling industry of lumbering, railroading and maple sugaring out of 45,000 acres of Adirondack forest preserve in eastern New York. Beginning in about 1896, he privately built a railroad, railroad station, three dams, a boarding house and cabins for his employees and named the town Horseshoe and the company that did all of this the Horse Shoe Forestry Company.

Low's sugaring operation began in 1899 when he built his first steam-heated evaporator in the Maple Valley section of Horseshoe. This was not the typical bucket and horse-drawn sled sugaring operation. Rather, pipes and troughs brought sap from 10,000 maples to collection points near the railroad line where it was loaded into galvanized tanks on flatbed train cars and hauled to the evaporator. By 1907, three sugarbushes operated—Maple Valley, Wake Robin and Grasse River—and each had steam-heated evaporators. The sap flowed into the sugarhouse from receiving tanks at one end and left the other end as syrup—a continuous, assembly line of sap to syrup. Horse Shoe syrup was stored in barrels made in the Horse Shoe stave mill and bottled in glass jars embossed with the Horse Shoe Forestry Co. name or made into sugar. At its peak operation, Horse Shoe made 20,000 gallons of syrup.

In the off-season, Low used his huge evaporators to make wild blueberry and wild raspberry jam. He bottled spring water and shipped it to New York City in bottles labeled Adirondack Mts. Virgin Forest Springs. He cleared 200 acres of land for a potato

Installed at George Cary's Highland Farm near St. Johnsbury, Vermont, circa 1925, the metal sap pipeline proved leaky, prone to freezing and vulnerable to passing deer.

farm, made wine from cherries, elderberries and grapes and built a stone grist mill for his Staff of Life cereals.

The fall of Low's Adirondack enterprises came in 1908, when most of the Horse Shoe Forestry Company was destroyed by fires set by sparks from a passing New York Central and Hudson River railroad engine. A telegram from Low on September 28,

A.A. Low, an entrepreneur who made maple sugaring into a big business, riding the personal railway he used to collect sap from three sugarbushes that were part of his Horse Shoe Forestry Company in New York's Adirondack Mountains.

1908, described the devastation: "Up all night with terrific fires. Situation still very critical. Loss appalling." With his dreams in shambles, Low retreated from the Adirondacks and died in Brooklyn four years later.

In Vermont, around 1886, a salesman for a Maine grocery-supply company reluctantly accepted a quantity of maple sugar in a barter arrangement and turned the deal into the first multimillion-dollar maple business. George C. Cary had made the deal with a North Craftsbury storekeeper, taking 1,500 pounds of sugar at 4½ cents a pound. Fortuitously, Cary met a salesman from a Virginia tobacco company who said he was currently paying 5 cents a pound for West Indian sugar to flavor their cut-plug chewing tobacco. Cary convinced the tobacco representative to try

maple sugar as a replacement, and before many years had passed, railroad carloads of maple sugar and syrup, from Vermont and Quebec, were heading south into the tobacco trade.

The Cary Maple Sugar Co. of St. Johnsbury, Vermont, and Lennoxville, Quebec, became North America's dominant buyer and seller of maple products, taking syrup or caked sugar from Canada, Ohio, Pennsylvania, New York and New England and manufacturing it into 60- to 70-pound maple-sugar cakes for the tobacco trade.

As the buyer of 90 percent of the wholesale sugar traded in the United States and Canada, Cary was widely referred to as the Maple King, and he personally acquired some 4,000 acres of land in North Danville, Vermont, where he set up a model sugaring operation with an amusement-park air. He brought Penobscot Indians from Maine to demonstrate the making of sugar without modern tools, he had Vermonters dressed as early settlers carrying wooden buckets on sap yokes and showed the progression of technology right up to a tin pipeline system that dazzled visitors in the 1920s.

Sadly, Cary's business ended in failure when the Depression and the refusal of the American Tobacco Co. to complete a huge sugar transaction forced him into bankruptcy in September 1931. The former grocery salesman who had become a self-made millionaire died two months later. Out of the remains of his company, two important businesses emerged: Maple Grove Farms, a leading manufacturer of maple candies and a major tourist attraction in St. Johnsbury, and American Maple Products of Newport, Vermont.

BEAUCE SUGAR

ROBERT COOMBS, JR., whose own family company is among the largest maple-candy producers, says that the scale of the Cary operation was something to behold. "I remember going there as a young boy with my father and seeing an entire warehouse filled with cakes of black sugar or Beauce sugar brought in from Quebec. It was being sprayed with water twice a day, which drained off and flowed down to a lower level to be collected and made into uniform bulk-sugar cakes."

Various other attempts at large-scale sugaring have generally proved short-lived. An exception is the ambitious operation of the late Adin Reynolds of Aniwa, Wisconsin, who began expanding the family sugaring business in the early 1950s. In its peak years, if demand is high, Reynolds Sugarbush boils the sap from 100,000 taps. His son, Lynn Reynolds, who serves as president of the North American Maple Syrup Council and the International Maple Syrup Institute, says, "We have about 5,000 taps of our own, and we buy the rest of the sap. You need to have the technology and a sort of milk-plant atmosphere to

sustain this level of production." Reynolds says that reverse-osmosis sugar concentrators, vapor compression and steam syrup finishing allows them to process up to 2,000 gallons of sap an hour. Reynolds admits that his family operation is a bit of an anomaly: "We've had to cut back in recent years because of the (Quebec) syrup surplus, but we have the geographic advantage of being able to ship most of our production to the West, where syrup isn't made."

According to Robert Coombs, whose own family operation grew as high as 25,000 taps, one of New England's largest at the time, the nature of the tree and fluky spring weather conspire to keep most sugarmaking operations small and honest.

"You have to remember that in most years the bulk of the business comes from five good days," he says. "The season is usually spread over six weeks, but more than half your sap comes from five good flows, and it's just too much hassle and too much to handle all at once if you have too many taps to manage."

If the Depression brought an end to the Cary empire, it also marked a period of decline in commercial maple production. While maple syrup became more and more of a special-occasion delicacy in the cities, it nonetheless remained the cheap, everyday sweetener for many households in rural areas and small towns.In a lovely account of sugaring near Cooperstown in upstate New York in the 1930s, published in *The Conservationist* in 1989, Niles Eggleston recalls that farmers who had moved to town had not all left their sugaring skills behind:

"In Milford, all the streets were lined with trees and a majority were hard maples. In the spring, every one was tapped with makeshift containers such as honey pails or cooking utensils hanging on nails to catch the sap. School children walking along the street would sample the sweet nectar but otherwise not disturb the operation. People in town depended on syrup as well as their garden to survive. They boiled down the sap on their stoves within their homes. Whether the damage all the steam caused to the plaster was a trade-off is a moot point."

Eggleston's own family lived on a farm where he says 110 to 150 taps gave them up to 100 gallons of syrup in the good years. As was the custom in many areas, the two town doctors got the first-run, extra-light syrup, while others paid $1.50 a gallon for the "good" syrup in 1935. The family ate its own share of their harvest, as well:

"We had pancakes with syrup every morning, used it as a side dish, soaked bread in it, poured it over ice cream and on cakes. We consumed 20 gallons per year in our own home."

HIGHER TECH

BY THE 1960S, the American countryside was fast losing its self-sufficient spirit, along with its unspoiled, farm-upon-farm look. Dairy farming, the economic mainstay for the majority of serious maple producers, was an industry in decline. Bigger herds and bigger, higher-producing Holstein cows meant that fewer and fewer dairy farms were needed to meet demands. Land was being sold to developers and homebuilders. Sugarhouses everywhere settled into disuse and decay.

By the early 1970s, the decline in syrup production was reaching alarming proportions, and not a few worried sugarmakers foresaw an end to their industry. Even for those remaining on the farm, the end of the ever-ready supply of free family labor and eager farm hands made sap-gathering an impossibly expensive proposition, given the price of syrup.

Then a series of events brought an abrupt turn-around. Plastic pipeline had begun to come of age, more than a decade after the first patent was awarded to Nelson Griggs of Montpelier, Vermont, in 1959, triggering a flurry of improvements by Everett Soule, George Breen of the 3M Company and Robert Lamb of Bernhard's Bay, New York, whose Naturalflow tubing would become an industry pacesetter. Farmers were immediately interested in this curious technology—various tin-pipe and other gravity systems had been tried on and off from as early as 1915—but this new plastic system appeared sensible and affordable.

These early pipeline systems, however, were proving trouble-prone, with sap production and syrup quality dropping in many sugarbushes. Then the energy crisis of the early 1970s stopped the world in its tracks. Fearing the escalating costs of cutting and hauling firewood, gathering sap and, where oil burners had replaced wood-fired arches, fueling the evaporators, farmers saw potential doom for a financially marginal business. With sugarbushes being cut for lumber and the Japanese on a maple-buying spree to construct bowling alleys, the maple industry reacted. Equipment companies made energy-saving a new, urgent priority, and state and provincial agriculture departments threw new resources into research and development of energy-efficient maple technologies. Pipeline problems were solved, and vacuum pumps added to improve production, especially during "weeping runs"—the slowest running days of the season. Evaporators were speeded up, often by scavenging waste heat from the escaping steam and using it to preheat the sap. Reverse-osmosis units used a high-tech filter membrane to allow sugarmakers to squeeze a portion of the water out of the sap before boiling, thus reducing evaporation fuel costs and late-night hours spent in the sugarhouse. In Quebec, with huge tracts of untapped maples growing on Crown Land, farmers were given financial incentives to modernize their production methods and increase their number of taps, using the government-owned trees.

The result was a fresh start for sugaring both among farmers, who could now make commercial quantities of syrup without a small army of help to gather buckets, and their neighbors who held non-farm jobs. Shorter boiling times allowed moonlighting and weekend sugarmakers to get into the picture, and they now make a significant portion of the syrup produced in many areas.

"Spring is the mischief in me," said Robert Frost, and an old-time sugar-on-snow party was a rite of emergence from winter's isolation and a time to celebrate spring's arrival.

"The schoolteacher, the guy who works for the phone company, the dentist whose grandfather had a sugarhouse—this is the fastest growing part of the industry," says one equipment dealer. "The bigger producers are still the driving force of the evaporator and equipment industry, but the hobbyists and small operators are where the growth is."

Syrup production today is approximately 1.6 million gallons in a good year—which 1992 was—in the United States. (The peak year in history, 1860, by comparison, showed U.S. production at the same level of syrup as today, but with an additional 40 million pounds of hard sugar—the equivalent of 6.6 million gallons of syrup in total.) In Quebec, whose bulk producers are capable of swamping the market with syrup, 1992 production exceeded 4.5 million gallons—almost triple the total U.S. production.

According to André Morin, spokesman for a new Quebec maple-products marketing group, that province and Agriculture Canada are planning new, large-scale generic promotion efforts to encourage the 90 or 95 percent of North American consumers who have never tasted real maple syrup to put it on their shopping lists. In addition, Morin predicts that the overproduction and stockpiling of syrup in Quebec will become a thing of the past.

Given that Quebec's accumulated syrup surplus amounted to 28 million pounds in 1993—enough to cover a football field, four barrels deep—other maple-producing provinces and states are greeting Morin's promises of a new marketing attitude in Quebec with optimism.

MAPLE'S NEXT CENTURY

WHILE PRODUCTION has rebounded in recent years and optimism has returned to the ranks of serious sugarmakers, there are those who believe that maple sugaring may have its toughest century ahead.

Speaking to an international group of sugarmakers at Vermont's annual Maplerama, Gregory R. Passewitz, a marketing specialist with Ohio State University, warned the audience, "You are not selling maple syrup. If you think you are just selling syrup, and if you think that as long as you make high-quality syrup you

While technology has eliminated much of the drudgery and speeded up the sugarmaking process, many smaller producers and amateur sugarmakers cling to techniques and simple hand-gathering methods not much evolved from those of a century ago.

will be O.K., you may be in for a rude awakening.

"What we are selling is Americana or Canadiana. We are selling handmade. We are selling nostalgia. We are selling purity. We are selling romance.

"We have to face the fact that many of the people who grew up with maple syrup are getting older and consuming less and less. We are selling a product that many people think of only as pancake topping. Not many people eat pancakes for breakfast every day, or even every week, anymore. There is absolutely no way that we expect pancakes to maintain or increase the market for maple syrup.

"How well we succeed in the future depends on how well we pass on the values of this handmade, old-fashioned, pure, native product. If we can get them out to the country, out to visit the sugarhouse, we usually have them with us for life. But the population and demographics of North America are changing so fast that we can't underestimate the challenge ahead of us."

SITTING IN A CIRCLE at the feet of an Abenaki storyteller known as Wolfsong, a group of elementary-school Vermonters recently spent a gloomy winter Saturday morning in the corner of a community bookstore, listening to Indian legends and myths. They sat gravely, a page out of the Patagonia catalogue with their Gore-tex and Synchilla parkas nestled around their waists, a band of Nintendo-generation kids spellbound by the tale of Glooskap and the maple trees.

"We have to teach them," Wolfsong quietly told me later, "or the old stories and the old respect for the Earth will be gone." Sadly, the future of maple sugaring is far from certain, given the pressures on rural land and challenges of marketing a product as primi-

Lessons of the maples: "We have to teach the children," says Abenaki storyteller Wolfsong, "or the old stories and the old respect for the Earth will be gone."

tive as anything on the modern supermarket shelf. "What would you expect to see here if you came back in a hundred years?" I asked Don Harlow, standing in the old family sugarhouse in Putney, Vermont. "Condominiums," he answered.

Other sugarmakers are more optimistic, but none minimizes the marketing tasks ahead. "We need to get the message across that tapping the trees is one of the most sustainable, responsible uses of this resource," says David Marvin. "It's one way of profitably preserving stands of maples that might otherwise be subject to clearing or development."

Although their approaches differ, Wolfsong the storyteller and Marvin the sugarmaker are unanimous on one point: the great maples face a threat of modern society forgetting their value. Those who truly care will take the time to pass on the history, the legends and an appreciation for sugaring's rich traditions. "If we tell them today," says Wolfsong, "maybe they will tell their own children someday, and the story will never be lost again." ❧

CHAPTER 3

THE SUGARMAKERS

*"The sugar-man wears many hats. He is weatherman
and woodcutter, trail-blazer and tree expert,
transporter, pipe-fitter, cook and chemist, demonstrator,
processor, packager and retail merchant."*

— PIONEER VALLEY ASSOCIATION
NORTHAMPTON, MASSACHUSETTS

FOR SOME, it's the first caw of a returning crow or the first drop of water melting from the tip of an icicle in a prismatic explosion of brilliant sunlight. For Maddy Harlow of Putney, Vermont, the excitement truly starts with a surefire sign: "One morning you look out and see water running alongside the road. You know the sap's got to be running, too, and somebody always hollers, 'Time to go sugarin'!'"

"If there's one thing about sugaring," says her husband, Don, "it's that it can't wait. You have to go by your feelings about when to tap, and you have to be ready. It can start anytime in February or March, and you start seeing the signs and know it's about to start running."

It is a moment quite unlike any other in the farm year, a silent wake-up call heard only by sugarmakers that sets off weeks of living at the beck and call of the thermometer, barometer and the enigmatic sap flows of the sugar maple. In the days of rural party-line telephones, not so long past in many regions of maple country, the first run of the season was

Two faces of maple: farm sign, **above;** *97-year-old sugar-maker Ray Grimes,* **left,** *testing syrup with a hydrometer.*

one of those occasions—like a barn fire or other event of overriding community import—that set the lines crackling. Beatrice Buszek, in her cookbook *The Sugarbush Connection,* records the spirit of this annual moment in her rural New Brunswick community: "Then it is that the party lines go humming mad . . . Sap's runnin'! Runnin'! Runnin'! It's runnin' good."

While the modern sugarmaker must be prepared for this day well in advance, with trees tapped, pipelines cleaned and sugarhouse at the ready, the early rush to get buckets in place and catch the rich first run of sap is a memory most sugarmakers still share.

The rhythmic ping of sap hitting the bare bottoms of metal buckets is a sound etched in the memories of anyone who has sugared the old-fashioned way. It

"Sap's runnin'! Sap's runnin'! Let's go sugarin'!"

is a sound that carries for amazing distances on a still March day deep in the countryside, and it is loaded with nuances that the city observer would scarcely understand. "The sound of dollars dropping," is the pithy assessment of old-time sugarmakers. For family farms, this was the sound of precious income—money that would be greatly welcomed after a long winter: money to buy seed, to pay the taxes, to square the accounts at the feed store. Many who grew up on farms remember that sugaring meant a new pair of boots or shoes for Easter.

"When sugaring time came," recalls Everett Willard, whose family sugared near Derby, Vermont, "we would notice different things on the table—maybe a ham or some fancy fruit—that were more ex-

Maple steam rising from an old sugarhouse, a universal welcome to friends, neighbors and even curious strangers to stop in and share the warmth. The open cupola in the peak of the roof keeps the sugarhouse from becoming a sweet Turkish bath.

With a break in the winter weather forecast, usually sometime in February or March, the urgent task of tapping begins. Horse-drawn sleds and metal buckets harken back more than a century, but are in no immediate danger of disappearing.

pensive than we usually had. My father had seven kids, and a lot of what we ate came right off the farm, but sugaring meant there was a little more money and some special treats would always appear."

The first drop of sap to run signals the start of what may be the most frenetic six weeks of the rural year, with nature momentarily opening a precious window that can close with terrible suddenness and finality.

"It's hard for people who don't sugar to understand," says Maddy Harlow, whose family runs Harlow's Sugarhouse, a landmark family farm that markets its own maple syrup, strawberries and apples. "It's a hurried feeling—when the sap is running, you have to gather and you have to boil. If you have to boil until three in the morning to get it all done, and then you have to start gathering again a few hours

later because the buckets are overflowing, that's just what you do."

Her annual diaries are a testament to the frenetic life of a maple-sugaring family when the sap is running. Sleepless nights. Late suppers with extra hands to feed—more beans and syrup into the crock, more potatoes and carrots into the stew. Corn fritters to make for the farmstand guests. Midafternoon catnaps for the boiler when there is a lull. Sudden cold snaps and the suspense of when it will all start again. Record-making days—156 gallons! Warm, worrisome nights that may signal the premature end of a season, as in 1992 when the temperatures suddenly soared and sugarmakers resignedly pulled their taps on one of the worst harvests in anyone's memory. Some who caught a fluky early run made out best, proving once again that it doesn't pay to try nature's patience.

The rhythms and intensities of getting the taps placed just as the sap starts to flow were neatly remembered in a 1947 children's text called *The Golden Almanac*, in which Dorothy Bennett wrote:

"It is rush, rush, rush once the sap has started to rise. Drill, drill, drill. Put in spout, put in spout. Hang on pail, hang on pail. Put on cover, put on cover. And start all over with more and more trees. There may be dozens, hundreds or even a thousand trees for one family to tend. It may be long after dark before they can stop to go home to dinner and to bed."

Tapping

WITH SUGARING there is no tomorrow," says northern Vermont sugarmaker Robert Howrigan of Fairfield. "It has to be today, or it's gone."

Howrigan is one of the living legends in the maple world, widely respected for his award-winning syrup, the zeal with which his family produces sugar, his loyalty to draft horses—his operation has five magnificent teams—and his timeless country values. Ask him about the sugar season, and he may just start by paying homage to the sugarmaking Howrigans before him.

"Our family has been in this area for seven generations, and they have always sugared," he says in an accent that is pure New England and that is all too quickly fading with his generation. "They tell the story about my grandfather, who was kind of a sickly man, come this time of year, and he'd be crippled up with rheumatism and arthritis and everything.

"But each year they'd get him on a double sled, and he'd get to the sugarhouse and he'd get the fire going. He'd get the heat from the arch and the steam, and he'd get some new maple syrup. Well, then he always said he was all set for another year.

"I'm sure you have heard about how the old Vermonters used to pile the old folks out in a snowbank to save food so they could survive the winter, but my grandfather came along after that era. . . . They say

Each bucket or pipeline spout requires a fresh taphole, about 2.5 inches deep, each year. With 2,000 to 4,000 taps to place, most family sugaring operations today favor labor-saving power tappers and sap-collecting pipelines.

he'd still be with us if they hadn't had a late Vermont spring one year, and he didn't get that new syrup early enough.

"Dad was a good sugarmaker," Howrigan continues. "Now a good sugarmaker, of course, he has to plan ahead. Dad was always ready, his wood was always stored and dry and repairs were taken care of. Dad was a super caretaker: harnesses, horses, equipment—they lasted with Dad." Howrigan says he and his family are still using a wooden sap trough that his grandfather hewed by hand in the late 1800s at the home farm. In effect, it is the frontier version of a pipe, and sap that has been drawn out of the sugar woods by teams of draft horses flows through it into the storage tank in the Howrigan sugarhouse. "It's been used every year," he says, "and I think it's an-

but as one of the first responsibilities of the younger helpers, it is remembered with great fondness. "Dad stayed on the sleigh, handed 'em to us and told us where they went. The boys scattered them, mostly one or two buckets to a tree. He had only one tree he allowed us to put three buckets to. He was very conservative—he was ahead of his time there."

While there are records of early white settlers studding single maples with dozens of taps—and photographic evidence of giant maples literally being tapped to death with dozens of spouts ringing their trunks—no sugarmaker today wants to be accused of overtapping his or her trees. One rule almost universally accepted is never to tap a tree less than 10 or 12 inches in diameter. (The old farmer's rule had it just right: "Never tap a tree smaller than the bucket you're putting to it.")

However, considerable debate has taken place over the past decade about other so-called tapping guidelines, with a number of foresters now suggesting that a general rule of thumb is never to place more than two taps in any single tree. Still in circulation are more liberal tapping rules—set by well-credentialed experts and government agencies—that allow up to four taps in big trees (more than three feet in diameter) and the subject is a contentious one.

"Our tapping guideline is to put out enough spouts to make a living," quips Don Harlow, whose wife Maddy quickly scolds, "Oh Don, you never overtap your trees." Harlow's sugarbush is blessed with many

other mark of Dad being a good caretaker, because each night when we'd get finished dumping for the day, he'd always have us turn it over so it wouldn't get sagged. It was quite a work of art and it's practical."

Howrigan says that, as children, he and his six brothers sometimes drove their father to distraction in anticipation of the sugaring season. "Oh gracious, we would tease Dad—he stored his buckets up over the kitchen where they would be dry and the tin wouldn't rust, and we'd tease him, 'When can we get the buckets out,' and he'd get sick of it after a while.

"My dad would tell us, 'When the sun comes in the east window and hits the seventh board on the wainscoting, you can bring the buckets down.' So then we'd have a big ceremony, we'd lug them down."

The next ritual—the scattering of the buckets throughout the sugarbush—has been replaced by the proliferation of plastic tubing in most sugarbushes,

> *"When the wind's in the West, the sap runs best . . .*
> *And when the wind's in the North, the sap runs forth.*
> *When the wind's in the South, the sap runs drouth . . .*
> *And when the wind's in the East, the sap runs least."*
>
> — OLD NEW ENGLAND FARM SONG

trees of substantial girth, and as another sugarmaker who still works with horses and metal buckets, he has an intimate knowledge of his maples.

"I've got one big tree that you could hang 12 buck-

ets from—and they'd all run over. I've got another tree that must be four feet in diameter, and if you hang one bucket it might get half full on a good day. You have to use some common sense."

David Marvin, a member of the International Maple Commission linking Canadian and American sugarmakers, is of a younger generation that more enthusiastically embraces the conservative tapping guidelines. Even he, however, says that there are many big, healthy maples that can continue to take three or four taps. "Our rule is that if a tree is 36 inches across and is overflowing two buckets, you add a third. Intelligent tapping is one of the least demanding uses you can make of this resource, and I'd be the last person to do anything I thought was shortening the life of the tree."

Whatever the tapping rules at work in a particular sugarbush, the placement of the taps is traditionally left to skilled hands who carefully avoid drilling too deep or too close to previous tapholes. Standard depth today is 2½ inches, with a ⁷⁄₁₆-inch hole angled slightly upward. The tapper watches the curl of fresh wood emerging from the taphole, being certain it is white and clean. Placing a tap in dark or blackened wood is an invitation to low production and off flavors in the finished syrup.

A spout—also known as a spile in many regions—is placed in the hole immediately and tapped snugly into place with a light hammer. If buckets are in use, a metal spout with a hook is the standard choice, while simpler hard-plastic or nylon spouts are placed if the bush has a pipeline-tubing system. It is crucial that the spout be inserted quickly, while the inner walls of the taphole are fresh and clean. The tapper doesn't want the wood to dry or become contaminated with microorganisms from the tree bark.

With too little profit in syrup to hire outside help, most farms look to the whole family to lend a hand for the 4-to-6-week sugaring season.

In smaller operations today, tapping may wait until the sap is actually about to flow, but in most instances, the placing of spouts must begin days or weeks in advance in order to catch the precious first run of the season. A typical serious family operation today numbers from 2,000 to 4,000 taps, and there are two schools of thought about when to tap.

The calendar watchers typically have a target date for all tapping to be done in their locale—the classic in Vermont being Town Meeting Day, or the first Tuesday after the first Monday of March. In Quebec and more northerly regions of Ontario, the season typically starts later, while sugarmakers in parts of Pennsylvania and Ohio may routinely begin tapping in late January.

Among the calendar watchers are the operations with tens of thousands of taps to place and miles and miles of tubing to check, repair and tighten. Knowing the approximate earliest-run date, these sugarmakers must calculate their workforce, the number of taps to be set and then work backward to the date when they must start to be ready in time. In this, they have one of the significant advantages of plastic tubing

---

Tapping a sap spout, also known as a spile in some regions, into place, left. Most trees will support one or two such taps.

systems, in that the tubing tends to prevent early-drilled tapholes from being invaded by microorganisms.

The second school of tapping comprises the nature and weather watchers, who are alert to all the signs, listening to all the forecasts and keeping a keen eye on the thermometer and barometer. "A sugarmaker can feel it in his bones," claimed Scott and Helen Nearing, who co-authored the *The Maple Sugar Book* in 1951. "When a farmer sees 'coon tracks in a snowbank," goes one old Canadian saying, "he begins looking at his sap pails."

PLUMBING THE TREES

THE MORNING everyone is waiting for brings with it a classic overnight shock to all natural systems in the frozen range of the sugar maple. From a freezing night, perhaps with temperatures in the low to mid 20s, thermometers surge into the high 30s or even into the 40s—the greater the mercurial whipsaw effect, the better the first run. A 15-degree swing in 12 hours will do the trick. It is often a blindingly bright day that reenergizes the northern world, bringing water cascading off rooftops, sending rivulets down icicles and forming sparkling puddles and streamlets everywhere. For the small-scale sugarmaker, it is the finest hour: a day when a fresh taphole will start dripping sap the moment the drill bit is retracted from the tree. "Two drops to the heartbeat" is the old sugarmakers' expression for a good, pulse-quickening flow. Affection for this sound and for the charm of the metal bucket (most are galvanized iron or aluminum today, not tin) runs deep, even in sugarmakers who have largely gone over to plastic-tubing systems.

With some 12,000 taps connected to an 80-mile network of plastic pipeline, David Marvin of Butter-

Spiderweb saplines: Like them or not, labor-saving plastic-tubing systems have saved the maple industry and are credited with causing less wear and tear on the trees.

nut Mountain Farm near Johnson, Vermont, would seem to have left the hand-gathering era behind, but he staunchly maintains several hundred buckets as part of his much larger tubing operation. "We tap about 500 buckets, and we can do those in about a day with two or three of us. I think we will always have buckets because they keep us honest and make us remember it isn't all romance, but mainly because we need to see what's going on. With buckets you can get a feel for the flow each day, each hour, but with tubing that's very, very difficult. The trees get all interconnected, and you don't really know how they are doing individually.

"We also use buckets because we have a number of good roadside trees, and trees my dad planted in 1959 and 1960 that are easier to get at with buckets.

"If I were tapping less then we do now and I could tap in a day or two, I think I would wait until I heard a forecast for some warm weather. But in the best of situations, we need a week to 10 days to tap everything. So we do it by the calendar and try to be ready by Town Meeting Day, and always want to be ready by the 10th of March. We tap all our tubing early, and then we tap our buckets after the first run."

GATHERING

L IKE IT OR NOT, tubing is here to stay—at least until a reverse wave of willing, cheap labor returns to the countryside eager to resume such demanding chores as gathering sap. Without tubing, traditional sugaring was in a sad decline in the 1970s, as farmers couldn't afford to hire seasonal help—or simply couldn't find help at any price with rural families getting smaller and the hired hand almost a thing of the past. In simplest terms, plastic tubing provided a sensible alternative to the most labor-intensive part of the sugarmaking process.

Gathering sap the traditional way at Don and Maddy Harlow's sugarbush near Putney, Vermont. An experienced team of horses virtually drives itself through the woods.

City-bred visitors to the sugar woods are routinely astonished to learn that what flows from the trees is a sparkling liquid with only a vague hint of sweetness. Highly perishable, the sap must be gathered often and boiled at once to make fine syrup.

A 16-quart bucket of sap, if full, weighs over 30 pounds, and a single gatherer might be expected to retrieve and dump 750 to 1,500 buckets in a day. Over bare, frozen ground, the task is workout enough; slogging through heavy snow or sucking mud, it becomes a test of stamina and character—especially when the sap runs day after day and the season stretches out to six or eight weeks. The sugarmaker may be beaming at the end, but the gatherers will know that the romance of syrupmaking has a darker side.

In times past, many farmers waited until their buckets were close to brimming before gathering the sap. Today, most quality-conscious sugarmakers try to gather daily, getting their sap in before microorganisms—bacteria and yeasts—become active. Fresh, cold sap makes the lighter-colored, finer-tasting syrup grades that fetch the premium prices. Bacterial action on sap converts the tree's natural sucrose to glucose and fructose, which tend to darken when heated and to produce the flavor of caramel, which can overpower the subtleties of great maple syrup.

Authors Helen and Scott Nearing were urban refugees in the 1940s who became dedicated sugarmakers and strong proponents of gathering sap daily. In 1943, they strapped on snowshoes—a necessity when snow is a barrier—on February 22 and didn't put them away until after the last day of gathering on April 23.

For ex-city types and self-taught sugarers, the Nearings made an impressive amount of syrup; they reported a total of 7,334 gallons from 1937 to 1947 — "from a yearly average of 3,250 buckets . . . Of this amount, 75 percent was Fancy grade. In 1942, the percentage of Fancy, on a crop of 515 gallons, was 94 percent.

"If conditions underfoot are average," they wrote, "one man can visit 50 to 75 buckets an hour, depending on the amount of sap in each bucket." Thus, in a 10-hour day of gathering half-full buckets, a single gatherer might heft 10,000 to 12,000 pounds of sap, all the while trekking a zigzag course uphill and down over sometimes uneven terrain, and having his or her own resources tapped by the snow or mud.

The Nearings eventually developed their own semi-pipeline system, with dumping stations placed strategically on the hillside above their sugarhouse near Jamaica, Vermont. Gatherers would pour the sap from buckets into funnels at various permanent standpipes, and gravity would speed the fluid downhill to storage tanks and on to their evaporator.

More typical at that time were sap-tank hauling sleds drawn by workhorses, and they are still found in surprising numbers of sugar operations—especially where the public is invited to visit and someone has kept alive a love for the big equines.

"The boys enjoy working with the horses," says Robert Howrigan. "We have five teams—and they don't tear up the soil like a tractor will. They'll paddle through and you'll never know they been there. And you can remote-control them; you'll speak to them and they'll move and stop while you dump the buckets and move from one tree to the next. A good team is a pleasure to work with. If you don't enjoy horses, well, that's another story."

Still, horses and buckets demand fit and willing help, not so easily come by in the Canadian and American countryside of the 1990s. "The labor costs, they're getting higher and higher, and it seems like there's less young people who want the challenge," says Howrigan, whose family uses both buckets and pipeline to produce high-quality bulk syrup for Dakin Farms. In the past, he says, it was easier to find young help—especially when school authorities sympathized with the needs of the sugaring farmers.

"If you didn't have any boys of your own, the neighbors did. We used to call it the mud vacation, but we had it tailored to sugaring too. That was the custom and we did it for years. Did it as long as I was in on the school board—21 years." He says, however, that not all young hands proved equal to the gathering task. "I've had young fellows who were stars on the football team, but they were a washout when it came to gathering sap. I think it's the cohesion of family unity that really allows us to take on this extra burden of work at this time of year to make some syrup. Our best boiler is a fellow my daughter met at college . . . and I have a son who's bought a farm down the road without the sugar. He comes in and helps us. I've got a brother-in-law, and he calls it his spring physical-fitness course. If you gathered any lard in the winter, you could get rid of it at sugaring time."

Trees and gravity are the resources of a sugarbush: a gathering team waits as sap flows downhill to the sugarhouse.

*A wood-fired inferno, the arch, or firebox, under a traditional evaporator
must be kept roaring if the day's sap harvest is to be finished in good time.
A heavy run may keep the fire going until the wee hours of the morning.*

Fireworks from "fast wood"—bone-dry fuel that burns intensely—escape the evaporator doors in a late-night session.

Howrigan also admits to positive feelings toward the pipeline systems that relentlessly bring in the sap—day and night, if it's running—and that have eased some of the load: "I guess at my age, I like to get up in the morning and find that tank of sap in the sugarhouse, before the horses get saddled up, so I appreciate the pipeline. It works good if it's well maintained, but the buckets have their place too."

Boiling

B Y GOSH, BOYS, I think we're gonna make a little syrup." These were the fateful words that started the 1963 sugaring season for Don Harlow's Uncle Frank, who had just installed a proud new evaporator in the family's barn-red sugarhouse that is a landmark near Putney, Vermont. Harlow says his uncle, who knew what he was doing, was "showin' off" for an earnest city-bred reporter who had been sent out to see the first syrup of the year made in the new rig.

The sap was running, and enough had already been gathered to feed the big King evaporator, which would have been any sugarmaker's pride and joy, with a big "$" cast into each of the heavy firebox doors.

"Well, Frank runs some sap into the new pans and gets a big, roaring fire going," recalls Harlow, "and in a few minutes she starts boiling like hell."

From here on, Uncle Frank and the newspaperman take over the dialogue:

"What's that sound?" asks the reporter.

"Oh," says Uncle Frank, in his best slow and patient old-Yankee-talkin'-to-a-city-fella voice, "that's the crackle of your good dry wood burnin' in the arch."

"And what's that bubbling?" asks the reporter.

"Now," says Uncle Frank, who has this routine polished to the fine patina of an old maple butterbowl, "that's your sap boiling and sending its fragrant steam off into the heavens,"

"Hmm," says the reporter after a few more minutes, "and what's *that* smell?"

"Now," sniffs Uncle Frank with a smile, "that's the fine flavor of maple syrup developing as the sugars concentrate."

"No," says the reporter, "it sort of smells like something burning . . ."

"Oh, that's the light caramel flavor coming out in the syrup," says Uncle Frank, who suddenly gets a strange look in his eye and decides to turn away from his audience and see how things are coming.

"Oh, s---!," says Uncle Frank. "That's the pan turning to charcoal."

It is in the sugarhouse, with a fire roaring in the firebox, sap literally jumping in the evaporator and heady clouds of maple steam billowing up that a sugarmaker's skills stand between a crop of liquid gold and blackened, sickening disaster.

"There's not a sugarmaker alive—if he's honest—that hasn't burned a pan," says Don Harlow, and the slim balancing act between success and expensive failure does nothing to detract from the excitement in all who are privileged to stand by a fully stoked evaporator. It is here that the gathered sap—thin and cold—meets the fire and, in a matter of 45 minutes or so, comes thickly out the syrup gate—30 times

Flowing like a molten river through the channels of the steaming pans, thin sap becomes syrup in about an hour.

sweeter and scalding hot. Imagine the contents of a steel drum holding 40 gallons of sap being rapidly reduced to fit into a one-gallon syrup container, and you start to appreciate the amount of heat and steam involved. Now imagine that you are standing in a room with a professional evaporator five or six feet wide and 16 feet long that is cranking through six or seven of these big barrels an hour, and you under-stand how the steam billowing up from a sugarhouse can be seen for miles. The big rigs that put out 300 to 400 gallons of water vapor an hour are familiar landmarks in sugaring season to pilots and knowl-edgeable truckers who, on a clear day, can sometimes spot a dozen or more maple plumes in a single vista.

In simplest terms, the typical sugarmaking evapo-rator consists of two flat metal pans sitting over a

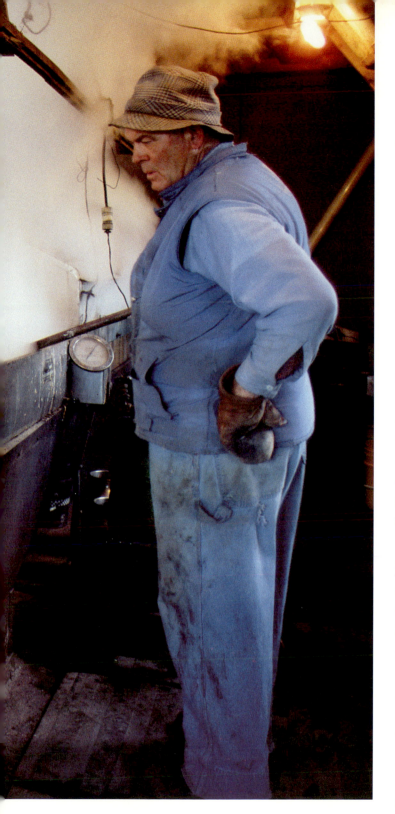

long firebox known as the arch. Cold sap enters the rear pan in a steady drizzle when the evaporator is at full tilt, with simple float valves used to maintain the fluid levels in the pans. The theory of modern syrup-making, which started to evolve after the American Civil War, is that boiling sap should progress steadily to syrup, without ever being re-mixed with cold sap, and not sit over the fire, turning brown, for hours.

To accomplish this, the evaporator is divided into multiple, interconnected channels, creating a maze that the sap must follow as it becomes hotter and hotter and ever more dense. The flue pan, or back pan, has a deeply channeled bottom that offers a tremendous surface area to the heat of the fire beneath. This pan requires only minimal attention but is the workhorse that drives off the greatest volume of water.

The front pan—known as the syrup or finishing pan— has a flat bottom, and it is here that the thickening sap finally turns to syrup. Although it is fed by a float valve that automatically allows sap to run in from the back pan whenever the level drops, experienced sugarmakers watch it with hawklike vigilance when syrup is nearing the finished stage. Like a hot, lazy river, the sap weaves through the channels, its boiling characteristics changing subtly as it goes.

It is here that the great maple flavor comes out with just the right amount of cooking time—too much and the sugars start to caramelize, the syrup darkens and a lower-grade product is made. It is a steamy, demanding job that is absolutely unforgiving of those who panic, grow inattentive or forget the consequences.

"I turned my back for a few minutes," one New England sugarmaker admitted to a friend at a post-season workshop this year, "and then I heard this 'blut, blut' and I barely got to it. I didn't burn it, but it was just sitting there ready to go."

"Ya can't get scared," mused the friend. "You've got to run the rig, not let the rig run you."

The sugarmaker is watching for telltale changes in the boiling pattern and development of color as the syrup stage nears. He regularly uses a long-handled strainer to skim foam that inevitably appears when even the cleanest sap is boiled. During the early part of the season, this scum is usually a bright white, but it yellows and darkens as the days and weeks pass.

The sugarmaker also has a syrup scoop at hand, to

Testing the state of things at the finishing end of his evaporator, sugarmaker Ralph Perry Jr. watches hot syrup starting to "apron" or drip in a sticky sheet from his scoop. At this stage, experience and a cool head help, as syrup burns very quickly.

move the thickened fluid along if necessary, and to test for doneness. The age-old indicator of finished syrup is a phenomenon known as "aproning," when the sugar-rich syrup comes off the upheld scoop in a slow curtain or sheet, rather than spilling freely as water or sap would. Because aproning is not a precise indicator of sugar density, a thermometer and hydrometer are employed to ensure perfect quality control.

The various measures of "perfect" are: syrup that boils at 7 degrees Fahrenheit above the boiling point of water (at the same time and location); syrup that weighs 11 pounds per gallon at a temperature of 60 degrees F; syrup with a Brix sweetness reading of 66.9 to 68.9; or syrup with a sweetness reading of 36 to 37 degrees Baumé.

Most typically, today, the sugarmaker will use both

an experienced eye to watch the boiling patterns, the start of aproning, and a thermometer and hydrometer to get an accurate density reading of the syrup as it is ready to be drawn off. (Syrup that is too thin may end up spoiling, while too-thick syrup will precipitate sugar crystals when it cools and sits in storage. These crystals are especially vexatious, as many consumers wrongly jump to the conclusion that broken glass has somehow gotten into their syrup—the crystals do look very much like shards of clear, broken glass.)

The person in charge of all this is called the boiler, and he or she is often the master of the whole operation. "My dad always did it," says Nate Danforth, referring to the legendary "Shorty" Danforth, who at six feet six inches cut an imposing figure in maple circles, where he is still remembered as one of the great Vermont sugarmakers. "He did the tapping with a big heavy power tapper that he invented. It was the first of its kind, as far as we knew, but it took the ruggedest guy to handle it." Danforth says the women of his family played other key roles during sugaring.

"My grandmother did a lot of boiling. She hung buckets, too, and she always corrected my grandfather when he called it a 'man and woman operation.' 'It's a two-man operation,' she would say."

If something goes wrong, best that it be one person, man or woman, who is responsible. Running an evaporator requires both a sense of calm and an alert mind that can juggle myriad variables and mental tasks: Is the fire hot enough? Too hot? How's the fuel supply? Is there enough sap in the storage tank to keep the pans filled? Are the gatherers keeping up? What's happening with the weather? Is the day's run over or are we in for an all-nighter? Are the various float valves working just right? Does the rig have hot spots or cold spots that need special attention? Is sugar sand—also known as nitre silica or malate of lime— building up and threatening to scorch? Is the cream or defoamer handy and still fresh?

The latter is a sugarmaker's panic button, used when a pan or section of a pan gets too hot and thick and turns into a seething mass of bubbles that will rise up and spill out of the pan, causing both a financial loss and an unholy mess. A fleck of cream or vegetable oil—just a tiny droplet—dripped into the foam will break the surface tension of the bubbles almost instantly, taking the life out of the threatening mass of hot syrup and giving the boiler a chance to recover control of the situation.

A piece of salt pork, suspended on a

string over the evaporator, used to serve the same purpose, but it has largely been supplanted by vegetable oil to avoid problems of rancidity, off flavors and objections from vegetarians.

"We once had a nice gentleman come in from New York or Boston, wanting to buy a couple of gallons

A seething pan nears the finished stage, **top,** *while the endless task of feeding the evaporator fire keeps helpers busy earning their next taste of new syrup.*

Scalding-hot harvest: Finished syrup must be filtered immediately after it comes off the evaporator to catch impurities and remove sugar sand, or nitre, a gritty substance that will otherwise precipitate in packaged syrup.

of syrup," says one sugarmaker who has now abandoned the use of pork belly suspended from a rafter on a string over the syrup pan. "He looked and looked at the piece of fat, seemed to be thinking about it, and then he thanked us and left. We finally realized he must have been Jewish and hadn't even considered that maple syrup could have been touched by pork."

Constantly in the back of the sugarmaker's mind is the knowledge that the more time the sap spends over the heat of the fire, the darker the final product. All syrup requires a certain amount of time to develop the characteristic colors and flavors, but too much time in the cooker can turn beautiful Fancy or Light Amber syrup to a less desirable, lower-value, darker grade.

An experienced sugarmaker will hit a rhythm, taking off a gallon or more of syrup at regular intervals of 20 to 30 minutes, depending on the capacity of the evaporator. The hot syrup goes into a clean syrup bucket or container and then immediately through a filter to remove any impurities and nitre. Although it can be a potent laxative if taken in quantity, nitre is

harmless, and some old-timers still think it adds to the flavor of syrup. Commercial sugarmakers who must strive for a crystal-clear product remove it, either with the use of felt or with paper filters.

SELF-TAUGHT SUGARMAKER

IF THE BOILING seems as intimidating as it is fascinating, it is also a set of skills that can be learned, even by a busy young mother who decides to start sugaring on an impulse.

"It was back during the World War when everything was rationed," recalls Marjorie Palmer of Hinesburg, Vermont. "I had small children, and we never had enough sugar. We owned a farm, but it was rented out, and I had never been in a sugarhouse in my life. I knew there were maples and some buckets at the farm, and I told my husband I wanted to start making syrup.

"He laughed and he said, 'Do you know anything about it?'

"I said, 'No, but I can read.'

"When you are young, you know, you try anything. The wife of the man who was running the farm said she would like to give it a try with me. Neither of us knew anything, but just like foolish kids, we went right to the top."

Palmer says she approached Dr. James Marvin, head of the University of Vermont's maple-research center, and then went to the manager of the Leader Evaporator Company. Both men were encouraging, and the two women—an undertaker's wife and a college student—were soon making their own maple syrup. "I'll tell you," laughs Marjorie Palmer, "we thought it was wonderful. It was pretty black syrup, but we thought it was just great."

This was the beginning of decades of boiling—she found partners and helpers

Vermont's version of the Ivory Tower: maple researcher Sumner Williams tests a boiling pan at the University of Vermont's working sugarhouse.

"A nectar almost sacred" is how one sugarmaker honored fine maple syrup, shown here at the "draw off" or point at which it emerges from the finishing pan of the evaporator. Syrup of proper density comes off the fire at about 217 degrees Fahrenheit.

to gather the sap—and the foundation for a reputation as a serious sugarmaker. She was, in fact, one of the first women accepted as an equal in the old-boy fraternity of Vermont sugarmakers. It wasn't, however, always easy.

"The old evaporators, they didn't have faucets. They had a bent pipe that came out at right angles, and you turned it down to draw off the hot syrup and back up to stop the flow. Well, one night when I was all alone, it broke off in my hand and the hot syrup was coming out—of course it poured down on me, but I knew I'd burn the evaporator up if I didn't plug the hole. I got it plugged with a stick, and I opened the doors of the arch and got most of the burning wood and threw it out in the snow. By the time I got this done, my foot was all burned. I couldn't wear a

shoe for months. I couldn't walk back down either, and at that time, I didn't have a snowmobile. I had to wait until somebody missed me and came up.

"Another time, I came out of the sugarhouse—it was probably 2:00 in the morning—and I had a lantern, but it was raining so hard it put the lantern out. I got lost coming down the hill. I couldn't find my way down, and finally I came out on a ledge by another farm. My car was down the road at the farm, and somehow I finally followed the ledge down. I couldn't see a thing, and I was so nervous."

Even this wasn't enough to discourage Palmer, who is now 85 and who sugared until a bout of ill health forced her to retire a few years ago. Her son has continued the tradition, and when a group of North American sugarmakers recently spent a day touring Vermont sugar-

The Sugarmakers

Day and night for up to six weeks each year, the sugarmaking family's life is at the beck and call of the weather and the unpredictable runs of sap.

houses, Palmer was among them, spry and looking under the hoods of newest evaporators and mingling with the next generation of master boilers.

"I love it, it's just part of me now," she says. "I even lay in bed sometimes at night and I think of when I was up in the old sugarhouse, being all by myself. I would look out the window and see the sugarbush and feel sad that I wasn't sharing it with someone. It is so beautiful with the sun in the snow and the shadow of the trees and the buckets.

"Sugaring is a wonderful experience . . . there is something about it, something that makes you feel so lucky to be doing it, lucky to be alive . . . There's just something about it."

THE SUGARHOUSE

AMONG THE KEENEST memories of the farm year are coming into the sugarhouse from a cold, starry night to be instantly enveloped in warmth and a wonderful cloud of maple steam tinged with the aroma of a hardwood fire.

"It's always been the sweetest-smelling job of the

year," says one dairyman who also sugars. "There's the new hay in June and good, fermented corn silage in the fall, but the sugarhouse when she's going full tilt is pretty hard to beat."

For rural neighbors, a steaming sugarhouse is also an open invitation. Noel Perrin, a Dartmouth professor who built himself a small sugaring operation in the early 1970s and wrote about it in *Amateur Sugar Maker,* was astonished at what happened the first time he fired up his new Grimm evaporator:

"You get a superb draft with an evaporator, and about two minutes later the first wisp of steam arose from the sap. A minute or two after that, the red paint began to blacken on the furnace doors, and at the same instant the first little wave of boiling began. Shortly thereafter the whole back pan went into a rolling boil, and a continuous eight-square-foot cloud of white steam began ascending to the steam vent and out both sides of it. I rushed out the door to see what it looked like from outside. . . . For some reason the sugarhouse reminded me of a Viking helmet, the great plumes of steam, now gold-colored in the sunlight, being the horns. This mass of steam coming out in perfect silence and then floating away on the wind also reminded me by an even looser association of a clipper ship leaving port with sails up. . . .

"Just after I finished skimming and putting a little more wood on the fire, I learned a new social fact about Vermont. I see no truth at all to the myth that New Englanders are taciturn—they love gossip as well as anyone I know—but the talk takes place mostly on neutral ground: in stores and barnyards, at auctions and church suppers. Your house is private.

The Nintendo generation meets one of North America's most primitive food-making rituals. Marketers wonder how maple's anachronistic character will fare in the future.

Vermonters are less likely to drop in unannounced for coffee than other Americans, or to have you over for the evening. There are about two hundred people in Thetford Center, and I would guess I know a hundred and ninety of them. But I have not been in more than a dozen houses, and most people have never been in mine.

"A different custom prevails for sugarhouses. Steam had been rolling out for about 15 minutes now, and people in the village had had time to see it. I don't say they came pouring out of their houses and down to visit, but one or two at a time a remarkable number did appear. . . . If I ever build another sugarhouse that's visible from a traveled road, I will make it considerably larger than eight feet by eleven."

As Perrin learned, a really well-planned sugarhouse has room for a small crowd and an armchair or two. If the warmth and fragrance act as a magnet, there is something more that is probably fundamental to the special affection sugarmaking seems to engender in all who experience it.

From the tree to a hot cup of just-finished syrup, a person can feel in control of a complete process, moving in simple steps from a watery raw material to a wonderfully rich, precious finished product in a matter of hours. Success comes from you and the tree, no additives or middlemen required.

To be sure, some who gather when sugar is being made are drawn by a sweet tooth. In times past, a new crop of maple came at the end of the dreariest part of the year for country families. Winter staples included potatoes and turnips, bread and beans and salt pork. The chickens had usually stopped laying and the cows were giving little milk. Fresh fruits and vegetables were months away. There may have been hard-caked maple sugar for topping the porridge, but the fresh taste of new maple syrup must have been an even more wonderful sensation than it is today.

"One time when our family was growing up," Robert Howrigan recalls, "it warmed up and we started boiling and we made the first ten gallons of syrup and we put it in a milk can and brought it into the back room of the house.

"Then the weather stayed froze for a week, and we couldn't sugar of course, and by the end of that week, that syrup was all gone. My mother used to make

sugar cakes, and we always kept syrup in pitchers on the table. I think there is something about new maple syrup that is kinda tempting. It's a good tonic, it does the work that needs to be done."

Many other sugarmakers remember eating syrup in quantities that city people might consider stupendous, given the retail value of the product. In this setting, maple syrup needs no pancake, and often as not is sipped out of a cup or eaten straight out of a bowl with a soup spoon. Enough syrup gets consumed by the sugarhouse crew that many start to crave antidotes to the sweetness: sour pickles, salty beef jerky, eggs boiled in the syrup pan, potatoes roasted in the coals of the arch.

Hard cider was the chaser of choice for some in decades past, and sap beer was made on some farms.

One year's syrup samples, **top,** *with a bottle for each day's production—lighter being better. Vermont sugarmaker Eustace Thomas,* **middle.** *Full-tilt boiling,* **bottom and right,** *can go on around the clock during exceptional runs.*

"Red" Whiting fills traditional half-gallon cans at Raymond Howrigan's busy sugarhouse. Packing syrup at 180 to 190 degrees Fahrenheit virtually assures no spoilage in a product that stores easily but retains its best flavor if kept in a freezer.

As a place for men to gather and socialize late at night, in dry, conservative rural communities, the sugarhouse served, if only for a brief time each year, as a special kind of sanctuary. Today, with women and children more commonly present, the old-boy atmosphere is not always to be found, but the tradition of dropping into someone's sugarhouse to taste the new crop and share a brew is alive and well.

LATE NIGHT IN THE SUGARHOUSE

I F A JUG OF SOMETHING is part of the late-night scene in some sugarhouses, others are strictly teetotal. "The men my dad hired were sometimes pretty rough looking," recalls Nate Danforth of Danforth's Sugarhouse in East Montpelier, Vermont. "I remember thinking they were pirates when I was a boy—they'd show up unshaven and pretty scruffy. You needed to promise some of them a fifth at the end of the week to get them to work, but Dad always had a strict rule for everyone during sugaring: No drinking."

Indeed, most men and women running an evaporator like to keep a clear head while drawing off finished syrup. Once the season is in full swing, boiling days can be long, starting sometime in the afternoon and often ending near midnight. In sugarhouses without the latest technological enhancements, and these are still the majority, a sugarmaker wants to get the day's tank or tanks of accumulated sap boiled, filtered and safely into storage drums.

With an enhanced superfast evaporator and/or a reverse-osmosis unit, which acts like a high-tech filter to wring water out of the sap and substantially speed up the boiling time, many sugarmakers today can count on being all cleaned up and home in time to catch the late news—and tomorrow's weather forecast.

Having new technology requires careful timing. Judging the flow of sap into the storage tanks, the sugarmaker sets the reverse-osmosis unit running and then can spend part of the day checking tap lines for vacuum leaks. "We can do it all with fewer people," says David Marvin, "but that doesn't mean we've taken all the work out. We have 80 miles of pipeline to walk, and we check each tree many times during the season." The freezing and thawing cycles can cause plastic fittings and taps to loosen, and sap can freeze, causing blockages in the system. Air leaks must be found and corrected, or the whole system can slow down. During lulls in the season, most sugarmakers take advantage of quiet days to wash their equipment, swabbing out all gathering and storage tanks to remove sap-loving bacteria.

By late afternoon or early evening on a typical day, with the reverse-osmosis unit having produced a goodly quantity of concentrated sap, the evaporator is fired up and the day's run is transformed into syrup. What used to take eight or ten hours may be done with less than half the boiling time. While visitors sometimes expect to find the sugarmaker filling pint, quart and gallon containers right out of the evaporator, virtually all syrup first goes into bulk containers for repacking under less hurried conditions.

Small producers may use easily managed five-gallon cans, but the standard for commercial producers is a 31-gallon drum that, at 381 pounds and somewhere around 200 degrees when filled, is a handful to maneuver. From here the syrup may have many fates, de-

pending on its quality and the marketing philosophy of its maker.

In some regions, most notably Quebec's maple-rich Beauce, virtually all production is sold in the drum at bulk, wholesale prices. Each spring the world's most productive maple region floods the processing center of Plessisville with a sea of syrup.

The better grades will be repackaged for retail trade, while the darker B and C or utility syrup will go to restaurants, food processors and tobacco companies. It will end up in canned baked beans, maple-flavored cereals, salad dressings, vinegars, barbecue sauces, aromatic pipe tobaccos and all manner of table syrups that introduce a hint of real maple flavor. Some will end up in the hands of naturopathic healers in Europe and health charlatans in the American South, where it is variously sold as an exotic curative or the foundation for a lemon-water-and-maple-syrup fasting diet.

Some is more legitimately destined to become granulated maple sugar, maple butter, maple cream or one

Checking the grade of a sample, Robert Howrigan enjoys a reputation for making prodigious quantities of premium light-colored syrup that fetches the best prices.

VERMONT
makes it
SPECIAL
MILK & MAPLE

form or another of maple candy. At Maple Grove Farm in St. Johnsbury, Vermont, the maple-candy capital of the world and a popular tourist attraction, prodigious quantities of syrup are converted into melt-in-your mouth candy maple leaves that find their way into the gift-shop trade throughout the country.

While the marketing of maple products is a year-round occupation and challenge for many, back at the farm and sugarhouse the boiling season usually ends with everyone breathing a weary sigh of relief. Just as it started, the weeks of boiling can stop abruptly and, if nature hasn't been generous, with disappointing finality. A balmy night can signal a hiatus or, if things fail to snap back into the freezing zone, the finish of another year.

The last batch of sap in warming conditions may be a "frog run," with the night sounds of spring peepers heralding the imminent arrival of spring. Also called the "bud run," this flow of sap was traditionally relegated to the farmhouse cellar for the making of maple vinegar. (Syrup made in the waning days of the season carries the taint of metabolites from the awakening tree—nutrients being mobilized to feed the leaf buds—and such off flavors are highly objectionable in syrup for the retail market. Syrup tagged as "metabolism" is borderline awful, and "buddy" is a term that applies to a product that should never reach the table.)

With full spring breaking and red-winged black-birds calling, the sugarmakers can pull their taps, rinse their equipment, flip the evaporator pans and latch the sugarhouse door for another year. With a crop of good syrup safely in drums, they can truly relax for the first time in weeks. A sense of relief, fulfillment and, when the season has been a long one, bone weariness sets in. A sentiment about this most special of country rituals and probably as old as sugaring itself will often be heard:

"Happy to see it come, happy to see it go." 🍁

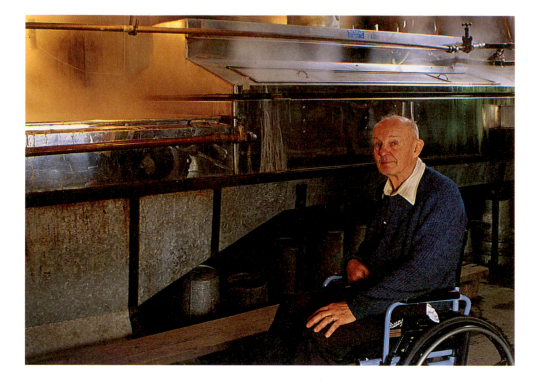

Maple Math
& Misperceptions

Harry Morse's primer for sugarhouse visitors

MY NAME is Harry Morse," says a distinguished voice that you don't quite expect to find in a dark, old Vermont sugarhouse talking to a busload of Israeli tourists. "Forty years ago, I was a dairy farmer." He lets the crowd adjust to the peculiar accent—there is something about it that makes one think of "proppa" British, brought gently but firmly down to earth—then continues his welcome.

"I got sick of milking cows . . . " Heads nod. Some of these guests may actually know the rigors of life on a dairy farm.

" . . . and my wife got sick of the smell of me after I had been milking the cows." The crowd smiles, charmed by the American lack of pretense.

"So, I stopped milking cows," he says. "Now I milk people."

The joke sets in, and this old Yankee farmer watches them exit laughing—all the way to the cash register.

This is the second time in three years that the same group from Israel has come to the Morse farm in the hills above Montpelier, and it is likely the second time some of them have heard the same line. Nonetheless, they go merrily away with their jugs of Morse Farm Pure Maple Syrup, not feeling the least bit milked by the 75-year-old man whose twinkling eyes signal a sense of humor and an honesty that speaks many languages.

Harry Morse is a sugarmaker's sugarmaker, a man who moved this sugarhouse with him when the family—going on eight generations of tree tappers—moved from one farm to another. Today he is slowed down by his health, and his son Burr manages much of the business, but Harry is still the master at passing on the lore and craft of making maple syrup to some 35,000 visitors a year. "People come here from Europe and Hawaii and California, and they have no idea how syrup is made. Many of them expect us to be boiling every day, especially the ones who come for the foliage in the autumn. They have the notion that syrup is made when the leaves turn color.

"Probably the biggest surprise for most," he continues, "is how much sap and fuel and work it takes to make a gallon of syrup. They usually have no idea that 40 gallons of sap go into the making of one gallon of syrup. They don't know it may only run for one month—or even just two weeks—a year, and that it only runs when we have freezing nights and warm days. They don't know that there's not a drop of real maple syrup in Aunt Jemima or Mrs. Butterworth's. And most of them have the idea that dark syrup is heavier. We explain that all syrup must be the same weight, by law."

Having sat in an unpadded old church pew in the rustic sugarhouse, hearing the story and, if the sap is running, getting a taste of syrup hot out of the evaporator, "they go away and never forget it." ❧

SUGARING BENCHMARKS

Averages & Equivalents

32–40 gallons of sap =	1 gallon of syrup
Sugar content of sap =	2%–2.75%
Sugar content of syrup =	66.5%
# taps / tree =	2–4
# taps / gallon of syrup =	2–4
25 gallons syrup =	1 cord wood burned
1 gallon syrup =	11 pounds
1 pound maple sugar =	8 gallons syrup
1 U.S. gallon =	3.785 liters
1 Imperial gallon =	4.546 liters

Comparative Calories

Maple Syrup	40/Tbsp. =	80/oz.
Molasses	40/Tbsp. =	80/oz.
Honey	45/Tbsp. =	90/oz.
Brown Sugar	53/Tbsp. =	106/oz.
Cane Sugar	55/Tbsp. =	109/oz.
Karo Corn Syrup	60/Tbsp. =	120/oz.

Production Leaders*

1.	Quebec	4,222,000
2.	Ontario	592,000
3.	Vermont	570,000
4.	New York	400,000
5.	Maine	153,000
6.	New Brunswick	109,000
7.	Wisconsin	100,000
8.	Pennsylvania	95,000
9.	New Hampshire	94,000
10.	Michigan	85,000

(*U.S. gallons of syrup, 1992 crop.)
[Sources: USDA, Agriculture Canada.]

Maple Syrup Content

Aunt Jemima® =	0%
Mrs. Butterworth's® =	0%
Log Cabin® =	2%
Vermont Maid® =	2%
Pure Maple Syrup =	100%

❦

CHAPTER 4

SHADE-TREE SUGARING

*A modest introduction to the
art of making maple syrup at home*

To MAKE RATTLESNAKE STEW," reads one of our favorite pioneer cookbook recipes, "first take one large or two medium rattlesnakes." For the would-be maple-syrup maker thinking about trying his or her hand at sugaring for the first time, getting past the initial step is often the most intimidating part. My own induction took place some twenty years ago, after I had spotted a box of bright metal sap spouts and several stacks of spanking-new buckets at the back of the hardware store around the corner from the newspaper offices where I worked.

Armed with a dozen sap spouts, a brace and bit and a rookie's mixture of enthusiasm and trepidation, I read a short booklet on the subject and rushed out to tap the assortment of maples that surrounded the old farmhouse I was renting at the time. The time of year was right, and no sooner had the taps gone in than the sap came spilling out. Not bad for a book-taught sugarmaker, I was thinking as I stood back to admire my first tapping job—the buckets were per-fectly set, lining the laneway and running along the dirt road that passed the front of the farm. I was thinking about running for the camera when a battle-

*A line of roadside maples, **above**, and a few sets of buckets, spouts and covers, **opposite**, are the starting essentials for backyard sugaring, a rapidly growing spring pastime.*

weary little Farmall tractor came chugging down the road pulling a load of wood in a wagon that looked like an original buckboard with bald Model A tires.

This was my nearest neighbor, and we were on fine, if somewhat stiff, terms: we shared a party line; he delivered me bone-dry firewood whenever needed; I provided him constant amusement as a city kid trying to teach himself country ways. The gleam in his eye as the old tractor coughed to a stop put me instantly on guard. What had I done now?

Making the moment last, he silently surveyed the yard, and his eyes danced with glee as he went through his handkerchief ritual, pulling out a grimy old red-and-black rag and deliberately clearing his nostrils, one side and then the other. He spat some tobacco juice into the ditch, feigned a quizzical expression and slowly composed the question he would be able to repeat for years to come:

"Tappin' some trees, eh?"

He let the question hang with a sense of timing I knew only too well.

"Never heard of anybody tappin' a soft maple before . . ."

Now, as it happened, I had just read that perfectly good syrup could be made from any of the large eastern maples, but it turned into yet another episode of the guy with the books and university degrees arguing in the face of hardscrabble country experience.

My old neighbor was right, of course. The silver and Manitoba maples weren't really worth the effort when 10 acres of prime sugar maples were going untapped just 100 yards down the road.

A DARKER SHADE OF MAPLE

PART OF THE FATE of those of us not born with a sap bucket in hand is surviving the first year or two of gaffes and embarrassments. Fortunately, if you can find a maple—almost any maple—success of sorts is virtually assured. Home syrupmaking is not only possible, it can be done mostly with found and scrounged gear, and the results are guaranteed to be profoundly satisfying.

Even the three gallons of dark stuff we made from the soft maples that first year seemed a wonderful crop indeed—full of maple flavor and making a glistening row of Ball canning jars. Then came the following spring, when operations moved to the real sugar maples. When the candy thermometer said that the first batch of the new season was finished, I at first thought something must be wrong. It was as pale as sweet clover honey. The taste, however, provided one of those eye-opening moments of a lifetime: it had the finest distillation of maple flavor I had ever tasted. It was beginner's luck Fancy syrup, full of complex tastes and a perfect maple bouquet—and it has kept me trying to tap at least a few trees every spring since.

In truth, most first batches of homemade syrup turn out a darker shade of Grade B (not something a serious sugarmaker aspires to), but the universal reaction from friends is almost sure to be wonderment. For the beginning sugarmaker, there is a never-to-be-forgotten sense of self-accomplishment. Even the funkier amateur syrup is far superior to the faux-maple table syrups the great American palate finds acceptable. The feat of making something as primitive and direct from nature as maple syrup strikes a deep chord for many of us, particularly in the digitized,

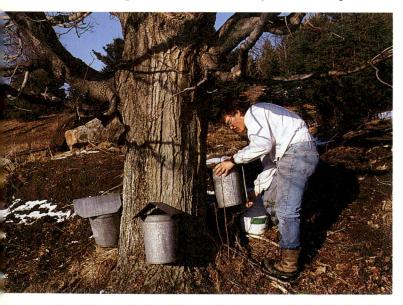

The south side of the maple may run earlier in the day, but experts recommend spreading taps to all compass points.

A healthy old maple growing in a yard can be what old-timers affectionately call a "sap cow"—easily outstripping the yield and sweetness of trees in a dense sugarbush. Experts recommend no more than two buckets for an aesthetically valuable tree.

microwaved, synthetic North American lives we lead.

Lest the fear of making mistakes and not having an expert instructor scare you away from the notion of making your own syrup, consider that, of the dozens of sugarmakers who directly and indirectly supplied information for this book, not one claimed to know everything about maple trees and making syrup. To the contrary, one of Vermont's most experienced sugarmakers recently stood before a roomful of his peers—from all over New England, Canada and the Midwest maple states—and said, "One of things about sugaring that you can just about count on is each season you're goin' to learn something new, no matter how long you've been at it." Heads nodded quietly in agreement, an amazing moment considering these were some of the greats of North American sugaring.

As with any endeavor dependent on nature's co-operation, sugaring demands humility; if you don't have it at the start, it will come with time. Making maple syrup also requires a certain amount of patience, character and ingenuity, but compared to other rural or folk-art endeavors, it is one that welcomes newcomers without exacting a high price of admission. For less than the cost of a gallon of syrup, one can be adequately equipped to make excellent quality syrup or maple sugar—albeit on a microscale.

Most of the equipment can be found around the house and begged or borrowed with little trouble. The biggest commitment will be your time. Even modest batches of syrup will necessitate spending some crisp late nights around a fire, bathed in maple steam. My guess is that the great majority of people who try it find themselves instantly, helplessly hooked. Sugaring is a timeless, priceless, once-a-year rite of spring that must be the most exuberant way to break all the physical and mental bonds of a northern winter.

The minimum requirement, as with the rattlesnake stew, may be the biggest stumbling block: you need at least one maple of 10 inches in diameter. The very best sap does come from the sugar maple (also known as the hard, rock, curly or bird's-eye maple) and the black maple (which some botanists classify as a hybrid or variant of the sugar maple), but resourcefulness is the sugarmaker's middle name, and you may certainly tap other maples if given no other choice. (See *Poor Man's Maples*, page 42.)

Adding to the first-year confusion is the fact that winter is the worst time of year to be identifying leafless trees, and there are some wickedly funny stories about city types putting taps in elms, walnuts and hickories. (Every once in a while you will see a telephone pole tapped here in Vermont. This is a form of Yankee old-boy humor aimed at befuddling the tourists, but it also serves as a sobering reminder to ask for advice if you can't figure out which trees to tap. If in doubt after comparing the bark and the leaves under your trees with a good field guide, swallow your pride and ask a neighbor who knows his trees.)

Contrary to conservative first instincts, starting small doesn't really mean restraining yourself to one tree and a single tap until you've learned the tricks. To have enough sap to boil with a margin of safety—and to end up with more than a cupful of syrup—a sensible minimum is four to six taps.

The good news for anyone planning to tap a tree growing in the yard or along a roadside is that these are far and away the best sap producers. The big, spreading crown of a so-called "open-grown" tree is many times larger than that of a typical sun-deprived sugarbush maple, and its summer leaf mass is able to generate significantly more carbohydrates to store for the next spring's sap run.

A few good-sized trees near the house can make for a decent crop of syrup for a single family. With just

Tapping, for the amateur, can wait until the first perfect sugarmaking day, when the sap is starting to run. After drilling, **top,** *the tapper lightly hammers a spout into place.*

three large maples in my own side yard, I have often been able to make more than two gallons of syrup. The universal rule of thumb is that each tap placed will yield about one quart of finished syrup if the weather is at all cooperative; a backyard sugarmaker can often do much better. In fact, tap for tap, the little producer can beat the big-time professional hands-down, just by sticking to the big, friendly sap-cow maples on nearby lawns and roadsides. If your property is bereft of sugar maples, look for a nearby string of tappable roadside trees, keeping in mind that you will have to be able to tromp back and forth to the taps lugging heavy containers of sap. Note obstructing fences, water-filled ditches and half-mile hikes over plowed fields or lawns that will be off-limits to any sap-gathering vehicle.

The determined would-be sugarmaker is almost

With the bucket hung from the spout and the lid slipped into place, **top,** *the sugarmaker is off to the next tree as drops of sap begin hitting the bucket ,"two drops to a heartbeat."*

but one *very rough* benchmark goes like this: Take the going retail price for a gallon of Grade A syrup and divide by 100 to get an estimation of a fair price to pay for a gallon of sap. Thus, if the syrup price is $30 a gallon, you might reasonably pay 30 cents for a gallon of average-density sap. Naturally, sweeter sap is worth more, and if you are buying more than a small quantity, it may be wise to test the density with a sap hydrometer and set the price according to local guidelines.

SIMPLIFIED TAPPING RULES

THERE ARE ARGUMENTS for and against tapping your prize shade trees, and the advice of Sumner Williams, assistant director of the University of Vermont's Proctor Maple Research Center, is succinct: "If I had an old specimen tree that I just couldn't stand to lose, I wouldn't tap it." If a tree is already weak or stressed for any reason, including advanced age, tapping could just add to its woes.

However, according to Williams and most knowledgeable backyard sugarmakers, the risk of hurting a maple by tapping are slight, if one follows a set of recommended tapping guidelines. Unfortunately, these rules vary from state to state and province to province. Local county foresters or departments of agriculture should have guidelines currently in use in your region. The following suggestions are representative of the new, generally more conservative tapping standards that are gaining acceptance.

Some sugarbush-management experts consider these guidelines too cautious. Ontario's Clarence Coons, for example, firmly believes that it is fine to tap a 10-inch tree, to use two taps on trees 12 to 18 inches in diameter and to place up to three or four taps on big, healthy trees. (See *Sugarbush Steward,* page 46.)

Nevertheless, there is definitely a growing sentiment among thoughtful sugarmakers who argue against placing no more than two taps on any single tree, no matter how large. (This is nothing new, really.

sure to find some kind of access to trees, as long as maples grow in the area. I've never been turned down by a neighbor when asking if I can poach on his or her maples; it helps to have easy-going farm neighbors with country ethics, and it also helps to offer to share the syrup. Many small-scale sugarers rent or lease pieces of sugarbush or come to barter arrangements with the owners. Many people will be happy to let you tap their trees just for a chance to watch what you are doing and to share a sampling of the first sugar-on-snow.

If all else fails, you can probably find a sugarmaker willing to sell fresh sap. To my mind, the tapping and gathering aren't to be missed, but some people are happy confining themselves to the boiling and finishing. Ask someone in the know what the going price for sap is; the calculations are a bit convoluted,

As early as 1878 a sermonizing Vermonter named L.C. Davis virtually charged his fellow farmers with cruelty to their trees if they put more than one tap on any tree. "Why will you abuse this most noble of trees, the sugar maple?" he asked.)

Scientific observations fail to support Davis's extreme position, but the choice of undertapping compared to the Tapping Guidelines is certainly the personal prerogative of any recreational sugarmaker. The family farmer with bank payments to meet and a big evaporator to keep fed is, obviously, under different pressures to produce as efficiently and intelligently as possible.

In any case, the backyard sugarmaker has one tremendously satisfying advantage over the big operators: we can wait until the very last minute to place our taps. While the operations with tens of thousands of taps must begin tapping weeks before the sap flows, we can afford the luxury of waiting for that perfect first day when the icicles start to drip and the mercury rockets up out of the freezing zone into the high 30s or 40s.

Bore a taphole in these conditions and you have one of the ultimate forms of instant gratification: sap will come spilling out the moment you withdraw the bit. Tap the spout or spile into place with a lightweight hammer, hang the bucket, and your sugar season is off and running. Kids—and you are missing at least half the fun if kids aren't around for this—will yelp with glee. If you don't have children at home,

do what the old country sugarmakers have always done: borrow some from the neighbors to share the excitement and lend a hand.

If you happen to miss the beginning of the season, do not despair. The run normally lasts four to six weeks, with breaks for freezing weather—day and night—when no sap flows. As long as the nighttime temperature drops crisply into the freezing zone and things thaw nicely the next day, the sap should still be running. The great fear among sugarmakers is a stretch of prematurely balmy days and nights. Once the trees start to bud and either the nighttime or daytime temperatures get too high, the sap flow turns "buddy"—giving syrup one of its most offensive natural flavors—and then shuts down as if a divine faucet has been twisted to the Off position for another year.

If *when* to tap is a relatively inexact science, *where* to tap is positively rife with conflicting advice. Although most older sugarmaking guides will tell you to place your taps on the sunny side of the tree and under a big branch, researchers have repeatedly demonstrated that the total yield per taphole over a season does not depend to any great extent on its relationship to overhanging limbs or any particular point of the compass. (The sun-warmed south side of the tree will run first, but researchers assure us that the north face will produce an equal quantity of sap over the course of a season.)

Do be sure to stay at least 6 inches to the left or right and at least 18 inches directly above or below

---

ENLIGHTENED TAPPING

🍁

1. **Tap no tree smaller than your bucket or less than 12 inches in diameter** (*36 inches minimum tape-measured circumference at chest height*).

2. **Place up to two taps on trees 18 inches or more in diameter** (*54 inches or more in circumference*).

3. **Two taps per tree is the maximum.**

4. **Never tap near a visible previous taphole.** (*Stay at least 6 inches to either side and 18 inches above or below an old taphole scar.*)

5. **Always used clean spouts.** (*Boil them the day you tap or dip in alcohol prior to tapping. Don't carry clean spouts in unwashed sap buckets.*)

6. **Place nothing in the tapholes at the end of the season.** (*Studies show that wooden plugs, corks or other devices may retard healing.*)

7. **If a tree is slow to heal—taking more than two years to close a taphole—consider not tapping or reducing the number of taps.**

Roadside trees hung with buckets are a sight to gladden the soul, but syrup from maples growing near heavily salted paved roads may have off flavors from the calcium or sodium chloride residues that run off and are readily taken up by the trees.

any visible old taphole. Otherwise, you will be close to or into unproductive wood. (In a healthy maple, a taphole should heal over in a year or two years. A tree that fails to cover its tapholes quickly may be under stress, or a naturally slow healer. In either case, it may be wise to cut back on tapping such a tree, especially if it is a prized specimen.)

Concentrating tapholes too close together can also threaten the health of the tree. If your bit produces curls of dark wood or anything other than fresh, clean sawdust, find another place to tap; discolored wood means two things: low sap flow and the chance of getting off-flavored syrup. (That dark wood may be part of an old tapping wound or a streak of rot that will feed more than pure sap into your bucket.)

The taphole standard diameter today is $7/16$ of an inch to accommodate both traditional metal spiles and plastic pipeline spouts. Standard carpenter's bits

in this size are available everywhere, and sugarmaking suppliers have special shortened versions. If a foray into the cellar turns up a dull, rusty old bit, either clean and sharpen it or get a new one: dull, dirty bits make for low production, quick invasion by bacteria and slow healing by the tree. A half-inch bit may be substituted, but be sure your spouts are big enough to fit tightly—the tapered aluminum types will work fine, but others will fit loosely and leak sap.

Angle the taphole slightly upward (between 5 and 10 degrees is right) to get gravity working for you, and do not drill more than 2½ inches deep. An old farmers' proverb says that the best sap comes from the shallow tap, and this happens to be true. For the finest quality sap, at the price of reduced volume, drill no deeper than 1½ inches. Holes deeper than 2½ inches can lead to health problems for the maple, providing an entry route for bacteria and fungus. A specialty

ENDURING BUCKETS

SWEET MAPLE

When wooden sap buckets were replaced by metal earlier in this century, some traditionalists said syrup would never taste as good again. Today, some small producers claim the best syrup comes from buckets rather than tubing.

tapping bit, short and very sharp, is a good investment.

Keep turning the bit as you withdraw it from the hole to extract the curled shavings. Using a twig, small pocketknife blade or a piece of hooked coat-hanger wire, remove any loose wood from the hole. (Do not blow into the taphole; researchers say you may introduce bacteria.) Quickly tap the spout or spile into place. Do not whale away at it: the spout should be snug, not driven into place for life. Glancing blows will damage the tree, and the less havoc you wreak the better.

The spouts or spiles themselves can usually be found at most farm-supply stores and hardware centers in maple-sugaring regions. If all you get are quizzical looks and dead-ends after a foray into the Yellow Pages, try a mail-order supplier (see Sources). In the maple business, these people are virtually all friendly, honest and reliable. If needed, you can have spouts, buckets and other paraphernalia on your doorstep by the next day via a commercial parcel service.

For the sugarmaker with time and frontier inclinations, homemade spouts are certainly not out of the question. A four-inch length of wooden dowel, a half-inch in diameter, can be clamped in a vise and bored through the center with a drill or hand-carving tools to make a simple spout. Likewise, a short length of naturally hollow sumac stem—the traditional spile used by some early sugarers—does quite nicely with the center pith poked out. In either case, the tree-end can have its edges smoothed and, if necessary, be tapered with a whittling knife. (If you fancy sitting by the fireplace on winter evenings carving completely handmade spouts, try using basswood

"Sap runs before a rain and after a snow" says an old maple dictum, and a shade-tree sugarmaker gets a first-hand lesson in nature's ebbs and flows.

for authenticity and ease of whittling.)

Most sugarmakers opt to buy their spouts, and the traditional metal types used for decades are de rigueur in these parts, but plastic versions may be more common in your region. Old cast-iron spouts are great if you can find them, and Dominion & Grimm has a new cast-aluminum version with classic lines called the Royal that is a lovely piece of work.

To my mind, used spouts and buckets are a great buy if you can find them, and working with still-good equipment from 30 or 50 years ago can be a real pleasure. Call a local sugarmaker or two, or contact one of the equipment suppliers listed in the back of this book. This equipment is not in short supply, if you know where to ask. (Consider that hundreds of thousands of buckets and metal spouts have gone out of service in the last 20 years. Given the country reluctance to throw such things away, most are probably tucked away in sheds and attics, waiting to be rescued.) At this writing, serviceable old galvanized or aluminum buckets with lids and spouts can be had from dealers in the range of $2 to $4 a set, depending on the source and the quantity you want. A bit of light surface rust shouldn't disqualify an otherwise sound bucket; sap is much less prone to pick up any sort of off flavors than finished syrup. Reject heavily rusted buckets, however, and think twice about buying any bucket that has been painted inside. If you do find painted buckets, be sure the paint used was lead-free and meant for contact with food products. (Grimm still makes its old-faithful galvanized buckets and covers from the original patterns, at about $8 for a factory-new set.)

I have most of my original aluminum buckets from 20 years ago, but there's no feeling of sentimental attachment; they love to sail away in winds that won't faze heavy galvanized buckets. I've heard from an old Quebec sugarmaker that plastic buckets make for lower-grade syrup, and they tend to freeze solid overnight and thaw out at a maddeningly slow pace. Likewise, the plastic bladders—such as the King Sap Sac—that commonly turn up in chain hardware stores are disliked by many amateurs. They are ugly—looking like nothing more than huge intravenous fluid bags—and can be devilishly tricky to clean, making them great bacteria breeders if they aren't scrupulously washed and disinfected. (The manufacturer claims that sunlight hitting the sap in the bags helps kill bacteria, but this is inconsistent with the ironclad rule of keeping sap as cold as possible.)

Perhaps the most common amateur substitute for good metal sap buckets is the opaque plastic gallon milk jug. These work, but are barely acceptable: a gallon can fill swiftly in a good run, and the jugs will overflow every time you turn your back unless someone is around to watch them all the time. (A real sap bucket holds two to four gallons.) Furthermore, the light plastic bottles dance around in the wind and can be tricky to hang; more often than not, you see them blowing around the yard rather than catching sap, and they are an indignity tacked to a proud old sugar maple.

Next to Godliness

One ingenious idea adapted by bucketless, budget-conscious amateurs is tapping with plastic spouts and running several short lengths of sap tubing into one recycled five-gallon food-grade plastic pail. Mini-pipeline systems of just 10 trees are not unheard of, allowing the sugarmaker to forget about buckets and gathering pails entirely. The pipeline taps are cheap (about three for a dollar) and can also be inserted before the season starts, because, with the pipeline in place, they don't allow a new taphole to dry out as quickly as one with an open metal spout. Correct pipeline installation is a bit tricky, and the advice of a dealer or experienced sugarmaker should be sought. The basic fact needed by someone putting up just a few taps with pipeline is that you must use gravity to keep the sap flowing; the pressure in the tree is not enough to force sap through a poorly hung line. In the sugarbush, a good plastic pipeline system is said to run "DTS"—downhill, tight and straight. Sagging lines tend to collect sap, which stagnates and becomes a wild breeding pool for bacteria and yeast.

Whatever taps, buckets and even pipeline you choose, everything should be sanitized before tapping begins. The taps, to begin with, are perfect little devices with which to inject microorganisms, bacteria and yeast spores into the fertile, vulnerable tree. Boil the metal ones and dip plastic pipeline spouts in alcohol or a weak (1:20) solution of unscented chlorine bleach and water. This is the same solution that some commercial producers use to disinfect pipeline. You absolutely *must* rinse the spouts well with clean, warm water after dipping. Contaminated spouts will cause your tap holes to "dry up" significantly sooner, cut your sap yield and introduce unwanted bacterial growth that will spread to buckets or pipeline and all your storage vessels. ("Drying up" occurs when multiplying bacteria accumulate to the point that the inner walls of the taphole become sealed off.)

GATHERING BASICS

YOU'LL BE A BETTER sugarmaker if you think of a bucket of sap as not much different from a pail of fresh cow's milk," says one award-winning sugarer whose farm produces both milk and maple syrup. Bacteria thrive in both milk and syrup but are kept in check by cleanliness and cold temperatures.

Sap should be gathered morning and night, if possible, to achieve the highest quality. In cold, overcast weather, sap may keep in the buckets for a day or two, but this isn't good practice. Once bacteria start multiplying in your buckets, maintaining quality gets harder and harder. Some gatherers throw out the piece of ice floating at the top of the sap bucket after a good, cold night. It is mostly water, but if gathered up with the sap, it will help keep things cold while the sap is waiting to be boiled and discourage bacteria growth. It is probably unwise to pour off the sap and leave the ice in the buckets, as tests have shown that after a few days, the ice can become a bacterial breeding ground.

Bucket covers make life much simpler, but you may have to wait for the first rain to prove that the expense was worth it. Walking through your sugar orchard on the morning after a hard rain and trying to decide whether to dump the buckets or to gather and take a chance on boiling rainwater all day will illustrate the beauty of good lids. (Advanced sugarmakers or technophiles will have a handy sap hydrometer or refractometer at this point to measure the sugar content of the cold sap. At a 1 percent concentration, it will take 86 gallons of sap to yield a gallon of syrup. (See page 29.)

Getting the sap from the tree to the fire may require some improvisation. Solutions range from well-cleaned canning kettles on a sled, a hand-pulled wagon (for those whose trees are a stone's throw from the backyard evaporator) to baffled sap tanks in the trunk or pickup for sugarmakers with miles to cover. Horses, snowmobiles and even dog teams are used to bring in the gathered sap.

In our own microscale operation, we just lug around five-gallon rigid blue plastic drinking-water containers, originally bought for camping and emergency water supplies, which have sturdy handles and screw-on caps to stop sap from sloshing out. A big funnel is handy to prevent spills between sap bucket and jug.

Maple equipment-supply houses have all manner of gathering and storage containers in food-grade plastic, often at very reasonable prices. Restaurants, dairies and small bakeries can also be good sources of white heavy-duty plastic buckets that have been used for bland foodstuffs. (Shun anything that has housed pickled herring, onions, Greek olives or anything with an assertive odor that will contaminate the sap.) Leader and Grimm, using their original patterns, both offer a series of attractive gathering buckets with tapered sides to contain the sap and an old-fashioned pouring lip that hearkens back a century or more.

Well-organized sugarmakers have a sap storage tank near the place where they boil. The best are shaded from the sun—the north or northwest side of a shed or other wall is best—and covered. Some sugarmakers also go one step further and insulate the storage tank in some way to keep it chilled. Old-timers used thick wooden Tomahawk tanks that kept the sap cold and fresh much longer than the galvanized metal and plastic that is standard today. Restaurant suppliers and sugarmaking-equipment dealers have all sorts of plastic barrels, food-grade garbage cans and vats that can be used. A virgin Rubbermaid 30-gallon garbage can reportedly will keep sap without affecting the flavor. A feed store can also supply sheep- or cattle-watering troughs that can serve to hold sap. Old steel milk cans are highly desirable sap holders, if you can find them in decent condition. These have the great advantage of being able to be moved close to the fire to preheat the sap before adding it to the evaporating pan.

Keep in mind, however, that gathered sap is best boiled down daily and not left overnight; if kept very cold, it may last 48 hours, but the really dedicated sugarmaker doesn't sleep until the day's sap has been boiled. Once fermentation starts, the potential of sap to produce delicately flavored syrup declines rapidly. (If using a storage container, it is wise to strain the cold sap as it arrives from the gathering, to remove the stray bark, lichen, sap moths and other debris. Filtering out bush debris right after gathering has been shown to bring the quality of the final syrup in commercial operations up one full grade, compared to leaving it floating in the sap. Multilayer cheesecloth or a clean, old cotton towel works adequately for this, but maple dealers now offer very convenient cone-shaped sap filters that are inexpensive and last several seasons.

White-collar and part-time sugarmakers will find compromise necessary at times, and some hard-pressed amateurs manage to get by boiling sap only on odd days or weekends by putting each day's yield into the freezer to prevent loss of quality. (Taking a lesson from the commercial outfits, one local amateur has rigged a small pump and ultraviolet sterilizer, bought for less than $200 from a marine-aquarium supplier, to prolong the freshness of his sap. The UV

Sap is best gathered daily, but if it can't be finished the same day, the amateur can freeze partially boiled batches and finish them as soon as it is convenient.

sterilizer is simply a fluid-tight tube surrounding a fluorescent-type UV-emitting bulb that kills microorganisms but doesn't change the composition of sap.)

EVAPORATING EQUIPMENT

HOW TO BOIL WILL DEPEND on a multitude of circumstances, including budget, backyard aesthetics and the ambitiousness of your entry into sugarmaking. While dreaming of buying a small evaporator and building a sugarhouse, we've lately been content with six or eight taps and

"There's more than one way to kill a cat besides soaking him in butter," says an old proverb that, roughly translated, means, "You can make some very good syrup without a single piece of expensive gear." Used buckets are cheap and abundant.

doing all the boiling entirely within our country kitchen. The first stage of evaporation happens on a Vermont Castings Encore airtight stove that cranks along all winter at one side of the room. More intense boiling and finishing take place on our propane-burning Findlay gas range.

Every other syrupmaking article and booklet will warn that boiling sap indoors is guaranteed to steam the wallpaper from your walls and/or coat your ceiling with a film of molasses. I'm not sure who first gave this advice, but I suspect it might be a scare tactic started by the friendly folks who bring us "Vermont Maid" from New Jersey. If wallpaper peels off this readily, I've never seen it do so when trying to strip the stuff from a wall.

It helps if your kitchen, like ours, is 200 years old and naturally drafty, and anyone with a new, airtight

home will want to exercise caution if evaporating indoors. However, by cracking open a few windows and/or running a ventilation fan, the steam problem can be easily overcome in most houses. This steam will fog the windows and fill the house with the aroma of maple, but it is not sugary or sticky and the odor is short-lived; maple steam is almost pure water vapor.

Boiling outdoors is the way we started, and it is a commonsense first choice of most sugarmakers with more than a handful of taps. The minimum-investment, assemble-in-minutes substitute for an arch (the firebox under an official evaporator) is concrete building blocks. Easily and inexpensively available from building-supply centers if you have to buy them, the blocks can be set together with no mortar to form a simple box support. Simply lay a steel grate over the blocks and set your pan or kettle on top. Anyone with a Yankee instinct for making do will figure out one way or another to contain a fire and support a container for boiling. Aim for real stability, however; a rickety old barbecue set or tumbling bricks can cause scalding hot sap to spill and burn bystanders.

The backyard evaporator is really just a hot, continuous fire with a large pan to hold the sap as it boils down into syrup. How this is achieved can be as simple as a camp stove bubbling sap in a heavy metal soup pot or as complex as a Rube Goldberg-approved assembly of old barrels and wood-stove parts from the town dump. (For a gallery of minimum-cost examples, see *Backyard Sugarin'*, by Rink Mann.)

Salvaged metal drums are a favorite of sugarmakers, and myriad designs have been made to work using the barrel either as firebox or evaporating pan. (If the latter, be sure to know the previous use of the drum. I wouldn't trust anything that had held agricultural chemicals or the like, especially when honey drums or old syrup barrels can be found.)

Big canning kettles or industrial-size soup pots can be pressed into service to serve as evaporating containers, and both the native tribes and early European settlers made formidable amounts of sugar in deep kettles that were hardly the ideal shape for evaporating. A real evaporator works well because it has a large bottom area to sit over the fire and a large surface area for steam to rise off the sap. Better than kettles are big, flat baking or roasting pans from restaurants or school cafeterias that may have been used for haunches of beef or making macaroni and cheese for multitudes. A common size is 18 by 24 inches and 4 to 6 inches deep. Light scorching or rust can usually be cleaned from used pans with steel wool and elbow grease. Stainless-steel pans or pots are best, if there is a choice. (It may help to know that imperfections in the sap-boiling pan may go unnoticed during most of the boiling process and never bother you if the finishing is done in small, perfect kitchen pans. Old scorch marks will, however, prove problematic if you try to finish syrup in the evaporator pan and will tend to cause burning time and time again.)

If you happen to live anywhere near a sugaring-equipment dealer, the very best choice of pans will be found there, either used or new models in small sizes. Even on a very tight budget, you may find a trade-in or "factory second" pan just right for learning to sugar.

With your syrupmaking skills advancing, you may even want to graduate to a multipan set-up. The first pan starts with fresh sap, which is usually moved with a scoop after it has been reduced by half or two-thirds. The second pan is used to take the thickened sap even closer to syrup. This method lets you avoid adding cold, thin sap to hot, concentrated sap, which tends to make for darker syrup.

Proximity to your wood supply is an important consideration, and some shelter from the wind is advisable. An old rule of thumb for sugarmakers with evaporators is a full cord (4 feet by 4 feet by 8 feet) of dry hardwood for each 25 gallons of syrup. Preheaters, reverse-osmosis and piggyback units have professional sugarmakers using much less wood today, but the less efficient home-boiling operation may require a half cord for each 5 gallons of finished syrup. Boiling sap is a great time to use up scrap lumber, knotty chunks of firewood, old fence posts, cheap slab wood and dead branches from your yard or sugarbush. Wooden shipping pallets, which burn hot and fast, are free for the taking at many warehouses. The only real caveat about firewood is to be sure the supply isn't green or soaking wet. A good quantity of "fast wood" or bone-dry lumber scrap is good to have on hand to start and freshen the fire.

BOILING TACTICS

SOME PEOPLE LOVE to boil right in the sugarbush and make sure the wood supply is there the autumn before, covered and dry, before the snow falls. A roof over the boiling area is a major step up, but it should be the least of your concerns for the first year or two.

And so, with a fresh supply of sap, a firebox of some

sort, an evaporating pan or kettle and a stack of dry wood, you light a match and become a sugarmaker. In the early stages of boiling—before the sap thickens close to the density of syrup—you can't boil too fast or get the fire too hot. Don't be content with a gentle simmer: it takes a strong, rolling boil to evaporate at a decent speed.

In the professional evaporators, sap depth is kept to an inch and a half or even less. The pro, however, has automatic float valves to keep sap flowing in as needed. Unless you are extremely vigilant, don't try to maintain a really shallow boil with rudimentary equipment. With the sap 6 or 8 inches deep, you can still run to the house for a short break without risking disaster.

My notion of the Indian or settler method, and the one for rank beginners, is to get your deep pot boiling and keep adding fresh sap as the level drops. Be sure the sap level is relatively high whenever you aren't paying close attention.

Throughout the boiling process, a scum will form atop the hot sap; skim this off from time to time with a sap strainer or a large slotted spoon covered in cheesecloth. Once all your sap for the day is condensed into one container, bring it down to a somewhat thickened state. Then, rather than try to finish it over a hard-to-regulate outdoor fire, pour the sap into a smaller kitchen vessel and bring it indoors to do the crucial last steps on the stovetop.

At this point, it's a good idea to pour the hot sap through a filter of some sort: multiple layers of cheesecloth, old cotton tea towels, paper coffee filters or a proper sap filter from a maple-supply house. Invariably, ash and other bits of debris will turn up, and you must get them out before things get thick and hard to strain. (A caution: new sap and syrup filters, or any cloth material other than cheesecloth, should be boiled before use to remove any manufacturing contaminants. We always rinse new cheesecloth in

scalding water for the same reason.)

From here on, it helps to stay close by the stove and use your hydrometer, candy thermometer or "aproning" test with a spoon frequently. Remember this old farmhouse syrup-finishing maxim: "A watched pot never boils over."

Syrup is done when it "aprons"—a folk-tech term for the formation of a sticky, sheetlike curtain of syrup that falls slowly from the edge of an upheld spoon or sap scoop. (Unfinished syrup spills freely like water.) At this point, it must be taken off the heat immediately; continued boiling will make for a syrup that is too dense and turns to sugar when it cools or forms sugar crystals in the bottom of the can or jar.

> *"A watched pot never boils over."*

Problems—or at least some exciting moments—lie ahead for the sugarmaker who misses the point when sap becomes syrup. There is a sort of flash point that syrup reaches just before it's done; in an instant, the boiling gets noticeably different, with fine bubbles that seem to strain upward through the thickening liquid. The color usually gets darker at this stage, but if you are making premium-grade light syrup, the nature of the bubbles is a better indicator than color.

If not handled with care, syrup at this point can turn into a seething mass of boiling liquid and foam that levitates out of the pan, cascading over the sides and, if you are boiling on your kitchen stove, into nooks and crannies you didn't know existed in and under your range. An unbelievable volume of fluid can foam out of a container in mere seconds. Experienced sugarmakers react to foaming emergencies in two ways: quickly adding some cooler, thinner sap or breaking the surface tension of the bubble mass with a touch of fat. The latter is an almost miraculous reaction, in which a mere drop of vegetable oil or cream or a speck of butter can tame a foaming pan or evaporator in an instant. A legendary precaution one can take is to suspend a piece of pork fat (as in the white

A small evaporating rig with a divided finishing pan that allows periodic drawing off of syrup, rather than finishing a whole batch at once. Equipment dealers usually have used pans for intermediate sugarmakers ready to graduate from kettle boiling.

band in a strip of uncooked bacon) on a string near the surface of the boiling sap. Dr. Mariafranca Morselli, one of the maple industry's toughest taste judges, recommends using fresh vegetable oil, such as a light olive or safflower oil; she feels that animal fats tend to turn rancid too quickly near the heat of the fire. Similarly, defoaming agents are notorious for causing off flavors, most often because of overuse or because they have lost their freshness. A small jar of oil is good for one season or less. "Whatever you use," says Sumner Williams of the Proctor Maple Research Center, "use as little as possible."

Burned syrup is heartbreaking, miserable stuff to clean up. The syrup left in the pan itself will caramelize and blacken with sickening speed, rendering the container useless unless caught in the early stages. Trying to remove sugar fused to metal is an ex-

hausting exercise with no guarantee of success. One possible remedy is to bring a layer of water in the scorched pan to a boil and then scrape while the boiling continues. However, even after repeated scrubbings, soakings and boilings, you may have to consider the surface of the pan damaged for life and useless for sugarmaking.

Not only is the final approach to finished syrup the most exciting step—the sap really is beginning to look, smell and taste like the real thing—but the one requiring the most attention. The sap will be bubbling along near the boiling point of water (212 degrees Fahrenheit at sea level) when suddenly the boiling point will start climbing. It is bona fide maple syrup when it boils at 7 degrees above the boiling point of water. (The altitude above sea level and the immediate barometric pressure both affect water's

boiling point; precise sugarmakers reestablish the boiling-point-of-water benchmark whenever the weather changes.)

To get measurements in this temperature range, a candy thermometer is required; these are stocked at most grocery and hardware stores. Serious sugarmakers don't trust mass-produced candy thermometers, though, and all maple suppliers offer nifty specialized sugarmaking thermometers, some of which allow you to set the prevailing boiling point of water at the beginning of a session.

Professionals who must adhere to more precise standards use a hydrometer, which measures the sugar density of the syrup on the Brix Scale or in degrees Baumé. Perfect maple syrup when boiling hot (210 to 219 degrees F) should measure 32 degrees Baumé or 59 degrees Brix—or float a hydrometer at the red line indicating this density.

The more accurate method of measuring finished density is to cool the syrup to 60 degrees Fahrenheit, when it should have a density of 36.0 Baumé or 66.9 Brix, depending on how your hydrometer is calibrated. If testing density at anything other than boiling (210 to 219 degrees F) or 60 degrees F, you must consult a reference table that shows relative densities of finished syrup at different temperatures. (See chart on page 136.)

Hydrometers are relatively inexpensive, but some states require that commercial sugarmakers use only approved, calibrated units from maple suppliers. Even these are relatively cheap, and, to my mind, an essential tool if you want to know that your syrup is truly the right density.

The only trick with a hydrometer is that it must be used with boiling-hot syrup to get the proper reading. Rather than fooling around with both a thermometer and a hydrometer and correcting for temperature variations, an obvious, foolproof method

Hot filtering is a must, and whatever material is used, it must be scrupulously odor-free, or off flavors will result.

calls for a simple tall, metal hydrometer cup, filled with hot syrup right out of the pot or evaporator. Keep your hydrometer at the ready, floating in a bucket of hot water to keep it clean.

(For backyard sugarmakers, a handy instrument called the hydrotherm will measure sugar density quickly and accurately at any temperature between the boiling point and the cold standard temperature of 60 degrees F. When the density is just right, the instrument floats in the syrup with the top of the red thermometer column at the same level as the surface of the fluid. The current $25 price tag is well worth the peace of mind in knowing that a pint of syrup given away to friends is not going to spoil or turn into a collection of crystals. The hydrotherm is not sanctioned for commercial use.)

If you have neither hydrometer nor candy thermometer and are making the syrup just for your own use, watch for the sap to start foaming up in the same manner as jelly, use the aproning test or just taste a slightly cooled sample of the syrup. If you think it seems right and is thick enough, remove it from the heat. (At this stage, some syrupmakers add milk, cream or egg whites to coagulate and trap any sediment in the batch. Purists regard this practice as crude and unnecessary. Obviously, any such mate-

Although a candy thermometer will suffice for home syrupmaking, a syrup hydrometer and hydrometer cup, left, are essential for anyone who wants syrup of the proper density.

rial must be skimmed off and/or filtered before bottling.)

Old-timers used to say the next step is to strain the syrup through an old felt hat. Depending on the state of your hat, you might use something else. The

SYRUP DENSITY CHART

Correct Hydrometer Readings
for Maple Syrup at Varying Temperatures

Degrees Fahrenheit	Degrees Baumé	Degrees Brix
209+	32.0	59.0
202+	32.25	59.5-
193+	32.5	60.0-
185	32.75	60.4+
176	33.0	60.9
167	33.25	61.4
158	33.5	61.9
149	33.75	62.4
140	34.0	62.9
130	34.25	63.4
120	34.5	63.9
110	34.75	64.4
100	35.0	64.9
90	35.25	65.4
80	35.5	65.9
70	35.75	66.4
60	36.0	66.9
50	36.25	67.4

NOTES:
1. Use only with hydrometers calibrated at 60 degrees F.
2. When using a hydrometer cup, fill until the foam runs over.
3. Lower hydrometer into syrup gently.
4. If syrup is not at the boiling point (209 degrees F or above), adjust the reading according to the scale above.
5. Readings taken below 50 degrees F are often inaccurate.

that appears in the final stage of boiling. Heavy felt syrup-strainers can be purchased, while many commercial outfits are moving to disposable paper filters. A multilayered nest of paper coffee filters is a possible substitute—but avoid using an old filter holder or coffee pot. Hot syrup is like a flavor magnet, and you could easily end up with Mocha Java Medium Amber.

You may also try to improvise with thick felt or stiff interfacing material from a fabric store, but beware treated materials, which have the potential of ruining all your work with chemicals or off flavors. (When in doubt, boil the filter material first.) Similarly, wash a felt syrup filter thoroughly after use—using only hot water without soap—and store in a dry, odorless environment. The felt will readily absorb any ambient odor—wood smoke, moth balls, aromatic cedar or Aunt Hattie's Victorian potpourri—and can easily ruin your first batch of syrup the next spring. Never store syrup filters in an airtight container or plastic bag.

Sooner or later, you will probably want to graduate to proper cone-shaped maple filters that make life much easier and are especially welcome if you are packaging in glass that will reveal any cloudiness or settled sugar-sand. Many sugarmakers today use a disposable paper prefilter inside a 5- or 8-quart felt or synthetic cone filter. They report that the paper does a better job of getting out the superfine particulate matter and assuring a crystal-clear final syrup. (The paper cones can be rinsed and reused several times, and they reduce the number of times the felt filter will have to washed.) Remember, all filtering must be done while the syrup is as hot as possible.

If your intention is to make maple sugar, wait un-

hot syrup should be allowed to flow through on its own; do not stir it through.

The object here is to remove nitre, also known as sugar sand or malate of lime, a fine, gritty precipitate

til the boiling point is 20 degrees F above that of water and then pour the syrup immediately into molds. (See *The Sweet Arts*, page 193.)

WELL-PACKAGED MAPLE

HOME SYRUPMAKERS usually have no trouble finding recycled containers for their first, small batches. Glass is the material of choice for both amateur and professional; it preserves color and flavor significantly longer than either metal cans or plastic jugs. (Henry Marckres, a Vermont maple inspector, says that Mason-type canning jars with rubber seals work fine; he suggests leaving the least possible headspace, or air at the top, which causes syrup to darken.) Glass also puts your syrup on display for all to see: if it is cloudy or is precipitating sugar crystals, the imperfections are immediately obvious. On the other hand, good syrup shows off its natural beauty best in sparkling clear glass.

Some traditionalists will have their syrup in tin and nothing else. " 'By gawd, my grandfather used tin and so did his father,' is something we all hear," says Marckres. Metal cans are, in fact, second to glass and not much better than the newest plastic jugs in their ability to keep syrup color from deteriorating in storage. High-density plastic syrup jugs, specially made for the maple industry, have been shown to hold flavor better than metal cans, and many staunch traditionalists are making the switch to plastic.

Although cases of spoiled maple syrup are relatively rare, the sugarmaker must ensure that any cans, jugs or jars are spotlessly clean before filling (sterilizing them with a boiling-water rinse as for canning is a good idea). Syrup is properly poured into containers at 180 to 190 degrees F. Immediately after capping,

turn your cans or bottles on their sides so that the hot syrup fills the top portion and sterilizes the inside of the cap and the topmost area of the container. Let cool with ample space between the containers. Stacked tin cans of syrup can stay very hot for an amazingly long time, making for poor-quality syrup. The phenomenon of crowded cans of hot syrup darkening a full grade—from Medium Amber to Dark Amber, for example—is known as "stack burn." The trick is to cool the containers as quickly as possible.

Many sugarmakers set the syrup out on a cold porch in an unheated shed to bring the temperature right down; some blow a stream of air from a fan over the cooling containers.

After cooling, store the syrup in an upright position in a cool place and refrigerate after opening. If you have any doubts about the syrup's density, freezing is the simplest way to prevent any chance of spoilage and to keep the syrup at its peak of quality. Many backyard sugarmakers freeze their entire crop and advise friends and relatives receiving the syrup to do the same. Unlike mistakes in canning other foodstuffs, spoilage in syrup has never resulted in anyone being poisoned. A really bad container is unmistakably inedible, usually smelling like rotten fruit or vinegar. Most often, the spoilage is nothing more than a layer of mold that forms in the cap. This mold can safely be peeled off and the syrup resterilized by bringing it briefly to 180 degrees (or even to a brief, light boil) and then rebottling it. This process may cause the syrup to darken, but shouldn't seriously harm the flavor.

The choicest grades of syrup are the lightest in color—not a deep brown as so many consumers be-

Syrup can, circa 1920.

lieve. In reality, most homemade syrup disappears with moans of satisfaction and relatively little discussion of how close it came to being Fancy or Light Amber. The majority of consumers, in fact, think they prefer the darker grades of syrup—mistakenly believing it is "heavier"—and good backyard syrup, unless it has a scorched or buddy taste, is almost always received with gusto.

Still, there are loftier goals for the sugarmaker who wants to compete with the best. (The fifth-generation sugarmakers will be happy to have you join the competition at the County Fair. One tip: keep your Prize Contender syrup in glass and keep it in the freezer.) The first run of sap usually produces the finest syrup and the color typically becomes darker and darker as the season progresses.

Tapped Out

REMEMBER TO REMOVE your spouts when the season draws to a close. (Do not plug the holes with anything. Maple researcher Sumner Williams says that open tapholes seem to heal faster and recommends "just letting Mother Nature take her course.") Wash the spouts well, and don't forget to boil them before reusing them the following spring. A scalding rinse of all buckets is also recommended, while those who have used plastic pipeline must now contend with the worst feature of this technology: forcing a cleaning solution through the system to remove traces of sugar and disinfect the lines. The disinfectant most commonly recommended for cleaning pipelines and other maple equipment is ordinary unscented household chlorine bleach, diluted at 1 part bleach to 20 parts water—never stronger. Galvanized metal must not be left in prolonged contact with the solution, or off flavors may be generated next season. Never, ever, use any type of fragrant detergent or soaps or any iodine-based dairy sanitizers on maple-sugaring equipment. According to the Vermont Department of Agriculture's Quality Control Manual, "Both have ruined the flavor of large quantities of syrup, rendering it totally unsalable." The bleach rinse must be flushed out with clean water, both to avoid off flavors and to help prevent squirrel damage, as the rodents seem to relish the chlorine salt residue left by the bleach rinse.

One effective home-devised cleaning solution that is currently gaining popularity is a mixture of one quart of red-wine vinegar in five gallons of water, followed by a water rinse. According to one sugarmaker who had serious squirrel problems prior to using vinegar, the rodents' interest in his tubing has decreased significantly. Those who cherish simplicity will also be pleased to know that some very accomplished sugarmakers routinely clean their equipment with nothing more than fresh water.

And so, the first sugaring season is over. Either you are terminally relieved or, more likely, maple is forever in your blood. Along the way, you've made something that gives a unique insight into the lives of the Indians and settlers who tapped the parents of these trees centuries ago. And, while the smoke was rising and your backyard sugar operation was in full swing, neighbors and friends will inevitably have drifted by to check out what all the activity and steam was about. A few of them snickered. Some had family stories or memories of sugaring and even a useful hint or two. Most couldn't resist throwing a stick on the fire or stirring the boiling sap. Each and every one hungered for a taste of the steaming syrup—the pure, eternal essence of spring in maple country. 🍁

A standard grading kit is an essential tool for the serious amateur or professional syrupmaker.

BACK TO BASICS, MAPLE EDITION

A refresher course in the pursuit of flavor—and lightness

STANDING BEFORE A ROOMFUL of seated sugarmakers, mostly professionals but with a healthy smattering of "backyarders," Extension Specialist George Cook puts a one-quart "Squeezable!" pop-top plastic bottle of Vermont Maid "syrup" on a table. A riff of grumbles reverberates in the crowd, as if the very shadow of evil has just passed over them. Waiting briefly for quiet, the rail-thin, high-cheeked agriculture agent places a smaller glass jar containing a pound of honey next to the Vermont Maid. A few quizzical expressions appear. Finally, holding a liquor minibottle—the airline single portion—he brings out 1½ ounces of pure maple syrup and, holding it like a pawn in a chess game, places it at the end of the line-up.

"This is how we stack up against the competition, folks, when you look at what the average North American consumer is using in a year," says Cook, who has come to take part in a sugaring workshop on a brilliant green Saturday morning in late spring.

"We are selling an anachronistic product. We talk a lot about the fact that Canada has three times the production of maple, and that 70 or 80 percent of their crop comes to the U.S." There are a few Canadians in the crowd, and everyone wonders where this might be going.

"But the real competition is Log Cabin and Aunt Jemima and Vermont Maid—all the table-syrup brands with little or no maple content," he says. "It's our job to make a product with consistent quality, because we know that once people taste the real thing, they appreciate the difference."

Cook, who works out of the University of Vermont's Extension Offices in Morrisville, Vermont,

Retired science teacher Donald Moore with his pride and joy sugarhouse. Many builders say their only regret is in failing to include room for a few armchairs or even a sofa. "It's about the friendliest place you can go with your boots on," says one.

acknowledges that making great maple syrup is not always easy.

"There are few crops that are so weather-dependent. Most years, we have just four weeks of weather that can make or break a crop. Things can happen very fast, and every once in a while we have to stop and remind ourselves of the basics. Remember, we are selling *flavor.*"

The core of his message to the group is about to begin, but Cook first neatly includes himself as an ordinary sugarmaker who shares their struggles with weather, equipment and the vagaries of the sugarbush. "After work and on weekends, the kids and I get out in the sugarwoods and hang 65 taps. It's just a little operation, but I think it's important for kids to grow up knowing what it is to make maple syrup."

Cook has had his hand on a clear Plexiglas box filled with small squarish glass bottles of syrup, and now they come front and center. "Here are our daily samples from this last season, showing how we did from one day to the next." Twenty-odd little bottles flash in the light, and there seems to be a fair proportion of Fancy-Grade syrup—a showing that the full-time sugarmakers in the audience recognize as pretty good syrupmaking by anyone's standards. With his wife, two daughters and son, Cook makes about 25 gallons each year in his spare time and takes pride in ending up with mostly Fancy- and Medium-Amber-Grade syrup.

His credentials firmly in place, Cook proceeds to lay down a set of rules that beginners and old hands alike would do well to remember:

A Sugarmaker's Checklist

🍁

1. Be ready.
   - Be prepared to make the most of the fine early runs. Check, clean and, if necessary, repair or replace equipment, filters, hydrometer/thermometer and containers. Be sure you have enough dry wood or fuel for the season.
2. Start clean—stay clean.
   - Clean and scald your utensils.
3. Tap carefully.
   - Don't let inexperienced tappers work without supervision. Pay attention to detail when you place each tap.
   - Don't overtap; fewer taps can mean more syrup. Follow the Tapping Guidelines—no more than two taps per tree. "We don't want trees that look like porcupines."
   - Never place a tap in brown wood. "It may be a crack leading to a nest full of squirrel droppings."
   - Use a sharp bit. Stay 6 inches away from any old taphole.
   - Use all sides of the tree.
4. If using pipeline, make sure it's clean.
   - Disinfect with a solution of 20 parts water to one part bleach and flush well.
5. Gather often.
   - Sap is a perishable commodity. Get it in while it's cold and fresh.
6. Strain your sap.
   - Don't let sap ice sit in the buckets or storage tank too long.
7. Boil at once.
   "The most common problem backyard sugarmakers have is collecting a little bit each day and saving it up until they have time to boil on the weekend. Then they end up with stuff that looks like blackstrap molasses and wonder why."
8. Boil until it's all in.
   - Finish each run as soon as possible.
9. Use only food-grade containers and pails.
10. Use a reliable hydrometer and thermometer.

11. If you have a lull, take the opportunity to rinse the equipment.
    "We've seen sugarmakers turning out Medium Amber get right back to Fancy (Light Amber) by cleaning their equipment."
12. Use fresh defoamer and don't overdo it.
13. Keep evaporator pans clean.
14. Never burn used oil in an oil-fired arch.
    - It's illegal.
15. Be sure your syrup is the right density at draw-off.
    - Use a properly calibrated hydrometer/thermometer.
    - At 210 degrees Fahrenheit or above, finished syrup should measure:
      32 degrees Baumé or
      59 degrees Brix
16. Filter syrup while still hot to prevent cloudy syrup.
17. Be sure filters are not a source of off flavors.
    - Store filters in a clean, dry place away from any odors. Do not store airtight or they will get musty.
    - Wash new filters in hot water and give them a sniff test. If in doubt about a filter, wash again in hot water or replace. Bad filters can cause very expensive mistakes.
18. If selling syrup, recheck the density when cooled to 60 degrees F.
    - Use the official chart to measure at cooled temperature levels, adjusted.
      At 60 degrees F: 36 to 37 degrees Baumé.
      At 60 degrees F: 66.9 to 68.9 degrees Brix.
19. Package syrup at 180 to 190 degrees F.
    - Cold-packing syrup is the leading cause of spoilage.
20. Clean and rinse all equipment at the end of the season.
    - If using a disinfectant, rinse thoroughly. (Rodents are attracted to salts left in pipelines by chlorine-bleach disinfecting solutions.)

A Serious Case of Maple

*Evaporator fever, and other thoughts on
becoming a real sugarmaker*

For some, it is inevitable: one look at a new Lightning or Hurricane or King evaporator—all gleaming stainless steel and bright copper, every bit hand-bent, hand-cast, hand-assembled, hand-rubbed—and the dream of a sugarhouse of one's own takes root.

The leap from backyard sugaring to buying a true evaporator is, fortunately, not the most expensive exercise in weekend adventuring one will ever consider. Because sugaring is still firmly tied to the parsimonious Yankee farmer's budget, a fully equipped small sugarhouse with a brand-new hobbyist-scale evaporator can be had for about the same price as a decent riding lawn mower.

Marriage partners may be inclined to classify this as just another Big Kid's Toy, and a spouse who doesn't share one's passion for sugaring probably won't be smitten on the spot by the looks of a racy new 2-by-6 raised-flue beauty with sap preheater, wood-saver blower and an automatic draw-off thrown in—just for efficiency's sake. (He or she might even liken Evaporator Infatuation to falling for a car or tractor, complete with its own array of turbo-charged options and irresistible bells and whistles.)

He or she would be wrong, of course, especially if the maples are there to be tapped and if the labor is free. Given maples, manpower and a ready market, some very convincing arguments can be made on behalf of the evaporator. As one first line of defense, just compare the relative costs and benefits of the following late-winter weekend choices: standing in ski-lift lines, watching pro golf on television, or making some unbeatable maple syrup that friends and neighbors will feel privileged to be able to buy.

"For rural people with maple trees, sugaring can have fantastic income possibilities," says Clarence Coons of the Ontario Ministry of Agriculture. "The public demand is there—especially when you can get people to come out and visit and see syrup being made. I'd say the ability of the sugarbush and the sugarhouse to draw visitors is unmatched by any other farming activity."

Realistically, however, one needs a few years of microscale sugaring and the understanding of the amount of work involved before making a commitment to buy an evaporator and increase production. The threshold for justifying an entry-level unit is somewhere between 25 and 50 taps, which means having access to a reasonable stand of sugar maples. You'll have to be ready to cut and haul firewood, although the enhanced efficiency of an evaporator brings the amount of fuel needed down to the range of one cord per 25 gallons of syrup. And you will need a ready market for the syrup and a willingness to live up to tougher standards of finishing, grading and packing than you have enjoyed when doing it for personal consumption and gift-giving.

The most common first evaporator for serious backyard sugarmakers is one constructed from a steel drum. Typically, a heavy-duty used drum is put up on legs, given a cast-iron door for feeding the fire, and opened up to create a platform for a galvanized or stainless-steel evaporating pan.

Nate Danforth, Vermont's leading independent maple-equipment dealer, says that the sale of barrel evaporators and components, along with other small evaporators, is currently the liveliest segment of the maple-equipment business. "A thousand taps that yield 250 gallons of marketable syrup can be a nice little income for a rural family," says Danforth. "If everyone pitches in to get it made and get it sold, there can be a good return—especially if you can sell a good percentage of the crop in smaller (more profitable) containers, such as pints."

A fourth-generation sugarmaker with an engineering degree from the University of Vermont, Danforth is optimistic about the maple business, but he is also the antithesis of a car salesman, preferring to lose a sale rather than feel he's pressured anyone into buying more equipment than he or she needs—or can handle.

"An inexpensive barrel evaporator is not a bad investment," he says, standing next to a barrel-arch unit neatly crafted from a used steel drum that once transported Chinese honey. At $439, it seems a reasonable entry-level unit, a major improvement over most primitive backyard boiling rigs.

"There's nothing wrong with this design," says Danforth, "and we get a lot of people who want to make their own. You can buy the firedoor kit separately, and most any welder can make a sim-

An amateur sugarmaker's dream: a 2-by-6-foot raised-flue Lightning model evaporator from Small Brothers.

ple arch from a heavy-duty barrel. The main thing we like to advise the do-it-yourselfers is to buy a good evaporator pan. We hear too many horror stories about homemade pans."

Danforth, who didn't trade his Vermont twang for a university education, says that home-rigged pans have a history of warping or failing at high temperatures, with soldered joints coming loose and creating hot, sticky floods. A complete barrel-arch rig with a 24-by-33-inch stainless-steel pan sells in the $425-to-$550 range, depending on options. However, the pan alone can be had for about $250 and is clearly the part you aren't likely to cobble together on your own workbench.

"With a pan like this," says Danforth, indicating the three interconnected sap compartments, "you can simulate the operation and characteristics of a professional evaporator. With the preheater [a metal box with a float valve that sits above the back of the pan], you can have a constant drizzle of warmed sap. If you have a steady, hot fire, you can have a continuous flow (from sap to nearly finished syrup) with regular sugaring-off every 30 minutes or so, as with the big evaporators."

The operator must move the thickening sap along the evaporating route with a stainless-steel sap scoop, and Danforth says the small size of the unit makes it more demanding of attention than the bigger, more

Engineer and independent equipment dealer Nate Danforth: "A couple of hundred taps can represent a nice little financial return for a rural family if they sell pints to friends and acquaintances. I can't think of a better way for a family to work together and for children to experience the excitement and rewards of work."

forgiving evaporators. "You have to keep an eye on things, and you might have to move your sap around if one spot starts to thicken faster than it should. You learn to judge how close it is to finished syrup by the color and the bubbles—more by the bubbles if the syrup is going to be light." Clearly, one could learn some of the finer points of running an evaporator with this modest pan.

Brass fittings on diagonally opposite corners allow the syrup or near-syrup to be removed conveniently through one of the draw-off faucets. Sugar-sand, nitre or calcium malate tends to be deposited near these points of exit and these will cause problems if allowed to accumulate. "We call this the poor man's reverse-flow evaporator. Every day you can pick the pan up (before lighting the fire) and turn it to change the flow and allow you to clean out the nitre around the draw-off." (The flow of hot sap will actually clean the nitre on the inactive side for you.)

Whether buying or making one's own barrel arch, Danforth strongly urges the sugarmaker to cover the firebox bottom with sand or, better yet, line it with firebricks. "A heavy-duty barrel should last 10 or 15 years, if it's bricked up, but it can burn through in just three years with no protection."

The Leader Evaporator Company offers a barrel-type evaporator called the Half-Pint that has a deep-bellied arch made of 18-gauge black iron. With a list price of $595, it is pricier than the units using recycled barrels, but it probably has more years of service built into its heavy firebox.

Gearing Up

NEXT UP IN THE EQUIPMENT hierarchy is a true sugarmaking evaporator, a so-called Two-by-Four or Two-by-Six rig. All the manufacturers have them, and they are variously designated as Hobbyist, Sportsman or Junior models. Danforth says that for something in the range of $1,100 to $2,100, one can buy an evaporator with a real cast-iron arch, superior fire control and the potential to outlast its owner.

The low end of the price range brings an economical *flat* pan, a 24-by-48-inch unit that will handle between 50 and 100 taps (Danforth cautions that such estimates of capacity are affected by many variables, including the productivity of your trees, the fuel to be used and your skill at managing an evaporator). With the more efficient *flue pan*, which sits at the rear of the unit and has a deeply ridged bottom that can bring icy sap to a boil in about 20 minutes, one might run 75 to 200 taps.

Having a flue pan is like adding gears to a bicycle, with the potential to double or triple the evaporation speed of a simple flat pan. The choice is obviously up to the sugarmaker and his or her wallet, says Danforth, who says he still sells galvanized pans but recommends stainless. (Most dealers will accept trade-ins, taking an older galvanized pan in partial exchange for stainless, or a simple flat pan for a faster flue pan. Some very good deals can be had on this used equipment.)

Prior to the early 1980s, evaporator pans were mostly made of English tin, but stainless steel is now the professional standard, being much easier to clean, not prone to rusting and more easily refinished if surface damage occurs. Danforth says there are also health concerns about boiling in galvanized pans, and he advises evaporator shoppers to try and make sure that lead-free solder has been used in any model they are considering.

Brand loyalty among evaporator owners is similar to the division of faith between Ford and Chevy pickup drivers in any group of farmers. The primary dividing line between the two camps is the preferred position of the flues in the back pan, and it is a choice the first-time buyer must also face.

Essentially, in the *drop-flue* types, as made by the Leader Evaporator Company and Dominion & Grimm, the bottom of the flue pan hangs deep down in the arch, directly in the path of the flames and heat from the burning fire.

The *raised-flue* style, from G.H. Grimm, Small Brothers and Waterloo, has the rear pan elevated above the level of the front or syrup pan. In this design, heat is directed up into the flues by baffles as it moves from the fire back toward the chimney..

In certain well-known sugaring families and in certain regions, the superiority of one type over the other is almost an article of faith. Robert Howrigan, head of one of Vermont's most respected maple dynasties, is a King man, and proud of it. The King, made by Leader, and other drop-flue models are generally believed to be faster—if somewhat touchier to handle.

"I've sugared all my life, and I've sold them all," says Nate Danforth, "and the truth is that there is not a great deal of difference between the two types." He credits the drop-flue with increased boiling speed near the front of the flue pan because of the method of heat transfer, but says the raised-flue types tend to boil more evenly and be more durable. "They have inherently more solid construction, and if I were looking to buy a 20- or 25-year-old drop-flue, I'd sure check it for any structural weakness."

Danforth says the reputation for speed in the drop-flue evaporators was built in years past, when the raised-flue types generally had shallow, 5-inch flues, compared to the 7-inch standard today. He says that proper bricking of a raised-flue evaporator arch is also extremely important. "A properly designed and bricked raised-flue model can be just as fast as a drop-flue—times have changed in this respect."

For the less-experienced sugarmaker, a raised-flue evaporator offers more control, a bigger flue pan and an emergency safety valve: if the front syrup pan gets too hot and is about to scorch, the operator can easily flood it with cooler sap from the higher back pan. Danforth also points out that tests of stack temperature—the heat escaping up the chimney—show that the raised-flue models tend to extract energy more efficiently. For drop-flue believers, however, flat-out speed is something you grow accustomed to, and if the old King is a bit of a hair-trigger handful, well, that's what sugarin' is all about.

Buying an evaporator is likely a once-in-a-lifetime event, and Danforth's advice is to purchase from a dealer who is well established in the business and who offers the best possible service. While many commercial sugarmakers are what he calls "paper dealers"—authorized representatives of a particular factory but having no inventory themselves—he

counsels that you may be better off with a supplier who can produce a spare part on a Sunday morning or who will answer the phone in off-hour emergencies.

He says that far-flung buyers who may be 700 miles from the nearest evaporator showroom can still make informed decisions. "Put in some time on the telephone," he suggests. "Call the factories and some dealers. Ask a lot of questions."

Buying directly from a factory is not, he says, a guaranteed route to the best price. The independent dealers can often make better deals—and "throw in a big bundle of service." (Freebies are part of this game, and the buyer should always ask for a free scoop and strainer, along with a good package price on any other equipment. A free or very cheap set of buckets, lids and taps, if you need them, is an easy gesture for most dealers to make.)

GOING PRO

Unlike the automobile trade, there are no notorious lemons in the new-evaporator business, and those with experience in buying and selling evaporators say the only really bad deals are used rigs foisted off on gullible newcomers. "Auctions are the worst," says Danforth. "In the heat of the bidding, some pretty questionable equipment gets sold to people who are going to be terribly disappointed. Some used evaporators are a bad deal at any price."

If in doubt, do what most farmers do: buy new.

"We don't have a single evaporator made up ahead of time," says G.H Grimm's general manager John Record. "We'll start your evaporator when the order comes in. In a factory or warehouse, it would only get dusty and scratched if it sat around for months. When somebody buys a new evaporator, you know, he wants it all spit-and-polish new. It may not look that way for long, but you might only get a new one of these once in a lifetime."

Next to the showroom-perfect evaporators, the most overwhelming temptation in a sugarmaking

Most small-scale syrupmakers have no problem selling all they can produce to neighbors, friends and work acquaintances, but marketing to the general public introduces responsibilities of grading, packing and labeling that cannot be ignored.

supply house may be the big, brightly enameled metal farm signs proclaiming PURE MAPLE SYRUP FOR SALE HERE. Before tacking one of these beauties to the tree in the yard or toting a trunkload of your maple pride-and-joy to the little store down the road, consider that asking the public to purchase your product introduces a series of complexities that the back-yard sugarmaker can blithely ignore.

The nearest county extension agent or department of agriculture should be able to supply the prevailing rules and regulations that you will be expected to follow. Some states and provinces are more rigorous that others: Vermont, which has the equivalent of maple Mounties prowling the state, includes little warnings such as this in its guide for sugarmakers:

"REMEMBER: Low-density syrup is ILLEGAL!"

In reality, maple-quality inspectors spend most of their time educating sugarmakers about avoiding grade violations, rather than simply handing out fines and penalties. This is a friendly, honest business for the most part, but important considerations for would-be syrup sellers include:

1. Grading & Labeling.

You must be able to grade and label your syrup accurately using the color scale approved for your province or state. You will need to learn to use a color-grading kit or colorimeter; this will take some experience, and a second opinion from a veteran is always a good idea if you are uncertain.

As a professional sugarmaker, saying that your product is "approximately Medium Amber" is simply not good enough. The color of your syrup must be lighter than or equal to the grade standard in your state or province.

Now for the tough news: Your syrup must be graded properly to begin with and it must be able to hold its grade level while on the merchant's shelf. Unless the quality of your syrup is exceptional, it will tend to darken over time, especially if stored in plastic or ceramic jugs. (In certain states, an inspector may pluck any can of syrup from any retail shelf at any time to check that the grade advertised is accurate.) Here is the friendly warning you'll find in your quality-control manual: "REMEMBER! The law allows NO TOLERANCE for color change."

The trick here is to pack your syrup in batches, just enough to meet market demand for two or, at most, three months. Keep your bulk syrup cool and under tight seal prior to packing. These lessons come hard. "When we packed all our remaining syrup in nice, new plastic jugs one July," admits one very successful retailer marketer, "it had gone dark and lost a lot of flavor by Christmas."

The label must also bear the correct weight or volume and your name and address, including zip or postal code.

As a commercial sugarmaker, you will learn to live (or die) by the grades. "A common misperception is that 'just about like Grade-whatever' will be close enough," says Nate Danforth. "Don't try telling that to an inspector." According to maple inspector Henry Marckres, about 95 percent of the violations noted in Vermont last year were for syrups that did not meet the stated grade color standard. The maximum fine for such a misrepresentation in Vermont is $1,000, if the state chooses to impose it.

2. Hot-pack canning and bottling, with a tamper-proof inner seal.

A customer who finds spoiled syrup or mold growing in one of your containers will not be a happy customer. If you don't get an angry call, someone else might. A visit from state inspectors may very likely follow. You must be packing your syrup at a temperature of 180 degrees to ensure that no live bacteria can survive in the container. (The can, jug or bottle must be turned on its side during cooling to ensure that

the inside of the cap and air space is also sterile.)

Containers must be "clean, sanitary and free from rust," with some type of approved "tamper-proof" seal and a cap or other closing mechanism that is airtight.

Remember the plastic syringe someone claimed to have found in a can of Diet Pepsi? When you start packing syrup for sale, you become as vulnerable as the Pepsi company. Finding appropriate containers with some sort of seal that will show evidence of tampering will become your very real responsibility.

3. Exact weight and measure.

A gallon of syrup for legal trade must weigh exactly 11 pounds (not counting the weight of the container) at 60 degrees F and measure exactly 231 cubic inches. The syrup must show a sugar concentration of 36 Baumé at the same 60-degree temperature. Syrup that is lighter or heavier will not pass inspection.

Your containers must contain no less—and no more—syrup than the container size indicates. This requires some planning; a gallon of hot-packed syrup at 180 degrees measures 237 cubic inches but shrinks to the proper 231 inches at 60 degrees. The containers used must be able to accommodate this changing volume.

Still undeterred? Send for catalogues from the maple suppliers listed in the back of this book. Cottage-scale syrupmaking is a thriving little industry, and all the proper containers, labels, tools and signs are readily available from maple-equipment suppliers. (See page 210.)

THINK THRICE

START SMALL BY FIRST selling to friends and co-workers who aren't likely to call in Federal agents if they think your Dark Amber is actually borderline Grade B; if, on the other hand, they come back for more, you may have a future in

Seasoned hands have one unanimous suggestion for any neophyte buying an evaporator for the first time: Swallow your pride and ask an experienced sugarmaker to help you through the first session or two. There are tricks to handling a seething mass of foaming syrup, and they are best learned at the elbow of an expert. The expensive alternative is a scorched rig.

the maple industry.

The most popular container size for many marketers is the pint, and where most sugarmakers used to sell gallons, they are now suggesting half-gallons, because these are easier for the buyer to handle and store. (A gallon can, once opened and partially emptied, is more likely to lose quality because of the large airspace created.)

Among the ersatz ceramic jugs, which you may want to call "high-density resin" rather than plastic, the Sugarhill XL model is the one many sugarmakers seem to like best. It is the first to have a glasslike hardened surface to help prevent oxidation, and early research results give it improved marks. (Oxidation-resistant plastic containers will likely become the industry standard, says one major syrup marketer.)

You may wish to ask your clients to save the containers for reuse; this type of plastic can be put into re-

cycling or, for small operations, visually inspected, sterilized with hot water, given a fresh new cap and inner seal and resold.

LAST WORDS

YOU CAN TELL a young sugarmaker," says one veteran of burned pans and fermented cans of syrup, "but you can't tell him much."

Learning from an old hand and not making all the predictable mistakes is the way most self-taught sugarmakers would do it if they had to do it over again. When Nate Danforth delivers a professional-level evaporator to a relative neophyte, his strongest advice is this: "Have a veteran sugarmaker on hand for the first boil or two. Those years of experience may be needed to sense when the float has not been adjusted properly and you are about to go dry in the flue pan or to recognize that you actually have syrup in the middle section of the front pan that has to be pushed around before it scorches."

Most sugarmakers love nothing better than helping a rookie set up, adjust and "sweeten the pans" for the first time. Indeed, most owe a debt to some earlier teacher who helped them through the first white-knuckle sessions. "Don't be proud," counsels Danforth. "Ask for help—you'll be doing both of yourselves a favor. There is a lot of pride and hard-earned knowledge in that old sugarmaker just down the road. I know more than one greenhorn who was saved by inviting an old-timer to join in. There's a saying you'll hear sooner or later: 'Old sugarmakers never die—they just evaporate.'"

charcoal in the bottom of my boiling can. You probably can't know how this feels until you've done it yourself. For a few days, it seemed like the end of the world. Then, to my surprise, my dad took me down to the Leader Evaporator Company. We met a gentleman there who had made me a 2-by-2 galvanized evaporator pan to boil with—a real sugaring pan that I continued to use until I had to go away to school. He had heard the story from my father about me burning up my garbage can, and this pan he made was a slick rig, with a nice brass draw-off faucet. I still have it, and we still use it for heating syrup. I don't know if my father paid for it, or if it was a gift from his friend at the factory, but I'll never for-

PRICING BENCHMARKS

Starting with the gallon price, experienced syrup marketers often use the following percentages to figure the pricing of smaller container sizes:

GALLON (hypothetical price)		$30.00
Half Gallon	57% of gallon price	$17.10
Quart	30% of gallon price	$9.00
Pint	19% of gallon price	$5.70
Half Pint	11% of gallon price	$3.30

FINALLY, FOR THOSE WHO LIKE to aim high and dream the sweetest dreams, there is a short story about an 11-year-old boy named David Marvin who decided he wanted to make his own syrup.

"I got excited about tapping some trees around my home in the late fifties," he recalls, "and I set up an arch with a garbage can as an evaporator and my dad got buckets and spouts for me. I was trying to use a simple batch method, and I stoked the fire with wood each night before I went to bed and left the can with a load of sap to simmer. Each morning it would be fine, and I'd come home from school to empty my buckets and start boiling again.

"Well, one morning I went out and it was just all

get the day I got it."

Today, Marvin, in his late forties heads up Butternut Mountain Farm in Johnson, Vermont, one of North America's leading family-owned maple-marketing companies. It didn't hurt that his father was Dr. James Marvin, one of the grand old men of maple research and one of the best-liked gentlemen in the industry. But going from a kid-scale pan to a farm with 12,000 taps—not to mention a seat on the board of directors of the Leader Evaporator Company— David Marvin is one indication of just where a little experimentation with a backyard evaporator can lead.

"I'm not sure if it's a disease or a bad habit," he laughs. "Maple is our life." 🍁

A Taste of Vermont

FANCY GRADE   GRADE A MEDIUM   GRADE A DARK   GRADE B

❦

CHAPTER 5

A TASTE OF SPRING

*"You can bribe anyone in Washington
with a quart of maple syrup."*
– SENATOR GEORGE AIKEN

THE FIRST SIGN that sugaring season has arrived on our mountainside is the predawn sound of cars bottoming out in their uphill rush toward the nearby maple research center. All year long, technicians, politicians, reporters, students and scientists from as far away as Germany and China travel to Mt. Mansfield to visit the University of Vermont's half-million-dollar laboratory dedicated to the study of sugaring and the sugar maple. But sometime in early March, just when the ground has thawed enough to make the road rutted, muddy and virtually impassable, the sap begins to run. For the next six weeks, if it is a good season, vacuum pumps draw the yield from more than 1,000 trees through a network of colored plastic tubing that makes the forest look like a giant experiment-in-progress. The sap swishes down the mountainside, ducks briefly under the road and into the brand-new wood-frame sugarhouse, where the boiling goes on nearly all night.

Jouncing up the road to join in the sugaring activities, few visitors notice the dilapidated shack they must pass near the bottom of the hill. Above the door, the sign reads, "Reg and Marcel's Maple Producd's Established 1989." The

A taste known to as few as one in ten consumers, pure maple syrup is the quintessential North American country delicacy.

Marcel LeGrand stokes the fire in his Underhill, Vermont, sugar shack. Eschewing modern methods and technologies, LeGrand makes syrup with a loyal following among rural neighbors who have favorite maple recipes for every occasion.

spelling may be idiosyncratic, but when it comes to the finer points of maple syrup and its economics, the owner, Marcel LeGrand, and his partner, Reginald Potvin, can teach the experts up the hill a thing or two. Crammed around the perimeter of the evaporator, with the door cracked open, Marcel's relatives and assorted other locals gather to grouse about town politics, while the two sugarmakers carry on with the tricky business of reducing sap to syrup.

Not the least of the attractions here are the refreshments: a never-ending supply of beer, fried venison, crisp, sweet watermelon pickles made by Marcel's wife, Gladys, all the maple syrup you can drink and a traditional sugarhouse specialty—hard-boiled eggs cooked in maple sap.

A little larger than a hen house, the sugar shack is a patchwork of donations, in which Marcel claims to have invested "nothing but the Budweiser." He inherited the evaporator from his stepfather. The metal sides of the building are cast-offs from the nearby offices of IBM, the fiberglass roof was scrounged from the dump, and the concrete floor was poured by a friend who stopped by with some leftover cement mix in his truck. One day last year, two men in a delivery truck, seeing the shack with the steam roiling out of it, concluded that they had arrived at the country's foremost maple research center, unloaded a huge plate-glass window and drove away.

For their part, the professionals at the Proctor Maple Research Center are impressed by the flavor of the backyard sugarmakers' syrup. "Experience over education," jokes Marcel. By the end of the season, the two men will have made something on the order of $1,000 worth of syrup. It will be gone well before next spring, sold to relatives and neighbors for $30 a gallon, without so much as a dollar spent on advertising.

Romance & Reality

Every year, I buy two gallons from Marcel: one of Fancy, the lightest and most delicate syrup, made from the first run of the season, and the other of the strongest kind he makes, Dark Amber. I serve the Fancy over pancakes, where its sprightly flavor stands out. The Dark Amber, which has a more pronounced maple tang, is better for cooking. But other than for pancakes, I am careful how I use maple—and not only because it is expensive.

The real reason is that maple syrup is not as easy to cook with as the thousands of books and pamphlets put out by the producers would have you believe. Depending on the recipe, it can be the best or the worst of ingredients. "People use maple syrup as if it's Karo or molasses. But it's not as versatile as Karo nor as distinctive as molasses," says Jim Dodge, author of *Baking With Jim Dodge*, who grew up in New Hampshire and has been cooking with maple syrup since childhood.

Caught up in the romance of maple, I made some dreadful dishes before I learned this. I soon discovered that too much credulity doesn't pay when cooking with maple syrup. (Part of the problem, one sugarmaker confided to me, is that recipes in books by maple-sugar producers often call for more syrup than necessary for a simple reason: to sell more.) Poured indiscriminately over onions, carrots, chicken and even potatoes, as some recipes recommend, it tastes gruesomely sweet. On the grill, or cooked at too high a temperature, it chars if you turn your back for a second. Baked at too low a temperature, it is sticky. If you add too much, it makes baked goods gluey. In other recipes, its flavor is merely lost, drowned out by the aggressive tastes of walnuts, cinnamon or brown sugar.

But in the right proportion, paired with the right foods, it seasons breads, spareribs, vegetables and even seafood, adding not only sweetness but a singular character and piquancy that can be duplicated by no other ingredient. Once you find a good maple recipe, it is likely to replace all other versions in your file. I've never made any other dinner roll since I found Gladys Elviken's Potato Rolls, feathery light and elusively sweet, made with mashed potatoes and maple syrup, from Virginia Bentley's *Bentley Farm Cookbook*. Maple-Pecan Scones, from a recipe by Brenda Larocque, a sugarmaker from Athelstan, Quebec, are the richest, butteriest and most delectable I've tasted. After many frustrating years of trying to cook a duck to rival the ones I've eaten in restaurants, I finally happened onto skillet-roasted duck with maple and bourbon sauce that is scrumptious. If I could make only one eggplant dish for the rest of my life, I'd have to choose the Szechwan Eggplant of San Francisco cookbook author Joyce Jue: hot, sweet and totally addictive, subtly seasoned with maple. A locally made batch of syrup is also the world's best house gift. "You can bribe anyone in Washington with a quart of maple syrup," Vermont Senator George Aiken is said to have once observed.

Although promotional pamphlets tout maple in a series of distinctly "upscale" elaborate recipes—in puff pastry, in rabbit loin with chanterelle mushrooms and in venison scaloppine with chestnuts—most people use it in just one way: over pancakes or waffles. In fact, maple syrup is best in its simplest guise, as a natural sauce, added almost as an afterthought: baked as a glaze over ham; poured into the hollow of a winter squash with a little salt, pepper and lemon juice then baked; splashed over grapefruit and briefly broiled; or drizzled into holes poked in bread pudding.

Cooking with maple syrup, however, can be tricky, since its distinctive flavor makes it less a generic sweetener than a complex ingredient in its own right. "Maple syrup is more difficult to integrate into dishes other than desserts because it's powerful and it's sweet," says Ted Fondulas, owner of the nationally acclaimed Hemingway's Restaurant in Killington,

Vermont. Instead of likening maple syrup to granulated sugar, Fondulas compares it to Jack Daniels whiskey because of its strong character.

It's easiest to start experimenting with maple in desserts that don't depend on exact proportions. Although too sweet for my taste, a beloved and simple North Country specialty is a sort of cobbler made by pouring maple syrup into the bottom of a pan, placing biscuit dough on top and baking it. Maple syrup also makes a delicious sauce for flambéed bananas, baked apples, upside-down cake and crème brûlée.

Many cookbooks blithely recommend substituting maple syrup for granulated sugar in baked goods by using three-fourths as much syrup as sugar and reducing the amount of liquid by 3 tablespoons, while leaving oil, eggs and flavorings the same. (Baking times may have to be adjusted slightly since maple syrup browns faster than sugar.) These guidelines, however, are far from foolproof, because baking is a precise art and because maple syrup is a very different commodity from sugar, with its own rules that the books usually don't tell you about.

Sweet Balances

My own breakthrough in cooking with maple syrup came when I stumbled onto a recipe in a church cookbook for maple-cream pie accented with black pepper. "Don't omit the pepper," the recipe warned. "It is important for flavor." That turned out to be the case. The pepper not only curbed the richness of the cream and butter but brought out the bite that is the distinguishing feature of real maple syrup. In *The Maple Syrup Cookbook*, Ken Haedrich includes a Quebec recipe for a maple-sugar pie similar to the one that spiked my interest: instead of pepper, it adds a little brewed tea and cider vinegar.

Even in the realm of desserts, the most successful recipes pair maple either with ingredients that counter its sweetness—pepper, lemon juice, bourbon or vinegar—or paradoxically, with full-flavored fatty foods—butter, cream, bacon and nuts—that play its richness to the hilt. With breads, the same principle holds. Maple syrup seems to go best with ingredients that act as foils: cornmeal, whole-wheat flour, oatmeal and coffee, or in the case of my favorite rolls, with potatoes, whose earthiness provides the right contrast to maple.

Even more than sugar, maple syrup requires the best ingredients. In a disheartening trend, many post-World War II community cookbooks call for shortening, margarine and Cool Whip in maple recipes. These fats leave a greasy, unpleasant taste in the mouth when combined with maple syrup. Only the full flavor of butter or cream will do.

Although maple syrup has a strong, distinctive flavor on its own, it is easily overwhelmed by other ingredients. Recipes that contain lots of different spices hide its flavor: you may as well use white sugar. Although nuts are delicious with maple, walnuts are usually too strong. For that reason, traditional recipes call for milder butternuts. Pecans, which are more available, are also a good match for the taste of maple.

One place where the liquidity of maple syrup is a distinct advantage is in mixed drinks. It not only smooths out the raw edges of the liquor but is a lot easier to use than the traditional sugar syrup, which has to be boiled, then thoroughly cooled before use. Although the combination sounded forced to me at first, maple syrup goes surprisingly well with bourbon. The best whiskey sour I've ever tasted is a mixture of grapefruit juice, orange juice and lemon juice, with maple mellowing and bringing together the sharp flavors. At Hemingway's, the simplest maple concoction is a perennial favorite: hot buttered rum, a glidingly smooth blend of cider, rum, maple and butter.

When properly used in savory dishes, maple syrup lends an undertone rather than a bludgeoning sweetness. The trick is to use a light hand. In their book *The Thrill of the Grill*, Chris Schlesinger and John Willoughby transform an ordinary center-cut ham steak by grilling it and brushing it with maple syrup

"Maple is like a spice, more like vanilla or garlic than sugar," says chef and innkeeper Beau Benson, whose celebrated kitchen at the Cobble House Inn turns out an inventive array of maple fare, like Maple-Seasoned Salmon With Rosemary, **above.**

during the last minute of cooking, then serving it with a chunky applesauce sweetened with maple syrup and seasoned with orange juice, cinnamon, nutmeg and allspice. Maple syrup goes admirably with other salty or strong-flavored meats like duck and corned-beef brisket.

But it is equally appropriate for milder-tasting foods like chicken, salmon and even scallops. One recipe that turns up in many sugarmakers' cookbooks is disarmingly easy and can't be improved upon. You skewer a scallop on a toothpick, coil a piece of bacon around it, brush it with maple syrup and broil it briefly. Maple holds its own in soy-sauce marinades, too, forming a slightly crunchy, slightly sweet crust on salmon or chicken, sealing in the juices of the fish or fowl as it caramelizes on the grill.

Maple syrup has long been a favorite addition to sweet vegetables like carrots, winter squash, parsnips and sweet potatoes. But it can take on vegetables with more spunk, too: red cabbage with apples or mashed turnips with butter, salt and pepper. A tablespoon dribbled over brussels sprouts after cooking is an unlikely sounding but perfect final touch. In salad dressings, maple syrup contributes both sweetness and vim, especially in combination with balsamic vinegar, whose mellow acidity provides just the right counterpoint.

Cobble House Secrets

In Gaysville, Vermont, where nearly every lawn sports a sign "Pure Vermont Maple Syrup Sold Here," Beau Benson, chef/owner of Cobble House Inn, gives an adept demonstration of just how versatile maple can be in the hands of a master. Benson uses maple much the same way French

chefs use butter, adding a jot at the end to her main-dish sauces. In her cooking, maple functions more as a seasoning and thickener than a sweetener, melding the flavors. "Maple is like a spice or flavoring— more like garlic or vanilla than like sugar," she says.

Benson uses about 40 gallons of syrup a year, in traditional dishes like baked beans, barbecue sauce and over homegrown, home-cured ham. She also utilizes it in plenty of less traditional ways: over cornmeal-sausage turkey stuffing, in creamed onions and in an almost unlimited range of inventive sautés, with chicken, pork, fish and seafood. Practically the only food Benson doesn't add a little maple to is beef, though she finds it compatible with the gamier taste of venison.

The maple is always added with restraint so it does not dominate.

Mouthwatering, old-fashioned Maple Dumplings are a signature dessert made by Kathryn Palmer, **above,** *who helps run one of Vermont's best-known family sugaring places near Waitsfield.* **Opposite page,** *topping vanilla ice cream with good, light syrup makes a favored dessert in many sugarmaking families.*

"Real people do not cover their food with maple," Benson says firmly. Otherwise, the ingredients are improvisational, with guests selecting their own combinations of fruit and herbs to go with whatever meat, fish or shellfish they prefer. The proportions are freewheeling; if too much liquid is added, the sauce is simply cooked a little longer to thicken it. The charm of these meals is that they can be prepared in moments without advance notice, and I had no trouble duplicating Benson's results at home without a precise recipe.

One of Cobble House's most popular dinners is a maple-seasoned salmon with rosemary-orange glaze, in which swordfish, scallops or snapper may be substituted. To make it, Benson takes a salmon fillet, browns it, splashes in some orange juice and a little Chardonnay, sprinkles in fresh rosemary, shallots and finally adds some maple syrup. For a variation on the

same dish, she uses chicken breast, with chicken stock in place of the orange juice. Or, Benson may pound a pork tenderloin into a thin cutlet, sauté it in butter, add brandy and demi-glaze—concentrated veal stock—and stir in a little crabapple jelly and maple syrup at the end. Or she may take a cutlet of venison, brown it in butter, add brandy and demi-glaze, then some homemade cranberry conserve made with maple syrup, and at the end, a little more maple.

Benson's barbecue sauce, a sweet, fiery concoction made in the height of tomato season, is a production worthy of the effort. First, she fills her 18-quart canning pot with crushed tomatoes from her garden that she has put through her Victorio strainer. To this, she adds about 5 chopped raw onions, 3 whole heads of raw garlic, about 1½ cups of Cajun spices made by combining various commercial blends, half a package of canning ketchup mix to thicken it (found in supermarkets throughout the summer), and the inevitable finishing touch, an entire quart of maple syrup. Benson cooks the sauce for 4 to 5 hours, stirring it carefully every 5 or 10 minutes and adding Kosher salt to taste at the end. Because of its high ratio of maple syrup, the sauce burns readily, both in the pot while it is cooking and on the grill. For that reason, Benson generally cooks her chicken or ribs in the oven until they are about halfway done, then paints them with the barbecue sauce and finishes them on the grill for the last half hour, watching them carefully.

For all these dishes, Benson prefers the darker grades of syrup, Grade A Dark Amber or the still more flavorful B grade. "I don't like Fancy; it's very weak and sweet, like pouring honey over dishes," she says. On the other hand, C-grade syrup, which is sold only in bulk for commercial use, is too dark: "It's like molasses and gets bitter and chocolaty tasting."

Taste Testing

When you live surrounded by maple trees and neighbors who stay up until all hours of the night boiling sap, it's heresy even to think about cooking with anything but pure maple syrup. But since imitation syrups cost one-third as much, I had always wondered whether the cheaper brands might make acceptable substitutes in cooking. Somewhat against my better judgment, I decided to put the matter to a test.

I asked a friend to prepare three unlabeled versions of my favorite black-pepper maple-sugar pie, one with pure maple syrup (Dark Amber), one with a commercial brand of syrup containing only 5 percent maple syrup and one with 2 percent. None of the five people whom I recruited for my taste test had any particular expertise in maple. As an impartial investigator, even I didn't know which pie was which when we gathered for the tasting.

One pie was visibly darker and richer in color. It had a pronounced maple kick. The other two were lighter colored, pasty and runny; the taste was as bland as the appearance. Mindful that consumers often prefer the stronger flavor of imitation syrup, I was afraid we had been fooled by an impostor. But in a vindication of recipes that insist on pure maple syrup, the winning pie turned out to be the one using real maple syrup. Everyone in the group had immediately identified the more pronounced flavor as true maple.

I store my maple syrup in the refrigerator, where it keeps nicely. If mold does develop, the syrup can be boiled and strained through cheesecloth, and it will be perfectly good. If the syrup crystallizes, it can be restored to a pourable consistency by setting the container in hot water until the crystals dissolve. You can also preserve maple syrup by pouring it into clean canning jars, allowing room for expansion, and placing it in the freezer, where it will keep for years. I've never needed to do that, though. In my house, maple syrup doesn't last anywhere near that long. ❧

—*Rux Martin*

SWEET MAPLE

CLASSIC
RECIPES

🍁

*Traditional & contemporary favorites
from the private collections of sugarmakers,
country inns & award-winning maple cooks*

Baked Eggs in Maple Toast Cups

THIS SPECIAL BREAKFAST is reminiscent of the sugarmakers' custom of boiling an egg in maple syrup in the evaporator. The syrup crisps the toasts and lends a hint of sweetness, and the eggs are served freestanding in the toast cups. The recipe comes from my well-thumbed copy of *The Official Vermont Maple Cookbook,* a pamphlet published by the Vermont Department of Agriculture.

- 3 **tablespoons butter, plus more for greasing muffin cups**
- 3 **tablespoons maple syrup**
- 6 **slices sandwich bread, crusts removed**
- 3 **slices bacon, cooked until crisp, crumbled**
- 6 **large eggs**
  Salt and freshly ground black pepper

Preheat oven to 400 degrees F. Butter 6 large muffin cups. In a small saucepan, melt butter and add syrup. Flatten bread with a rolling pin. Brush it with syrup mixture and pat slices into prepared muffin cups. Sprinkle bacon bits into bottom of each bread-lined cup. Break an egg into each cup, add salt and pepper to taste and bake for approximately 15 minutes, or until eggs are set. Run a knife around sides of muffin cups to loosen bread and gently lift out toast cups. Serve immediately.

SERVES 3 TO 6

Maple-Walnut Quick Bread

A DELIGHTFUL COMBINATION in a slightly sweet quick bread, good for breakfast, snacks, dessert or gift giving. The recipe is from Chef Michel Le Borgne of the New England Culinary Institute.

- 1 **cup maple syrup, plus 1 tablespoon more for glazing**
- 2 **tablespoons melted butter**
- 1 **large egg, beaten**
  Grated rind from 1 lemon
- 2½ **cups all-purpose flour**
- 3 **teaspoons baking powder**
- ½ **teaspoon baking soda**
- ¼ **teaspoon salt**
- ¾ **cup chopped walnuts**
- ¾ **cup orange juice**

Preheat oven to 350 degrees F. Grease a 9-x-5-x-3-inch loaf pan. Beat together 1 cup maple syrup, butter, egg and lemon rind. In a separate bowl, sift dry ingredients together and add walnuts, tossing to coat them with flour. Stir dry ingredients into syrup mixture and stir in orange juice.

Pour batter into prepared pan and bake for 1 hour, or until a toothpick inserted in the center comes out clean and bread has begun to pull away from sides of pan. Cool on a rack. After bread has cooled, brush with remaining 1 tablespoon maple syrup.

MAKES ONE 9-X-5-X-3-INCH LOAF

Maple-Pecan Scones

THE ULTIMATE IN SCONES. Adapted from a recipe in *Maplemania,* by Brenda Larocque, an Athelstan, Quebec, sugarmaker, these crumbly, buttery scones have a distinct maple flavor. Cream makes them exceptionally tender and rich.

To order *Maplemania,* write: Beavermeadow Farm, 883 Ridge Road, Athelstan, Quebec J0S 1A0. The book is $6.50 in Canada; $6.00 in the U.S., plus shipping.

- 3 **cups all-purpose flour**
- 1 **cup chopped pecans**
- 1½ **tablespoons baking powder**
- ¾ **teaspoon salt**
- ¾ **cup (1½ sticks) cold unsalted butter**
- ⅔ **cup maple syrup, plus more for brushing scones**
- ⅓ **cup heavy cream**

Preheat oven to 350 degrees F. Grease and flour a 9-x-13-inch baking sheet. In a large bowl, with a fork, stir together flour, pecans, baking powder and salt. Cut in butter until it resembles coarse meal. In a medium bowl, whisk together maple syrup and cream. Make a well in the center of dry ingredients and slowly pour in liquid ingredients, combining with swift strokes just until the dough clings together. The dough will be firm. Roll out about 2 inches thick on a lightly floured surface; the scones will not rise much higher than this in the oven. Cut scones with a 3-inch round biscuit cutter and place on prepared baking sheet about 2 inches apart. Brush tops with additional maple syrup. Bake for 15 to 20 minutes, or until tops are lightly browned. Transfer to a rack to cool. The scones may be served warm or at room temperature.

MAKES 11 LARGE SCONES

Maple Butter

THIS FOOLPROOF FROSTING-LIKE SPREAD, which can be mixed in minutes, is particularly delicious on sturdy whole-grain breads, provided you can prevent the family from eating it all straight from the bowl.

- 1 **cup maple syrup**
- ¾ **cup (1½ sticks) butter**

Cook maple syrup in a small heavy-bottomed saucepan over low heat, without stirring, until it reaches soft-ball stage (234 degrees F on a candy-making thermometer). Stir in butter. Pour mixture into a deep bowl and beat with an electric mixer until thick and creamy, about 4 minutes.

MAKES 1¾ CUPS

Gladys Elviken's Potato Rolls

🍁

"STRONG MEN HAVE BEEN KNOWN to weep for joy when first biting into one of these," wrote Virginia Bentley in her *Bentley Farm Cookbook* (Houghton Mifflin, 1974). Bentley's nephew, Sumner Williams, assistant director of the University of Vermont's Proctor Maple Research Center, further improved this recipe by substituting maple syrup for the original sugar. Mashed potatoes make the rolls feathery light, and the subtle earthiness of the potatoes is a perfect foil for the maple syrup. Serve with ham at Easter or with Dakin Farm Baked Beans (page 178). Freeze any extra in plastic bags.

2   **large potatoes, peeled and cubed**
1   **package active dry yeast**
½   **cup lukewarm water**
⅔   **cup maple syrup**
1   **cup (2 sticks) butter, melted**
4   **large eggs, well beaten**
2   **teaspoons salt**
     Approximately 6 cups all-purpose flour

Cook potatoes in boiling salted water until tender. Drain, reserving ¾ cup potato water, and mash. While potatoes are cooking, dissolve yeast in a small bowl in ½ cup lukewarm water until foamy, about 10 minutes. In a large bowl, combine yeast mixture, mashed potatoes, reserved warm potato water and maple syrup. Let stand in a warm place until spongy, about ½ hour.

Using a wooden spoon, stir into the yeast sponge the butter, eggs, salt and enough flour to make a soft dough. Mix thoroughly, turning out dough onto counter and mixing with your hands to combine completely. Wash out bowl, dry and butter it lightly. Place dough in bowl, cover and let rise in a warm place until doubled in size, about 2 to 3 hours.

After dough has doubled, turn it out onto a lightly floured board and knead lightly. The less flour you use, the lighter the rolls will be. Roll dough out about 1 inch thick and cut into rounds with a 2½-inch cutter or the rim of an inverted glass. Place rolls on two buttered baking sheets, about 1½ inches apart to allow for rising. Let rise in a warm place until doubled in size, about 1 hour.

Preheat oven to 425 degrees F. Bake rolls in middle or top of oven for 10 to 12 minutes, until tops are pale golden brown. Watch carefully so bottoms don't burn. Serve hot.

MAKES 4 DOZEN ROLLS

Maple-Walnut Sticky Buns

✦

THESE TENDER, SWEET ROLLS rise quickly in a warm kitchen and require only a half hour to bake. The recipe was contributed by Joan White, a sugarmaker from Underhill, Vermont.

ROLLS

1¼	cups milk
4	tablespoons (½ stick) butter
3¼	cups all-purpose flour
¼	cup sugar
1	teaspoon salt
2	packages active dry yeast
1	large egg, beaten

TOPPING

¾	cup (1½ sticks) butter
1	cup dark maple syrup
3	tablespoons light corn syrup
1	cup chopped walnuts

To make rolls: In a small saucepan, heat milk and butter until very warm (120 to 130 degrees F). In a large bowl, combine warm milk mixture, 2 cups flour, sugar, salt, yeast and egg. With an electric mixer, beat 4 minutes on medium speed. By hand, stir in remaining 1¼ cups flour to form a stiff batter. Cover and let rise in a warm place until light and doubled in size, about 30 to 45 minutes. Generously grease a 9-x-11-inch baking pan.

To make topping: Heat butter, maple syrup and corn syrup in a small saucepan, stirring. Stir in walnuts. Spoon topping mixture into prepared baking pan.

To assemble: Stir down dough. Drop dough by tablespoons onto topping in one layer and let rise in a warm place until doubled, about 20 to 30 minutes. While it rises, preheat oven to 350 degrees F. Bake for 25 to 30 minutes, or until a toothpick inserted in the center comes out clean. Invert onto a serving plate. Serve warm or cool.

MAKES 20 ROLLS

"As much as I like maple syrup, though, I never became as addicted as Uncle Arthur, who poured it over nearly everything he ate, including mashed potatoes, macaroni, sausage and apple pie."

— LEWIS HILL
Fetched-Up Yankee
(Globe-Pequot, 1990)

Maple-Oatmeal Bread

COFFEE GENTLES the aggressive sweetness of the maple syrup in this excellent sandwich loaf. The recipe, from a pamphlet of prize-winning maple festival entries, has produced more than its share of blue-ribbon winners.

1   cup hot coffee
¾   cup maple syrup
½   cup boiling water
⅓   cup butter
1   cup old-fashioned rolled oats
¼   cup sugar
2   teaspoons salt
2   packages active dry yeast
¼   cup lukewarm water
2   large eggs, well beaten
5½   cups all-purpose flour

In a large bowl, combine coffee, maple syrup, boiling water, butter, oats, sugar and salt and let mixture cool to lukewarm. Dissolve yeast in ¼ cup lukewarm water and let stand about 10 minutes until foamy. Add to maple-syrup mixture. Stir in eggs. Gradually add flour, 1 cup at a time, stirring the first 4 cups in with a wooden spoon, then mixing in the rest with your hands. Place dough in a greased bowl, cover and let rise in a warm place until doubled in size, about 1 hour. Turn dough out on a lightly floured surface, knead lightly, shape into loaves and place in two greased 9-x-5-x-3-inch loaf pans. Let rise about 1 hour, until dough reaches top of pans.

Preheat oven to 350 degrees F. Bake loaves for about 55 minutes, or until tops are light brown and bread has pulled away from sides of pans. Cool on a rack before slicing.

MAKES 2 LOAVES

Maple Brown Bread

CORNMEAL AND MAPLE combine in this quick bread, which tastes like Boston Brown Bread. Serve with Dakin Farm Baked Beans (page 178) or toast it for breakfast. This outstanding recipe is adapted from one in *The Official Vermont Maple Cookbook*.

1¾   cups whole-wheat flour (unsifted)
1   cup yellow cornmeal
1   teaspoon salt
1   teaspoon baking soda
½-¾ cup raisins, depending on the sweetness
     desired

2   cups buttermilk
¾   cup maple syrup

Preheat oven to 350 degrees F. Grease two 4-x-8-x-2-inch loaf pans. In a large bowl, stir together whole-wheat flour, cornmeal, salt, baking soda and raisins. In a medium bowl, combine buttermilk and maple syrup and stir into cornmeal mixture. Mix thoroughly and pour into prepared loaf pans. Bake for about 1 hour, or until bread begins to pull away from sides of pans. Cool on a rack.

MAKES 2 SMALL LOAVES

Windridge Inn's Cinnamon Raisin Loaf

❧

ESPECIALLY ON THE WEEKENDS, residents of towns near Jeffersonville, Vermont, drive for miles to pick up a fresh loaf of this specialty of the Windridge Inn. It is a particularly light raisin bread, veined with cinnamon and slathered with a thick glaze.

BREAD

1	package active dry yeast
¼	cup warm water
1	cup milk, scalded
¼	cup sugar
1	teaspoon salt
4	tablespoons (½ stick) butter
1	large egg
4-5	cups all-purpose flour
½	cup raisins
2	tablespoons maple syrup
1	teaspoon ground cinnamon

GLAZE

6	tablespoons (¾ stick) butter, softened
1	pound confectioners' sugar
½-¾	cup maple syrup

To make bread: Have all ingredients at 75 degrees F. In a large bowl, dissolve yeast in ¼ cup warm water and let stand until foamy, about 10 minutes.

Meanwhile, place scalded milk in a medium bowl and beat in sugar, salt, butter and egg. Let cool to lukewarm. When milk mixture has cooled, add it to yeast mixture and beat in 3 cups flour, 1 cup at a time. Knead for 5 to 12 minutes, adding 1 to 2 cups more flour as needed. Place dough in a large greased bowl, cover and let rise in a warm place until doubled in size.

Grease two 9-x-5-x-3-inch loaf pans. Punch dough down and knead in raisins. Let dough rise again, covered, in a warm place, until nearly doubled. Roll out on a lightly floured surface into a ½-inch-thick 12-by-16-inch rectangle. Brush with maple syrup and sprinkle with cinnamon. Starting with a long side, roll dough up and slice into 1-inch pinwheels. Place rolls side by side on end, 8 to each prepared pan, so that they form a loaf shape, and let rise again, covered, in a warm place.

Preheat oven to 350 degrees F. Bake for 25 to 30 minutes, or until breads begin to shrink from sides of pans.

To make glaze: While bread is baking, beat butter and sugar together. Add syrup slowly, beating until mixture is fluffy. Spread glaze on while loaves are still warm and in their pans. Cool on a rack.

MAKES 2 LOAVES

Maple-Apple Pecan Ring

🍁

This coffee cake is equally good for breakfast or dessert. It comes from Underhill, Vermont, sugarmaker Joan White, who has won many cooking contests with her maple-syrup recipes.

CAKE

2½	cups all-purpose flour
1	teaspoon baking soda
1	teaspoon baking powder
1	teaspoon ground cinnamon
½	teaspoon ground nutmeg
½	teaspoon salt
1	cup sugar
¾	cup maple syrup
½	cup vegetable oil
2	large eggs, lightly beaten
2	cups peeled, cored and chopped apples
¼	cup chopped pecans

TOPPING

½	cup confectioners' sugar
½	cup maple syrup
¼	cup chopped pecans

To make cake: Preheat oven to 350 degrees F. Grease and flour a 12-cup Bundt pan. Stir together flour, baking soda, baking powder, cinnamon, nutmeg and salt; set aside. In a large bowl, beat together sugar, maple syrup, oil and eggs. Stir in dry ingredients, then apples and nuts and mix until just combined. Pour into prepared pan and bake for 55 to 60 minutes, or until a toothpick inserted in the cake comes out clean. Cool on a rack, but invert onto a plate while still slightly warm.

To make topping: Stir together sugar, maple syrup and pecans and drizzle over top of warm cake.

MAKES ONE 8-INCH BUNDT CAKE

Maple Whiskey Sours

🍁

MAPLE SYRUP mellows the harshness of the liquor and fruit juice better than white sugar does. It is also more convenient, since you don't have to go to the trouble of dissolving sugar in water to make sugar syrup. The result is smooth, fruity, yet not overly sweet. For best results, use freshly squeezed fruit juice. A variation made with rye whiskey is more tart.
Variation: 3 parts rye whiskey, 2 parts lemon juice, 2 parts grapefruit juice, 1 part maple syrup.

4	jiggers (8 ounces) bourbon whiskey
1	jigger (2 ounces) orange juice
1	jigger (2 ounces) grapefruit juice
1	jigger (2 ounces) lemon juice
1	jigger (2 ounces) maple syrup
	Ice

Combine all ingredients except ice in a cocktail shaker. Dividing evenly, pour into two ice-filled glasses.

MAKES 2 LARGE DRINKS

Hemingway's Hot Buttered Maple Rum

✺

THIS CONCOCTION, one of the most popular offerings at Hemingway's restaurant in Killington, Vermont, is perfect for serving after skiing or for soothing a sore throat.

½ cup apple cider
½ cup hot water
2 tablespoons dark maple syrup

2 tablespoons butter
1½ ounces Myers's dark rum
¼ teaspoon freshly grated nutmeg

Heat cider, hot water, maple syrup and butter in a small saucepan until butter is melted. Stir in rum. Pour into a mug and float nutmeg on top.

SERVES 1

Maple-Broiled Scallops

✺

THE APPETIZER OF CHOICE among sugarmakers: sweet scallops wrapped in crunchy bacon and basted with maple syrup. Don't try improving upon this recipe by adding garlic, green pepper, water chestnuts or anything else. It's perfect just as is.

1 pound lean bacon, cut into 3- to-4-inch lengths
2 pounds sea scallops
Maple syrup, about ¼ cup

Preheat broiler. Wrap a bacon slice around each scallop and secure with a toothpick. Place on a wire rack on a baking sheet. Brush with maple syrup. Broil for 3 to 5 minutes about 4 inches from the heat source, turn, brush with more maple syrup and broil for 2 to 3 minutes more, until bacon begins to crisp. Serve at once.

SERVES 10 TO 12 AS AN APPETIZER
OR 6 AS A MAIN DISH

Maple-Cured Salmon (Gravlax)
With Maple-Mustard Sauce

EVERY HOLIDAY, I serve gravlax, salmon cured in salt, maple sugar and dill, as a light lunch or appetizer before dinner. Adapted from a recipe in *The New York Times*, it substitutes maple sugar for the original white sugar. The sauce, which can be made in 3 minutes or less, sets off the delicate salmon nicely. Be sure to use only the very freshest salmon for this recipe and begin curing it 3 to 4 days before you plan to serve it.

To mail-order maple sugar, see page 211.

SALMON

2   pounds center-cut fresh salmon, skin on, cut in half horizontally

2   tablespoons maple sugar

1⅓ tablespoons coarsely ground black pepper

1   tablespoon salt, preferably Kosher

1   large bunch chopped fresh dill, plus more for garnish

2   lemons, sliced, for garnish

MAPLE-MUSTARD SAUCE

2   tablespoons Dijon-style mustard

2   tablespoons maple syrup

2   tablespoons cider vinegar

6   tablespoons corn oil

1   heaping tablespoon chopped fresh dill (reserved from above)

To prepare salmon: Remove all bones from salmon, using pliers or tweezers if necessary. Wash and wipe pliers dry. Combine maple sugar, pepper and salt and pat on salmon flesh. Coarsely chop 1 bunch of dill (reserve 1 heaping tablespoon for sauce) and sprinkle over fish. Place salmon halves with flesh sides together and wrap tightly in plastic wrap, then in foil. Place salmon in an enamel or glass container (a Dutch oven works nicely) and put a brick or other heavy weight on top of fish. Refrigerate for 3 to 4 days, turning salmon occasionally.

Just before serving, scrape seasoning mixture off salmon with a sharp knife. Place salmon on a bed of fresh dill garnished with lemon slices. Slice salmon thinly on the diagonal, leaving the skin behind.

To make sauce: In a small bowl, stir together mustard, maple syrup and vinegar. Whisk in oil slowly. Stir in dill. (The sauce will keep for 1 week or more in the refrigerator.)

Serve slices of salmon with a dollop of Maple-Mustard Sauce on the side.

SERVES 10 AS AN APPETIZER

Maple Teriyaki Salmon

ADAPTED FROM A RECIPE of Vermont Senator and Mrs. Patrick Leahy, this teriyaki sauce has a delicate, round fullness that enhances salmon. It's also excellent for grilling chicken or tuna.

MAPLE TERIYAKI

⅓	cup maple syrup
⅓	cup dry white wine
3	tablespoons soy sauce
1	small onion, minced
2	cloves garlic, minced
	Freshly ground black pepper
4	salmon steaks, about 1 inch thick

To make teriyaki: Combine maple syrup, white wine, soy sauce, onion, garlic and black pepper in a shallow nonaluminum bowl large enough to hold steaks.

To prepare salmon: Marinate salmon steaks for 1 to 3 hours in the refrigerator (overnight is too long). About ½ hour before grilling or broiling, remove salmon from marinade and let salmon come to room temperature. Grill over hot coals or broil, basting with the marinade, until done, about 5 minutes per side.

SERVES 4

Cobble House Maple-Seasoned Salmon With Rosemary-Orange Glaze

THIS IS THE MOST FREQUENTLY requested recipe at Cobble House Inn, in Gaysville, Vermont.
Variation: Substitute 1 whole boneless chicken breast, pounded flat, for the salmon, ¼ cup chicken stock for the orange juice and omit the rosemary.

2	tablespoons all-purpose flour
	Salt and freshly ground black pepper
½-¾	pound salmon fillet, about ½-¾ inch thick, skinned
1	tablespoon butter
½	cup freshly squeezed orange juice
¼	cup Chardonnay
½	teaspoon chopped fresh rosemary
1	tablespoon minced shallots
1	tablespoon maple syrup

In a shallow bowl, combine flour, salt and pepper. Dredge salmon fillet in flour mixture, brush off excess flour and set aside. In a skillet, melt butter over medium heat. Add salmon and sauté for 1 to 2 minutes per side. Add orange juice, Chardonnay, rosemary and shallots and boil until liquid is reduced by half, about 3 minutes. Stir in maple syrup. Cut salmon in half and serve topped with sauce.

SERVES 2

Maple Roast Chicken With Winter Vegetables

🍁

THE SKIN GETS CRISP AND DARK, and the vegetables turn sweet and soft. The recipe is by restaurateur and cookbook author Jim Dodge.

2   tablespoons butter
1   roasting chicken, about 6-7 pounds
½   teaspoon Kosher salt
¼   teaspoon freshly ground black pepper
4   carrots, peeled, trimmed and cut into 3-inch chunks
4   parsnips, peeled, trimmed and cut into 3-inch chunks
4   stalks celery, trimmed and cut into 3-inch chunks
4   onions, peeled and quartered
½   teaspoon dried rosemary
⅓   cup maple syrup

Place rack of oven on lowest level and preheat oven to 400 degrees F. Melt butter in a small saucepan. Brush over breast of chicken and sprinkle with salt and pepper. Spread vegetables evenly in a roasting pan. Place chicken on top and sprinkle with rosemary. Place in oven and baste about every 10 minutes with maple syrup. When you run out of syrup, use pan juices for basting. Roast until tender and the juices run clear when thigh is pierced with a fork and skin is golden brown and crisp, about 1½ to 2 hours. Let stand 10 minutes before carving. Remove chicken to the center of a large serving platter. Surround chicken with cooked vegetables. Serve at once.

SERVES 4 TO 6

"Grandma stood by the brass kettle and with the big wooden spoon she poured hot syrup on each plate of snow. It cooled into soft candy, and as fast as it cooled they ate it. They could eat all they wanted, for maple sugar never hurt anybody.
When they had eaten the soft maple candy until they could eat no more, then they helped themselves from the long table loaded with pumpkin pies and dried berry pies and cookies and cakes. There was salt-rising bread, too, and cold boiled pork, and pickles. Oh, how sour the pickles were."

— LAURA INGALLS WILDER
Little House in the Big Woods

Sautéed Chicken Breast With Maple & Spices

ALTHOUGH THIS DISH IS EASY enough to make even on a busy weekday, it tastes as if it took hours to prepare. What makes it special is the sauce, which tastes like a tomato compote. Slightly bitter saffron balances the sweetness of tomatoes and maple syrup. The combination was devised by Chef Michel Le Borgne of the New England Culinary Institute in Montpelier, Vermont.

3	tablespoons maple syrup
2	teaspoons soy sauce
2	teaspoons coriander seeds
3	tablespoons butter
1	onion, finely chopped
2	tomatoes, peeled, seeded and chopped
	Pinch thread saffron
2	boneless whole chicken breasts
	Salt and freshly ground black pepper
1	tablespoon red-wine vinegar

Combine maple syrup, soy sauce and coriander seeds and set aside. In a heavy saucepan, melt 1 tablespoon butter. Add onion and sauté until translucent. Add tomatoes and saffron. Sauté until almost dry. Set aside.

Season chicken breasts with salt and pepper. In a skillet, sauté chicken in remaining 2 tablespoons butter over medium-high heat until three-quarters done, about 3 minutes. Add maple-soy mixture, reduce heat and cook 1 minute. With a slotted spoon, remove chicken to a plate and keep warm. Add tomato-saffron mixture and vinegar to skillet and cook over medium-low heat, stirring, to reduce sauce slightly. Add salt and pepper to taste.

To serve, divide sauce among four plates, slice chicken breasts and arrange slices on top of sauce.

SERVES 4

"When made in such small quantities—that is, quickly from the first run of sap and properly treated—it has a wild delicacy of flavor that no other sweet can match. What you smell in freshly cut maple-wood, or taste in the blossom of the tree, is in it. It is, indeed, the distilled essence of the tree."

— JOHN BURROUGHS
Signs and Seasons (1886)

Skillet-Roasted Duck With Maple-Bourbon Sauce

MANY RECIPES FOR DUCK call for using only the breast—impractical for the home cook as well as a great waste of the legs and thighs. Roasted in a skillet, this duck is economical, simple to make and becomes sweet and crisp in the hot oven. The roasting time will vary depending on the size of the duck and on whether you prefer it rare or well done. Serve with brussels sprouts, mashed turnips and mashed potatoes, the last topped with the sauce.

One 4-to-5-pound duck, excess fat removed

1	**carrot**
1	**onion, halved**
	Whole black peppercorns
2	**cups water**
1	**firm apple, cored and halved**
	Salt and freshly ground black pepper
¼	**cup maple syrup**
¼	**cup bourbon whiskey**
3	**tablespoons balsamic vinegar**

Preheat oven to 400 degrees F. Make stock: Cut wings and neck from duck and place in a medium saucepan with giblets (do not use the liver), carrot, onion, a few peppercorns and water. Bring water to a boil and simmer, uncovered, for about 30 to 40 minutes while you prepare duck.

Rinse inside of duck with water and stuff with apple. Truss legs with kitchen string and salt and pepper the skin. Heat a cast-iron skillet and sear duck over medium-high heat on all sides. Transfer duck, still in skillet, to oven and roast for about 50 minutes to 1 hour, depending on size of duck, draining excess fat midway through cooking. Remove skillet from oven and increase heat to 425 degrees.

Strain stock into a bowl and place in refrigerator. Pour off all but about 1 tablespoon of fat from skillet. In a small bowl, combine maple syrup, bourbon and vinegar. Brush some of the mixture on duck, return skillet to oven and roast for 30 minutes longer, basting frequently with maple-syrup mixture.

Remove duck from skillet to a cutting board. Pour off all but about 2 tablespoons drippings. Skim fat from refrigerated stock and pour 1½ cups stock into skillet, stirring to scrape up any browned bits. Boil until sauce has thickened slightly.

Serve sauce over duck and accompany with mashed potatoes.

SERVES 2 TO 4

Braised Corned-Beef Brisket
With Maple & Bourbon

YOU'LL ABANDON CORNED BEEF and cabbage entirely once you taste this. The flavors of the salty meat and maple work off one another beautifully. The recipe has been slightly adapted from one by Chef Michel Le Borgne of the New England Culinary Institute in Montpelier, Vermont.

1   corned-beef brisket, about 4 pounds, rinsed
1   cup maple syrup
¼   cup bourbon whiskey

Preheat oven to 325 degrees F. Place brisket in a Dutch oven and bake for ½ hour, uncovered. Reduce heat to 275 degrees and bake, covered, for an additional 2½ hours. Discard all liquid in pan except ½ cup. Add maple syrup and bourbon and continue baking, uncovered, basting brisket until glazed, about ½ hour. Let brisket rest for 10 to 15 minutes before slicing.

SERVES 8 TO 10

Maple-Barbecued Pork Ribs

WATCH THESE RIBS like a hawk: they burn easily. The recipe comes from restaurateur Jim Dodge. To reduce cooking time on the grill and thus the risk of burning, first parboil the ribs in boiling water for 10 minutes. Then marinate the cooked ribs for at least 8 hours or overnight and grill them for only about 10 minutes per side.

1   rack spareribs (about 4 pounds)
1   teaspoon freshly ground black pepper
½   teaspoon salt
⅔   cup maple syrup
2   tablespoons rice-wine vinegar
1   tablespoon soy sauce

Rub ribs with pepper and salt. Place in a shallow nonaluminum pan. In a small bowl, mix together maple syrup, vinegar and soy sauce. Pour over ribs, cover and chill overnight, turning occasionally.

Remove ribs from pan and grill over moderately hot coals, turning and basting ribs so they cook evenly on both sides, about 20 minutes per side, or until done. Do not let them burn.

SERVES 4

Cobble House Cranberry Relish

BEAU BENSON, CHEF and owner of Cobble House Inn, in Gaysville, Vermont, serves this relish at Thanksgiving and uses it in sautés with chicken, pork or venison. It is sweet-tart and fruity.

2   **pounds fresh or frozen cranberries, picked over**
2   **cups sugar**
2   **cups water**
2   **navel oranges**
2   **cups peeled, cored and chopped fresh pineapple, or canned**
2   **medium apples, peeled, cored and chopped**
1   **pear, peeled, cored and chopped**
1   **cup chopped dates**
1   **cup golden raisins**
½   **cup maple syrup**
¼   **cup Southern Comfort**
3   **tablespoons cider vinegar**

Mix cranberries, sugar and water in a large non-aluminum pot and bring to a boil. Simmer until thick, stirring, about 20 minutes.

Meanwhile, remove zest from oranges with a vegetable peeler and mince. Remove and discard pith from oranges and chop fruit. Place chopped oranges and zest in a large bowl, add remaining ingredients and toss well. Add to cranberries and simmer for 15 minutes, or until fruit is softened. (The relish will keep for up to 1 month, tightly covered, in the refrigerator.)

MAKES 12 CUPS

Maple Syrup & Balsamic Vinegar Dressing

MY BEST SALAD DRESSING comes from a cookbook published by St. Paul's Church in Burlington, Vermont. Balsamic vinegar and fruity olive oil are ideal complements to the sweetness of maple.

1   **teaspoon dry mustard**
½   **teaspoon dried basil**
3   **tablespoons balsamic vinegar**
2   **tablespoons maple syrup**
1   **tablespoon lemon juice**
1   **clove garlic, minced**
1   **cup extra-virgin olive oil**
1   **teaspoon salt**
¼   **teaspoon freshly ground black pepper**

In a small bowl, combine mustard and basil. Whisk in vinegar, maple syrup, lemon juice and garlic. Whisk in olive oil, and continue whisking until the dressing is emulsified. Taste and season with salt and pepper. (The dressing will keep, covered, in the refrigerator for several weeks.)

MAKES 1¼ CUPS

Vermont Spinach Salad

THE CIDER VINEGAR in this dressing echoes the taste of the apple in the salad. The dressing can be made slightly sweet or tart, according to taste. One of the best things about this salad—apart from its combination of flavors—is that it's excellent for winter, when good tomatoes are but a memory. The combination was created by cookbook author and restaurateur Jim Dodge.

- 1   **pound spinach**
- 1   **large, firm red apple, unpeeled but cored**
- 1   **large hard-boiled egg**
- 6   **slices bacon (8 ounces), preferably cob-smoked, cooked until crisp**
- ¼   **pound extra-sharp Cheddar, grated, chopped or crumbled**
- ⅓   **cup maple syrup**
- ⅓-½ **cup cider vinegar**
- 2   **pinches Kosher salt**
     Freshly ground black pepper

Wash, dry and stem spinach and place in a serving bowl. Cut apple in half, cut each half into ½-inch chunks and add to spinach. Chop egg and crumble bacon and add to spinach. Toss until evenly distributed. Add cheese to spinach and toss.

In a small saucepan, whisk together maple syrup and ⅓ cup vinegar. Taste and add 1 to 2 more tablespoons vinegar, if desired. Add salt and pepper. Heat until warm. Pour warm dressing over spinach, toss and serve immediately.

SERVES 4 TO 6

Red Cabbage Braised With Maple Syrup

HERE IS MORE PROOF of the felicitous combination of bacon and maple. The recipe was created by Yves Labbé, chef of Cheval d'Or restaurant in Jeffersonville, Vermont, and was originally published by food writer Marialisa Calta. The cabbage is excellent served with duck, pork, chicken or, as Labbé does, with quail.

- 5   **slices bacon, minced**
- 1   **medium onion, minced**
- 1   **tart, medium-firm apple, peeled, cored and thinly sliced**
- 1   **pound red cabbage (about ½ head), outer leaves removed; cored and remainder finely shredded**
- 1   **bay leaf**
- ½   **cup maple syrup**
     Salt and freshly ground black pepper

Preheat oven to 350 degrees F. In a wide ovenproof saucepan or flameproof casserole large enough to hold all ingredients, sauté bacon until almost crisp. Pour off all but 1 tablespoon fat, add onion and sauté until translucent. Add remaining ingredients and cover. Transfer pan or casserole to oven and bake for ½ hour.

SERVES 4 TO 6

Eggplant Szechuan Style

THIS SLIGHTLY HOT, slightly sweet and totally addictive eggplant dish is adapted from a recipe by Joyce Jue of San Francisco, California, author of *Asian Appetizers*.

6   Japanese eggplants, peeled, or 2 medium regular eggplants, peeled
2   teaspoons salt
¼   cup chicken stock
2   tablespoons maple syrup
1   tablespoon soy sauce
¼   cup peanut oil
1   tablespoon minced garlic
2   teaspoons peeled, grated fresh gingerroot
¼   teaspoon hot-pepper flakes
3   scallions, chopped
1   tablespoon cider vinegar
1   tablespoon sesame oil

Cut eggplant into strips ½ x 2 inches. In a colander, toss eggplants with salt; drain 30 minutes over a bowl. Rinse and squeeze out excess water. Pat eggplant dry and set aside.

In a small bowl, mix chicken stock, maple syrup and soy sauce. Set aside. Preheat a wok over high heat until hot. Pour in 3 tablespoons peanut oil. Add eggplant in one layer and cook until tender and seared. Remove to a colander and drain over a bowl, reserving any juices.

Reduce heat to medium-high. Add remaining 1 tablespoon peanut oil, garlic, ginger and hot-pepper flakes. Cook gently but do not brown. Add half the scallions. Increase heat to high, add maple-soy mixture and any reserved eggplant juices and bring to a boil. Add eggplant and toss until most of the sauce is absorbed. Stir in vinegar and sesame oil. Remove to a serving dish and top with remaining scallions.

SERVES 4 AS AN APPETIZER OR SIDE DISH

Dakin Farm Baked Beans

THESE QUINTESSENTIAL New England-style baked beans are canned and sold by Dakin Farm in Ferrisburgh, Vermont. Kate Clifford, who makes them for company, likes to cook them on top of her wood-burning stove before baking them in the oven.

4   cups yellow-eye or soldier beans
½   teaspoon baking soda
½   pound salt pork, cubed or cut into pieces
1   medium onion, chopped
½   cup maple syrup
2   tablespoons prepared mustard, such as Dijon-style

2   teaspoons salt
½   teaspoon dry mustard

Wash and pick over beans, cover them with cold water and add baking soda. Soak overnight. Drain, rinse, place in an ovenproof pot, and stir in remaining ingredients and water to cover. Simmer, uncovered, over low heat for 1 hour, until beans are tender. Preheat oven to 325 degrees F. Bake beans, uncovered, for 1 to 1½ hours, or until tender, adding water as needed.

SERVES 10 TO 12

Maple Pecan Squares

THESE BARS, which have a delicate, buttery, tender, shortbread-cookie crust and a pecan-pie-type topping, go over big at bake sales, parties or Christmas-cookie exchanges.

CRUST

1¼ cups all-purpose flour
⅓ cup sugar
½ cup (1 stick) butter, softened

TOPPING

¾ cup maple syrup
⅔ cup sugar
2 large eggs, well beaten
2 tablespoons butter, melted
1½ teaspoons vanilla extract
2 tablespoons all-purpose flour
¼ teaspoon salt
1 cup pecans, chopped

To make crust: Preheat oven to 375 degrees F. Grease an 8- or 9-inch-square baking pan. Combine flour and sugar in a medium bowl. Cut in butter and blend until mixture resembles coarse meal. Press mixture into bottom of prepared pan. Bake for 15 minutes and set aside. Reduce oven temperature to 350 degrees.

To make topping: In a medium bowl, combine all ingredients except pecans. Beat well and stir in nuts. Pour pecan mixture over prepared crust and bake for 40 to 45 minutes, or until firm. Check the squares after 35 minutes to make sure they are not done early. Cool on a rack and cut into squares.

MAKES NINE 2½-INCH SQUARES OR FIFTEEN 1½-X-2½-INCH PIECES

Maple Oatmeal Cookies

CHILDREN WHO TASTE these cookies beg for more. They are from sugarer Sharon LaPorte of Underhill Center, Vermont.

Variation: Add ½ cup chopped nuts, raisins, chocolate or coconut to the dough.

1½ cups (3 sticks) butter, softened
1¾ cups maple syrup
1 cup sugar
2 large eggs
2 teaspoons vanilla extract
6 cups old-fashioned rolled oats
2 cups all-purpose flour
2 teaspoons baking soda
1 teaspoon salt

Preheat oven to 350 degrees F. Grease two 9-x-13-inch baking sheets. In a large bowl, beat together butter, maple syrup, sugar, eggs and vanilla. Stir in oats. In another bowl, stir together flour, baking soda and salt. Add dry ingredients to butter mixture and mix well. Drop by rounded teaspoonfuls about 2 inches apart onto prepared baking sheets and bake for 12 to 15 minutes.

MAKES APPROXIMATELY 70 COOKIES

Maple Layer Cake
With Maple Buttercream Frosting

THIS IS EVERYTHING YOU WANT from a home-baked cake. It is moist, with a tender, even crumb, and the maple flavor is rich and full. Though delicious on its own, it deserves nothing less than a buttercream frosting. The cake comes from Jan Siegrist's *Maple Sampler* (New England Press, Shelburne, Vermont, 1985); the frosting is a traditional French buttercream, but with maple syrup added.

CAKE

½	cup (1 stick) butter, softened
½	cup sugar
1	cup maple syrup
2	large eggs, well beaten
2½	cups all-purpose flour
2	teaspoons baking powder
1	teaspoon baking soda
½	teaspoon ground ginger
¼	teaspoon salt
1	cup hot water
1	teaspoon vanilla extract
½	cup chopped walnuts

MAPLE BUTTERCREAM FROSTING

1	cup (2 sticks) unsalted butter, softened
1	large egg plus 3 yolks
⅔	cup sugar
3	tablespoons water
3	tablespoons maple syrup

To make cake: Preheat oven to 350 degrees F. Grease and flour two 8- or 9-inch round cake pans.

In a large bowl, cream together butter and sugar. Beat in maple syrup. (The mixture will appear slightly curdled.) Beat in eggs. In a separate bowl, combine flour, baking powder, baking soda, ginger and salt. Add to butter-syrup mixture. Stir in hot water and vanilla and beat well. (The batter will be very liquid.) Stir in nuts. Divide between prepared cake pans. Bake for 30 to 35 minutes, or until a toothpick inserted in the centers comes out clean. Let cool in pans on wire racks for 10 minutes. Remove from pans and let cool while you make the frosting.

To make frosting: Cream butter until light and fluffy. In a separate bowl, beat egg and yolks. In a small heavy-bottomed saucepan, boil sugar and water together until mixture reaches soft-ball stage (236 to 238 degrees F on a candy thermometer or until a bit forms a pliable ball when dropped into ice water).

Using an electric beater, immediately beat boiling syrup into eggs. Set mixing bowl in a pan of not-quite-simmering water and continue beating for 4 to 5 minutes, or until mixture is light, foamy and doubled in bulk. (It will feel very hot to the touch.) Set bowl in cold water and continue beating until mixture is tepid. Beat egg mixture, a spoonful at a time, into creamed butter. Beat in maple syrup.

To assemble: When cakes are thoroughly cool, frost first layer, place second layer on top of first layer and frost top and sides.

MAKES ONE 8- OR 9-INCH TWO-LAYER CAKE, WITH 2 CUPS FROSTING

Maple Cream Cheesecake

Maple heaven in a velvety cheesecake. It comes from Carolyn Tandy, chef-owner of Emma's Restaurant in Jericho, Vermont.

CRUST

4	tablespoons (½ stick) butter, melted
1¾	cups graham cracker crumbs
3	tablespoons light brown sugar

CHEESECAKE

20	ounces (2½ eight-ounce packages) cream cheese, softened
½	cup sugar
3	large eggs
1	teaspoon vanilla extract
¼	cup all-purpose flour
¼	teaspoon baking soda
1	cup heavy cream
1	cup dark maple syrup

TOPPING

1	cup heavy cream
¼	cup maple syrup
	Chopped walnuts for garnish

To make crust: In a small bowl, stir together butter, graham cracker crumbs and brown sugar and press into bottom and sides of a 9-inch springform pan.

To make cheesecake: Preheat oven to 350 degrees F. In a large bowl, beat cream cheese until light and fluffy and beat in sugar and eggs, 1 at a time. Beat in vanilla. In a small bowl, stir together flour and baking soda. Add to cream-cheese mixture, mixing well. Mix in cream and maple syrup. Spoon into springform pan.

Bake until firm, about 1 hour, or until a toothpick inserted in the center comes out clean. When cheesecake is done, turn off oven and leave cake in oven for 1 hour, then remove from oven and cool on a rack for 30 minutes. Refrigerate. Remove the sides of the springform pan after the cake has cooled.

To make topping: Beat heavy cream until soft peaks form and beat in maple syrup. Frost the top of the chilled cake with cream and sprinkle with walnuts.

MAKES ONE 9-INCH CHEESECAKE

"Good God, how sweet are all things here!"

— CHARLES COTTON

Maple-Apple Pie

CRISP APPLES ARE the perfect match for the elegantly smooth taste of maple syrup in this pie by pastry chef Jim Dodge, author of *Baking With Jim Dodge*. Serve with chilled softly whipped heavy cream or with vanilla ice cream.

½	cup maple syrup
5	large apples, peeled and cored
10	tablespoons (1 stick plus 2 tablespoons) cold unsalted butter
1¼	cups unbleached all-purpose flour
½	teaspoon salt
¼	cup cold water

Lightly butter the bottom of a 9- or 10-inch glass pie pan. In a small saucepan, heat maple syrup over moderately high heat for about 3 minutes, or until syrup changes from a cream color to caramel. Pour syrup into bottom of pie pan, pouring a circle around the bottom edge and finishing in the center. Work quickly since the maple syrup will harden and become difficult to pour. It is not necessary to cover the bottom completely. Set aside.

Cut apples in half and then into ½-inch wedges. Melt 2 tablespoons butter in a large, heavy skillet over medium heat. Add apples and sauté until tender, about 5 minutes. Spoon into pie pan over maple syrup and arrange evenly.

Measure flour and salt into the bowl of a food processor. Cut remaining 8 tablespoons butter into 1-inch cubes and add to flour. Process until butter is cut into flour and the mixture resembles the texture of cornmeal. Add water and process until dough forms. Remove from the bowl to a lightly floured work surface. Dust top of dough with flour and roll it into a 12-inch circle. Fold in half and unfold over pie dish. Tuck edges down along inside of dish.

Bake in the middle of the lowest rack of oven for 15 minutes. Rotate the pie, so that it bakes evenly. Continue baking for 15 minutes more, or until crust is golden brown and firm to the touch. (If pie bubbles over during baking, slide a baking sheet under pie pan.) Have ready a serving plate large enough to cover top of pie pan. Remove pie from oven and let it cool on a rack for 5 minutes. Place serving plate upside down, covering top of pie. With your hands and a heavy kitchen towel or pot holders, secure plate against pie pan and turn it quickly upside down. Set it down on a table and remove pie pan. The pie will be upside down on serving plate.

MAKES ONE 9- OR 10-INCH SINGLE-CRUST PIE

Black-Peppered Maple-Cream Pie

❧

DO NOT OMIT THE PEPPER in this recipe; it is crucial for flavor. Serve the pie in small wedges, for it is very rich. This combination is slightly adapted from a recipe by Edith Foulds of Burlington, Vermont.

1½ cups heavy cream
⅓ cup all-purpose flour
1½ cups maple syrup (preferably light grade)
2 tablespoons butter
¼ teaspoon salt
¼ teaspoon freshly ground black pepper

One 9-inch unbaked pie shell

Preheat oven to 375 degrees F. In a heavy saucepan, whisk together cream and flour until smooth. Add maple syrup, butter, salt and pepper. Cook, stirring, over medium heat for 10 minutes, or until thickened. Do not let boil. Pour filling into pie shell and bake for 30 minutes, or until bubbling. Cool on a rack, then refrigerate until thoroughly cooled before serving.

MAKES ONE 9-INCH PIE

Maple-Apple Upside-Down Cake

❧

THE BOTTOM AND SIDES of this cake and the apples become encrusted with caramelized maple, while the rest of the cake remains moist and light. This is a fine, simple combination from one of the best maple cookbooks I know, *The Vermont Maple Syrup Cookbook*, edited by Reginald L. Muir (Phoenix Publishing, 1976), which is now out of print but available in libraries.

7 tablespoons butter, softened
½ cup maple syrup
2 medium apples, cored, unpeeled and cut into ½-inch slices
1½ cups all-purpose flour
2 teaspoons baking powder
1 teaspoon salt
¾ cup sugar
2 large eggs, separated
½ cup milk
Whipped cream (optional)

Preheat oven to 350 degrees F. Melt 3 tablespoons butter in an 8- or 9-inch-square baking pan. Pour maple syrup over butter and remove from heat. Arrange apples in the pan. In medium bowl, sift together flour, baking powder and salt. In a large bowl, cream remaining 4 tablespoons butter with ½ cup sugar and egg yolks until fluffy. Add dry ingredients and milk, alternating, to butter mixture. Beat egg whites until stiff; beat in remaining ¼ cup sugar. Fold whites gently into batter and spread batter over apples. Bake for 40 to 50 minutes, or until a toothpick inserted in the center comes out clean. Immediately remove cake from pan by inverting it over a serving plate. Serve warm with whipped cream, if desired.

SERVES 6

Maple Mousse

✦

VELVETY SMOOTH, this mousse, which tastes like a rich maple Bavarian cream, is a special-occasion favorite for a large gathering. Jennifer Adsit of Charlotte, Vermont, persuaded a sugarer in Lancaster, New Hampshire, to part with the recipe.

3	teaspoons (1½ envelopes) unflavored gelatin
½	cup cold water
4	large eggs, separated
1	cup maple syrup
½	cup light brown sugar
2	cups chilled heavy cream

Stir gelatin into cold water. Place in a 9-inch skillet and cook, stirring, over low heat until gelatin is dissolved, about 1 minute. Remove from heat. With an electric mixer, beat egg yolks until frothy. Pour maple syrup, then beaten egg yolks, into gelatin mixture and cook over low heat, stirring constantly, until mixture thickly coats a spoon. Remove from heat and pour into a large bowl. Stir in brown sugar. Stir intermittently until cooled to room temperature. Beat cream in a chilled bowl with chilled beaters until stiff. Beat egg whites in a separate large bowl until soft peaks form. When maple syrup-gelatin mixture has cooled, fold in whipped cream. Fold in egg whites gently. Refrigerate for at least 4 hours before serving.

SERVES 8 TO 10

Virginia Bentley's Old-Fashioned Maple Ice Cream

✦

ADAPTED FROM Virginia Bentley's *Bentley Farm Cookbook*, this ice cream has a subtle maple flavor. It's good with more maple syrup drizzled over the top.

1¼	cups maple syrup
4	large egg yolks
1½	tablespoons all-purpose flour
¼	teaspoon salt
3	cups milk, scalded
3	tablespoons vanilla extract
1	quart heavy cream

Combine ¾ cup maple syrup, egg yolks, flour and salt, stirring briskly, in the top of a double boiler; stir in scalded milk. Cook over boiling water until mixture just thickens. Remove from heat the instant it thickens. Strain through a sieve or whir in a blender. Add 1 tablespoon vanilla. Cover custard to prevent a skin from forming on top and chill. Place chilled custard in an ice cream freezer and add cream, remaining 2 tablespoons vanilla and remaining ½ cup maple syrup. Freeze following manufacturer's directions.

MAKES 2 QUARTS

Maple Crème Brûlée

❦

"IF I COULD ONLY EAT one dessert for the rest of my life, this is the one I would really want," says Ken Haedrich, author of *The Maple Syrup Cookbook* and *Country Baking*. The dessert has a large, dedicated following at Steve's, a restaurant in Rumney, New Hampshire, where Haedrich often makes it.

3	**cups heavy cream**
½	**cup maple syrup**
9	**large egg yolks**
1	**teaspoon vanilla extract**
6	**tablespoons light brown sugar**

Preheat oven to 325 degrees F. In a medium saucepan, heat cream and maple syrup over medium heat for about 5 minutes, stirring occasionally, until quite hot. Meanwhile, put egg yolks into a large mixing bowl and blend them with a wooden spoon. Stir about ½ cup hot-cream mixture into egg yolks. Slowly pour in remaining cream, stirring, then stir in vanilla extract. Strain mixture into a pitcher or large measuring cup.

Pour about ½ inch very hot water into a large shallow casserole and place it in the oven. Divide custard evenly among 6 individual ramekins or custard cups. Place cups in casserole, leaving room between them. Add a little more hot water, if necessary, so water comes about halfway up sides of cups. Tear off a sheet of foil a little longer than pan, shape it into a slight dome and place it over custards. Bake for approximately 50 minutes, until custards are just barely set. The centers may seem wobbly, but should not be liquid. Remove casserole from oven and place cups directly on a rack to cool. When cooled to room temperature, cover each one individually and refrigerate for at least 4 hours or up to 48 hours.

Just before serving, preheat broiler. Sieve about 1 tablespoon brown sugar over each custard. Quickly run custards under broiler to caramelize sugar, about a minute or two; sugar will melt and turn brown. Watch carefully so sugar does not burn. Serve at once.

MAKES 6 SERVINGS

"The first run, like first love, is always the best, always the fullest, always the sweetest."

— JOHN BURROUGHS
Winter Sunshine (1881)

Maple Flambéed Bananas

🍁

This variation on the classic dessert Bananas Foster takes less than 5 minutes to prepare yet has a rich, special-occasion taste. It's a favorite of Brenda Larocque, of Athelstan, Quebec, whose book *Maple-mania* is full of enticing maple recipes. To order a copy, see page 163.

¼   cup maple syrup
¼   cup heavy cream
2   tablespoons butter
¼   teaspoon ground nutmeg
¼   teaspoon ground cinnamon
4   firm bananas

2-4   tablespoons brandy
      Vanilla ice cream as an accompaniment

Combine maple syrup, cream, butter, nutmeg and cinnamon in a medium saucepan. Cook over medium heat until butter is melted and sauce is heated through. Peel bananas; slice in half lengthwise, then crosswise once. Add to sauce mixture and simmer 1 to 2 minutes. Turn banana mixture out of pan onto a serving platter. Heat brandy until warm; pour into a ladle. Carefully, averting your face, ignite brandy and pour over bananas. Serve with ice cream.

Serves 2 to 4

Maple Caramel Popcorn & Nuts

🍁

The ultimate snack for family gatherings in front of the VCR or for Halloween: popcorn and nuts mortared together with sugary chunks of maple-caramel brittle.

3   tablespoons corn oil
⅓   cup raw popcorn
1   cup roasted salted peanuts or mixture of peanuts and pecans
1   cup maple syrup
1   cup sugar
½   teaspoon white vinegar
2   tablespoons butter

Heat oil in a large, heavy skillet over medium-high heat until 1 kernel placed in oil pops. Add popcorn, cover skillet and heat, shaking pan, until all corn is popped. Place popcorn in a large buttered roasting pan, add nuts and toss.

Preheat oven to 200 degrees F.

In a heavy-bottomed medium saucepan, bring maple syrup, sugar and vinegar to a boil, stirring to dissolve sugar. Cook, without stirring, washing any crystals down sides of pan with a brush dipped in cold water, until a bit of syrup dropped into cold water forms a long thread, 240 degrees on a candy thermometer. Stir in butter until melted.

Pour caramel mixture over popcorn and mix gently. Bake for 1 hour. Cool and break apart into chunks.

Makes about 7 cups

Candymaking Tips

EXPERIENCED CANDYMAKERS *say it is almost impossible to recommend firm temperatures for different recipes. Among the factors influencing the outcome of a candy recipe in your kitchen are the weather (humidity and barometric pressure), your elevation above sea level and the specific maple syrup you are using. Keep in mind that the temperatures indicated in the recipes that follow are only benchmarks: the look and feel of the maple syrup are the best indicators for when the candy is ready.*

❧ Always use the freshest, light-grade syrup (Fancy or Light Amber in the U.S.; Light or Extra-Light in Canada). Darker grades and old syrup may not crystallize.

❧ On a sunny day, when the air pressure is high, boil the syrup approximately one degree higher; on a cloudy day, approximately one degree lower.

❧ When syrup is cooling, it must be left undisturbed, or large crystals will form, ruining the texture of the candy. Do not remove the candy thermometer from the pot at this stage, since even a small movement can affect the outcome; leave it clipped to the side.

❧ If the candy mixture "seizes" while you are beating it, try reheating it gently on top of the stove, stirring all the while, until the mixture becomes liquid again, then *immediately* pour it into the pan or other container.

Maple Taffy (Sugar on Snow)

❧

WITHOUT QUESTION, this maple confection—featured at impromptu sugarhouse parties throughout the north country during sugar season—is the simplest kind to make. The hot syrup is poured over a mound of fresh, clean snow, where it immediately stiffens and can be peeled off and eaten with forks or fingers. Traditional accompaniments are doughnuts and dill pickle spears to cut the sweetness.

The taffy can also be poured into microwave-proof containers, frozen, reheated in the microwave and poured over ice cream.

2 cups light-grade maple syrup (Fancy, Light Amber, Light or Extra-Light)

In a heavy-bottomed 4-quart pot, boil maple syrup on medium-high heat to 235 to 236 degrees F (to the higher temperature on a sunny day), stirring the surface occasionally to keep it from boiling over.

Immediately pour onto a mound of pristine, freshly fallen snow packed into a bowl or bowls and serve immediately, or pour into a freezer container and freeze for up to 1 year.

SERVES 4 TO 6

Maple-Cream Candy

✦

BEWARE: tasting this rich, creamy-tasting fudge even once will result in instant, lifelong addiction. Luckily, this is one of the simplest candies to make, since the addition of the cream makes it less temperamental than candies made with pure maple syrup alone. For this recipe, Brenda Larocque of Athelstan, Quebec, does not use a candy thermometer; she prefers to test the consistency by dropping a small amount into cold water.

2	cups light-grade maple syrup (Fancy, Light Amber, Light or Extra-Light)
1	cup half-and-half
½	cup chopped walnuts (optional)
1	teaspoon vanilla extract

Butter a 6-x-9-inch pan. In a heavy-bottomed 4-quart pot, boil maple syrup and half-and-half on medium-high heat, stirring occasionally to prevent it from sticking to the bottom, until the mixture reaches soft-ball consistency. At this stage, a bit of the mixture dropped into cold water can be easily massed into a pliable soft ball in the bottom of the glass with the fingers; if it immediately forms a small blob as it makes its way to the bottom, the mixture has been cooked too long.

Immediately place the pot in a sink filled with cold water to cool it rapidly. Cool to lukewarm, without touching, until the mixture is about 95 to 105 degrees F, or until you can comfortably hold the pot by the sides with your bare hands.

Beat in nuts, if using, and vanilla. Beat until the mixture becomes lighter in color, creamy and just begins to lose its gloss. When it is ready, the mixture should ribbon off the spoon and the ribbons should sit on top of the fudge rather than sinking back in. The mixture should just begin to "mound"—hold its shape—as you stir. Immediately turn it out into the pan. (If you have turned it out into the pan too early, stir it in the pan with a rubber spatula until it comes to the right consistency.)

Score into squares immediately and set aside to cool. Store in a tightly covered container.

MAKES ONE 6-X-9-INCH PAN

"The lips of my charmer are sweet as a hogshead of maple molasses."

—THOMAS FASSENDEN, 1806

Simple Maple-Sugar Leaves

✿

Although novices often assume that these confections are difficult to make, candymaker Brenda Larocque's recipe greatly simplifies the traditional procedure by omitting the time-consuming step of coating the candies with a crystalline shell of maple syrup. (In that process, the candies are dried for 12 hours and then immersed in the syrup for 6 more hours to cover minor imperfections and keep them from drying out during long storage.) Instead, Larocque boils the syrup for her candies a little longer so they resist moisture. Tiny white spots, indicating uneven drying, will sometimes appear; they in no way affect flavor.

2   cups light-grade maple syrup (Fancy, Light Amber, Light or Extra-Light)

In a heavy-bottomed 4-quart pot, boil maple syrup on medium-high heat to 235 to 245 degrees F (to the higher temperature on a sunny day), stirring the surface occasionally to keep it from boiling over.

Immediately remove the pot from the heat, leaving the thermometer clipped to the side, and place the pot on a wooden board to cool. Do not touch the syrup while it is cooling, or large crystals will form. Cool for 10 minutes, until the mixture is approximately 175 degrees.

Beat continuously with a wooden spoon until the mixture becomes lighter in color, thick and creamy and begins to lose its gloss, about 4 to 5 minutes.

Pour into rubber maple-sugar molds or a buttered pan. (Score into squares immediately if using a pan.) Set aside to cool. When candies are cool, turn the molds upside down and remove the candies. Store in a container on a cool, dry shelf for up to 1 month.

Makes 18 to 20 one-ounce maple leaves

"Each year I buy a quart of Canadian Club and stick it in the snow. You mix it with boiling sap, maybe ½ ounce per teacup of sap. Terrific. It's my gift for passersby . . . "

— Anonymous Sugarmaker,
Backyard Sugarin' by Rink Mann
(Countryman, 1991)

Maple Fudge

🍁

SOMEWHAT FIRMER in consistency than Maple Cream Candy (page 188), this fudge is sweeter and less rich.

2   cups light-grade maple syrup (Fancy, Light Amber, Light or Extra-Light)

Butter a 6-x-9-inch pan. In a heavy-bottomed 4-quart pot, boil maple syrup on medium-high heat to 238 to 240 degrees F (to the higher temperature on a sunny day), stirring the surface occasionally to keep it from boiling over.

Immediately remove the pot from the heat, leaving the thermometer clipped to the side, and place the pot in a sink filled with cold water to cool it rapidly.

Do not touch the syrup while it is cooling, or large crystals will form. When the syrup has cooled to approximately 125 degrees, immediately remove the pot from the cold water and beat the mixture with a wooden spoon until it becomes lighter in color, creamy and just begins to lose its gloss. When it is right, the mixture will just start to "mound"—hold its shape while being manipulated. (At this point, the mixture should still be pourable.)

Quickly turn it out into the prepared pan. Score into squares while still warm. Set aside to cool. Store in a tightly covered container.

MAKES ONE 6-X-9-INCH PAN

Maple Cream

🍁

IN MANY RESPECTS, maple cream is the trickiest of all the maple confections, but its amazing smoothness and sublime richness make it well worth mastering.

2   cups light-grade maple syrup (Fancy, Light Amber, Light or Extra-Light)

In a heavy-bottomed 4-quart pot, heat maple syrup on medium-high heat to 235 degrees F, stirring the surface occasionally to keep it from boiling over. Immediately remove the pot from the heat, leaving the thermometer clipped to the side, and place the pot in a sink filled with cold water to cool it rapidly. Do not touch the syrup while it is cooling, or large crystals will form.

When the mixture has cooled to approximately 125 degrees, remove the pot from the water and immediately beat the mixture with an electric mixer, scraping down the sides of the bowl. The syrup will gradually thicken, become lighter in color and begin to lose its glossy look. Continually test the mixture as you beat it by tasting and rolling a bit against the roof of your mouth. When it is ready, you will just begin to feel small crystals forming. Beating the mixture too long or failing to get it out of the pot in time will cause it to harden.

Quickly spoon the mixture into a glass or plastic container.

Store in the refrigerator for up to 3 months, or in the freezer for up to 1 year.

MAKES I CUP

Canadian Metric Equivalents

The following comparisons of Canadian metric and Imperial (U.S.) measures were developed by the Canadian government to provide benchmarks for the home cook. Because there is no exact equivalence for the Imperial cup or for ¼ and ½ teaspoons, however, converting from one system to the other may take a little experimenting, particularly in baking recipes, where exact proportions can be crucial. When making a recipe, don't skip back and forth between the two systems: work entirely in Canadian metric or in Imperial.*

Metric Symbols

Celsius:	C	gram:	g
liter:	L	centimeter:	cm
milliliter:	mL	millimeter:	mm
kilogram:	kg		

Temperature Conversion

	FAHRENHEIT	CELSIUS
Freezer storage	0	−18
Refrigerator storage	40	4
Yeast dough rising	85	30
Lukewarm liquid	110	45
Scalding liquids	175	80
Warming oven	200	100
	250	120
	275	140
	300	150
	325	160
	350	180
	375	190
	400	200
	425	220
	450	230
	475	240
Oven broiling, grilling	500	260

Small Measures

1mL	slightly less than ¼ teaspoon
2 mL	slightly less than ½ teaspoon
5 mL	1 teaspoon
15 mL	1 tablespoon
25 mL	1 tablespoon plus 2 teaspoons

Dry Measures

50 mL	slightly less than ¼ cup
125 mL	slightly more than ½ cup
250 mL	slightly more than 1 cup

Liquid Measures

250 mL	slightly more than 1 cup (8 fluid ounces)
500 mL	slightly more than 2 cups (16 fluid ounces)
1 L	approximately 1 Imperial quart minus 6 fluid ounces

Length

¼ inch	5 mm
½ inch	1 cm
¾ inch	2 cm
1 inch	2.5 cm
2 inches	5 cm
4 inches	10 cm

Weight

1 oz.	25 g
2 oz.	50 g
¼ lb.	125 g
½ lb.	250 g
1 lb.	500 g
2 lb.	1 kg
3 lb.	1.5 kg
5 lb.	2.2 kg

Source: Ontario Ministry of Agriculture and Food

Common Pan Sizes

UTENSIL	METRIC VOLUME AND SIZE	CLOSEST IMPERIAL SIZE
ROUND		
layer-cake pans	1 L (20 x 4 cm)	8 x 1½ inch
	1.2 L (23 x 4 cm)	9 x ½ inch
springform pans	2.5 L (23 cm diameter)	9 inch
	3 L (25 cm diameter)	10 inch
pie pans	750 mL (20 cm)	8 x 1¼ inch
	1 L (23 cm)	9 x ½ inch
	1.5 L (25 cm)	10 x 1¾ inch
casseroles	1 L (15 cm)	1 quart (6 inch)
	2 L (21 cm)	2 quart (8½ inch)
	3 L (25 cm)	3 quart (10 inch)
custard cups	150 mL (8 cm)	3 inch
	300 mL (11 cm)	4½ inch
SQUARE		
cake pans	2 L (20 x 5 cm)	8 x 2 inch
	2.5 L (23 x 5 cm)	9 x 2 inch
loaf pans	1.5 L (20 x 10 x 7 cm)	8 x 4 x 3 inches
	2 L (23 x 13 x 7 cm)	9 x 5 x 3 inches
jellyroll pan	2 L (40 x 25 x 2 cm)	15½ x 10½ x ¾ inch

Common Can and Package Sizes

VOLUME		MASS	
4 oz.	114 mL	4 oz.	113 g
10 oz.	284 mL	5 oz.	142 g
14 oz.	398 mL	6 oz.	170 g
28 oz.	796 mL	15 oz.	425 g

THE SWEET ARTS

Creams and leaves and fudges:
scrumptious lessons in home candymaking

I F YOU CAN'T MAKE CANDY, you haven't practiced enough." Like learning to ride a bicycle, the experienced candymakers will tell you, making maple confections takes patience, determination and a willingness to smile—or grit your teeth—through the first embarrassing attempts.

Unfortunately, most directions look deceptively simple: boil the lightest grade of maple syrup until it reaches 235 to 244 degrees F—depending on the kind of candy—cool and stir. But anyone who has tried to make those country-store-perfect maple-sugar leaves or even basic maple fudge, only to have the mixture turn to bedrock in the pan, knows there is more to this than reading a candymaking thermometer—or a cookbook.

In maple-syrup cookery, nothing is more subject to weather, temperature and other mysterious variables than candy, and nothing requires more culinary exactitude. Standard confectionery terms are really mere approximations of color and texture, and they seem folksy and friendly to a beginner. But behind instructions like "boil to the soft-ball stage" or "beat until the mixture begins to lose its gloss" is an unforgiving reality: A single degree on the thermometer can mean the difference between getting a velvety texture with just a touch of sugar crystal, and gritty, sandy ruination.

Practice is something that Brenda Larocque, a 42-year-old third-generation candymaker from Athelstan, Quebec, has gotten plenty of ever since she learned the art from her mother-in-law 15 years ago. Each year, Larocque and her husband, Herb, produce some 600 gallons of maple syrup from the trees on Beavermeadow Farm, Brenda Larocque's family homestead. Out of the season's light-grade syrup, which crystallizes more readily than darker grades, Larocque makes at least 3,000 maple-sugar leaves and log cabins, selling them for 60 cents apiece.

In addition to maple-sugar candy, Larocque makes all the other traditional maple confections: fudge, maple-cream candy (a divinely rich, smooth fudge with cream added), maple taffy (commonly known as "sugar-on-snow," or *la tire* in Quebec) and maple cream (which, despite its name, actually contains no cream at all), a soft, fudgelike spread made entirely of maple syrup, for slathering on bread.

Larocque accomplishes all this on her four-burner electric stove, using only small pots. Her special equipment is limited to a candy thermometer and rubber molds for the maple-sugar leaves. Making candy in small batches, she notes, has many advantages, even for an expert. Smaller pots mean greater control and easier rescue if by chance the maple syrup "seizes"—hardens in the pan—which can happen if

it is heated to the wrong temperature, or cooled or beaten for too long.

The secret to successful candymaking is not in the equipment but in knowing when the syrup looks and feels right during the cooking and cooling. "Maple syrup is real, real finicky stuff. It's the oddest product in the whole world," Larocque says. "It seems to have a mind of its own. You almost can't do candymaking by yourself. You have to see it done."

Even the indispensable candy thermometer is only an indicator of the right temperature. On a cloudy day, when the air pressure is lower, the water will evaporate from the syrup more easily than on a sunny day, when it must be boiled a degree or two higher.

Most of Larocque's confections are made from pure maple syrup with nothing else added, yet the texture of each is deliciously varied, depending on the way it is made. For maple-sugar leaves, for example, Larocque heats the syrup to approximately 244 degrees, transfers it to a wooden board—whose surface allows the mixture to crystallize *gradually*—then beats it for a short time with a wooden spoon. For fudge, however, the syrup is heated to a lower temperature (235 degrees) and it is cooled *rapidly* in cold water to *precisely* 125 degrees before being beaten with the spoon. For maple cream, on the other hand, the syrup is first heated to the same 235-degree temperature and cooled rapidly, but it is then beaten with an *electric mixer* until crystals *just* begin to form.

When cream is added to the maple syrup for maple-cream candy, which is one of the simplest and most delicious candies to make, the procedure is completely different. "Cream changes the chemical makeup entirely," Larocque says. For this, the syrup is cooked to "soft ball" (which Larocque tests this time not with a candy thermometer but by dropping a small amount into cold water) and then cooled rapidly and stirred with a spoon until it "begins to mound"—or assume some shape.

For all these confections, the maple syrup must remain undisturbed when it is cooling, since even the slightest stir will cause large crystals to form, creat-

Expert hands turn out perfect, sweet leaves by the trayful at Maple Grove Farms, North America's largest maple-candy manufacturer, using Canadian and American syrup.

syrup over clean snow or shaved ice. A quick bite when the syrup is still hot on top and icy below is a taste sensation.

ing a scratchy, granular texture. During the beating, having an iron arm helps but what really matters, Larocque says, is not speed but constancy—keeping the mixture moving—and knowing just when to stop.

Larocque acknowledges that candymaking often seems to require something more than skill and the right technique: a degree of luck. "Some days it just doesn't work. I stop when it doesn't." The worst time to make candy, according to the experts, is on humid, damp or rainy days, when the moisture in the air can drastically affect the texture of the confection.

There is no doubt that maple candymaking is both an art and a science—even experienced cooks can be humbled in their own kitchens during the first attempts. The final results when you get it right, however—the appreciative moans and the amazed disbelief: "You made *this* yourself?!"—can be worth all the failures and sacrificed syrup that are the price of learning this very special art.　🍁

—*Rux Martin*

Vermont Temporary Grading Samples

Fancy Grade A Medium Amber Grade A Dark Amber Grade B

U.S.D.A. Grading Samples

LIGHT AMBER MEDIUM AMBER DARK AMBER

COLOR STANDARDS FOR MAPLE SYRUP
ESTABLISHED BY UNITED STATES DEPARTMENT OF AGRICULTURE

Canadian Grading Samples

Extra Light Light Medium Amber

Samples shown for illustrative purposes only. Colors may have shifted in the printing process. Actual samples must be used for commercial grading.

A MAPLE BUYER'S GUIDE

Words of advice from the syrup sleuth and other experts

OVER THE YEARS, the grading system for maple syrup has changed periodically and varies between the U.S. and Canada and from state to state. Vermont, which makes two-thirds of the maple produced in New England, more than any other state in the country, has its own grades, the only state to do so. To the average consumer, the system is a bewildering jumble. "Even sugarmakers are confused by it," admits Sumner Williams, assistant director of the Proctor Maple Research Center in Underhill Center, Vermont, and an excellent maple cook who learned at the elbow of his aunt, cookbook author Virginia Bentley. "The public doesn't understand all those A's and B's and C's and numbers. Unless they're connoisseurs, they just look for the words 'Pure Maple Syrup.'"

In general, the darker the color, the more flavorful the syrup. For purposes of cooking, it's best to avoid the lightest grade, called variously Fancy, Grade A Light Amber or No. 1 Extra Light. Although it is too delicate and weak to hold up in regular cooking, its bouquet can be appreciated over pancakes or ice cream. Fresh extra-light syrup is also the only syrup recommended for candymaking.

At the other end of the spectrum, commercial C-grade syrup, which by law cannot be sold in less than 5-gallon containers and is used to flavor imitation syrups, is too heavy and molasses-like for good cooking. The mid-range syrups—Grade A Medium Amber and Grade A Dark Amber (No. 1 Light and No. 1 Medium in Canada)—which have more robust flavor with more caramel, and Grade B (No. 2 Amber in Canada), which has an even deeper caramel taste, are the best choices for stand-out maple flavor.

Nationally, syrup is graded according to color,

but in Vermont, by taste as well. Thus, a light, delicate syrup with the color of Fancy might have a dark flavor that would earn it a darker rating, or even a substandard rating if it contained off flavors, making its sale to consumers illegal.

Like vintners, sugarmakers tend to be wildly chauvinistic about the quality of their region's syrup, claiming that the colder nights make their syrup taste better, or that maples on mountainous terrain produce better-tasting sap than those on flatlands. Scientifically, none of this can be proven, according to Williams. "Maple trees don't know boundary lines. Nobody, regardless of palate, can tell the difference between Vermont, Pennsylvania and Canadian Fancy, when correctly processed and packaged."

Selling for about $30 per gallon, Fancy syrup costs $1 to $2 more per gallon than the other grades. Its arrival is heralded with roughly the same enthusiasm that greets the release of Beaujolais nouveau in France, with local restaurants sporting menu items like "Maple Sundae—First run syrup." The ability to make Fancy carries prestige.

"To the sugarmakers, you're not worth a hoot un-

Advertisement for an early New England blend of maple and cane syrups, which gained wide popularity in the late 1800s.

Open sugarhouse at Dakin Farm, with Sam Cutting Sr. passing out samples of syrup hot from the evaporator. Most sugarhouses welcome visitors during the busy season, often staging sugar-on-snow parties, tastings and horse-drawn sleighrides.

less you can make light or Fancy," says Williams. Despite all the mystique surrounding it, however, most people actually prefer the more assertive flavors of the darker grades, leading some sugarmakers to argue that the lighter grades should not cost more.

Sam Cutting, Sr., co-owner of Dakin Farm in Ferrisburgh, Vermont, which sells syrup by mail-order, sums up traditional thinking on the matter. While admitting that the best grade is a matter of taste, he defends the higher cost of light syrup, which requires pristine sap, scrupulously clean pipelines and boiling soon after the sap is collected. "If I can get paid the same for dark syrup, why should I stay up all night boiling?" he asks. "If you hold the sap overnight, it goes down a grade."

Regardless of grade, a good maple syrup is judged by its clarity of flavor—the absence of off-flavors.

The excess nutrients that flood into the tree just before the tree begins to bud produce a sour, bitter syrup that sugarmakers call "buddy." Williams uncorks a sample. To my untrained palate, it seems fine at first: potent and dark, with a heavy caramel taste. The aftertaste, however, is bitter and astringent enough to make my mouth pucker. Substandard syrup like this cannot be legally sold to consumers but is boiled into block sugar and exported to Japan, where it is used to sweeten tobacco. Sugarmakers have a host of terms for other offending flavors that result from faulty sugaring procedures: "barrel," "filter," "felt," "Clorox" and "soap."

In Vermont, the man charged with quality control is Henry Marckres, maple inspector of the Vermont Department of Agriculture, a sort of maple sleuth. When a syrup doesn't taste right, Marckres has the unhappy task of sampling it to pinpoint what may have caused the problem. Other states check the sanitation practices of maple-syrup producers, but Vermont is one of the few to inspect for flavor. So every day for the past 10 years, Marckres has visited every store across the state every year, opening the smallest container made by each sugarmaker, checking the grade, color and density and sampling it.

Marckres' work has brought him into contact with a good deal of syrup—his record is 932 tastings in a single day—and he is in great demand as a judge at festivals where he may taste 130 samples, pausing occasionally to refresh himself with a swallow of ginger ale, the preferred palate-cleanser of syrup tasters. He looks more like a burly sugarmaker than someone with a superior palate. "My father used to buy syrup and I went with him just tasting. If you taste syrup every day, you begin to notice things," he says. Earlier that day, he pulled some offending samples from the freezer at the Department of Agriculture, where they are stored until he can get around to them. He offers me a sip. Immediately my mouth is filled with a nasty complexity of flavors. This, he explains, is "metabolism" syrup. Its chocolaty aftertaste destroys all the maple flavor. This is the precursor of buddy syrup, produced when the season's temperatures have become too warm, causing the trees to put forth buds.

Another syrup has a sour flavor like apple cider gone bad. This one is "fermented." The sap has not been boiled long enough to give the syrup the proper density, Marckres explains. An overly light syrup will ferment; an overly heavy one will crystallize too readily. In Vermont, maple syrup must be of a higher density than in other states and in Canada, giving it, Marckres says, a more pronounced flavor.

The next syrup is even more wretched: chemical, thick, furry. This is "felt," produced when the sugarmaker strained the syrup through a new felt filter without rinsing it first. I am relieved when Marckres apologizes for not having "soap" or "Clorox" syrup on hand.

Instead, he gives me a sample from a bottle whose label says "Maple Syrup," but which lists apple juice, sugar, corn syrup and natural and artificial flavors as the ingredients. Viscous and unnaturally sweet, it is bitter as well. Adulterating maple syrup—substituting less expensive corn, cane or beet sugar for all or part of the maple and labeling it as real maple syrup—is illegal. Marckres shows me a jar marked "Vermont Frontier Maple Syrup," containing cane and corn sugar with molasses added for coloring, made by a Mississippi company, whose owners received a three-year jail term and a $150,000 fine for their fraudulent labeling.

However much sugarmakers may disagree about which grade is best and which region makes the best

Balloons and tastes of times past: crunchy, hot corn fritters swimming in maple syrup, a favorite at some sugarhouses.

syrup, they are militantly united against imitation syrup. In his office, Sumner Williams has a rogue's gallery of pseudosyrups: Aunt Jemima's, Hungry Jack, Mrs. Butterworth's, Maple Valley, Golden Griddle, Log Cabin and Vermont Maid (made in East Hanover, New Jersey)—all of which are a third the price of maple. Real maple syrup contains a single ingredient: maple syrup. "Nothing added and nothing taken away, except water," Williams says. In contrast, the fakes are ingredient-rich, containing mostly corn syrup and water, but also vanillin, sorbic acid, natural and artificial flavors, caramel color, cellulose gum and preservatives like dipotassium phosphate and sodium benzoate. Pure maple syrup, when it is added at all, makes up only between 2 and 5 percent of the contents, and it is of the cheapest C-grade quality.

Biochemically, real maple syrup is mostly sucrose, with a small portion of glucose and fructose. Corn syrup is made up of fructose, glucose and just a bit of sucrose. (Honey is half glucose and half fructose, with a little sucrose. But while honey is acid, maple syrup is alkaline.)

It isn't the sucrose that gives maple syrup its distinctive taste, but the "natural impurities" present in the sap, according to Mariafranca Morselli, research professor emerita of botany at the University of Vermont and an expert on the biochemistry and taste of syrup. Luckily for sugarmakers, the flavoring compounds in the syrup are so complex that they can't be duplicated chemically.

The flavorful components in maple sap are amino acids, organic acids and phenolic compounds, which are produced by the cells "when they are feeling sorry for themselves," under the normal stress of living, Morselli says. These flavorings make the syrup taste sweeter than other sugars, though it actually isn't. During the season, concentrations of some of these components rise in the sap, as the trees draw more nutrients from the soil, and when the sap is boiled, they can affect the taste of the syrup, producing off-flavors like the "metabolism" syrup I tasted with Marckres, and other flavors that sugarmakers identify variously as "nutty," "popcornish," "buttery" and finally "buddy."

At the same time, as bacteria begin to build up in the sap lines or in the storage tank, other biochemical changes in the sap occur that affect the color of the syrup and add caramel flavor. They cause the sucrose, which makes up 99 percent of Fancy syrup, to divide into two smaller molecules, fructose and glucose. These molecules do not crystallize as well as do those of sucrose, which is why the freshest Fancy syrup is best for maple-sugar candy.

To help identify syrups purporting to be "pure maple," Morselli devised a test that is now standard to detect the presence of cane or corn syrup in concen-

There is no mistaking the difference between pure maple syrup and imitation when they are tasted side by side. The maple has a dark, complex, almost wild undertone. What lingers on the palate is the zing, not the sweet, what John Burroughs in 1886 called "a wild delicacy of flavor." Next to it, the imitation is flat-tasting, heavy, gooey and cloying, deadening the tongue with its sweetness.

trations of over 20 percent. (In lesser concentrations, test results are too inconclusive to hold up in court.) While corn and sugar cane plants are monocotyledons, meaning they have one cotyledon per seed, the sugar maple is a dicotyledon, containing two cotyledons per seed. The two families of plants use carbon dioxide differently, and when the syrup is analyzed in the laboratory, the differences can be detected. Scientists are presently working to refine a test to identify adulteration with beet sugar, also a dicotyledon.

To keep pace with the rest of the food world, sugarmakers have developed some labeling and marketing savvy of their own. My neighbor still puts up his syrup in a square-sided tin with a colorful scene showing a sugarer carrying wooden sap buckets to waiting horses, with only the words "Pure Vermont Maple Syrup" on the side. But new laws could soon make nutritional analysis obligatory for large containers, so the consumer will be able to see at a glance that a tablespoon of maple syrup contains 40 calories, 29 grams of carbohydrates, a negligible amount of sodium and no protein, cholesterol or fat. One maple-syrup container in Sumner Williams's office advertises "Sodium Free." Can the words "No Cholesterol" be far behind?

Which container is best? Metal cans, with their folk-art painting on the side, have the nostalgic edge, but they also have an inner metal plug that is frustrating to pry off. (Though most people don't realize it, the best way to pour the syrup from a can is to tip it backwards or slightly to the side, so the syrup flows away from the container, without dribbling down the side.) Glass containers, available in a variety of cut-glass shapes, can be elegant-looking, and they show the color of the syrup, but they are breakable. In the last few years, small, squat plastic jugs have appeared on the scene. Though hardly as charismatic as the traditional tin containers, they are light, easy to open, pour easily and can be fitted with tamper-proof lids.

In a study on the effects of containers on the quality of maple syrup conducted by Morselli, a panel of 11 experts tasted syrup in plastic, tin and glass containers over the course of a year. After six months, the tasters detected metallic flavor in the syrup stored in tin. After a year of sampling the syrup in plastic jugs and glass containers, the tasters could not discern any change in flavor. Plastic, however, caused the syrup to darken in color because the container's slightly porous sides allowed oxidation to occur. Williams did a similar study with similar results: "Tin held color 2 to 1 over plastic, but plastic held flavor 2 to 1 over tin." All in all, he concludes, for color and flavor, "Glass is best." 🍁

—*Rux Martin*

GLOSSARY

"If you would think like a sugarmaker, first you must talk like a sugarmaker."

— ZEBEDIAH HOLBROOK

Acer (pronounced: ā-sir) Genus name for some 150 species of maple trees found throughout the world in the Northern Hemisphere, but most abundantly in Asia. *Acer* means sharp or pointed, in reference to the leaf shape.

anthocyanin Pigment found in maple leaves that is responsible for red coloration during autumn foliage season. In combination with yellow pigments, causes orange coloration and various shades of crimson.

aproning Visual indicator of correct consistency of maple syrup at its boiling point. If of a proper consistency for storage, syrup dripped from the edge of a spoon or other utensil will form a curtain or sheet, rather than spill off in droplets or a stream. (Also called sheeting.)

arch The elongated firebox of an evaporator. Originally formed of mortared brick and designed to contain a hot wood fire under the evaporating pans. Today, some arches are oil-fired.

ash pit Compartment under the grates in an evaporator arch where wood ash accumulates.

auger Hand tool consisting of a sharpened steel shank with a crosswise wooden or metal handle; used in the 1800s to bore tapholes, often with a diameter of ¾ or 1 inch.

Baumé (pronounced: bow-may) A standard scale used to measure sugar concentration in syrup. Developed by

Antoine Baumé in 1844. (Reading represents the specific gravity of a solution in degrees.)

Beauce The world's most important maple-syrup production region, along the St. Lawrence River in Quebec.

bit Sharp-edged steel screw used to drill or bore tapholes in maples. Standard size is 7/16 inch. Sometimes called a sugar-tree bit. Used in conjunction with a brace or power tapper.

black maple *Acer nigrum* Closely related to the sugar maple and considered by some botanists a subspecies, with the same fine-quality wood and sap-producing traits. Characterized by dark green, drooping leaves; most heavily concentrated in the U.S. midwestern states.

blackstrap Folk description of very dark, strongly flavored syrup, comparable to blackstrap molasses.

black sugar Very dark cake sugar produced in Quebec in the late eighteenth and early nineteenth centuries. (Also called "Beauce sugar.")

boiler The sugarmaker responsible for operating the evaporator. Usually the most experienced or most senior member of the sugarmaking team.

bole The main trunk of the tree.

boxelder *Acer negundo* Widespread, small to medium-sized maple species with an atypical leaf for the genus. A favorite of amateur sugarmakers where sugar maples are scarce. (Also called Manitoba maple or ash-leaved maple.)

boxing Crude method of tapping by early settlers: a large squarish cavity was hacked out of the tree. Massive sap flow resulted, but pioneers soon learned less damaging practices.

brace Hand tool used to hold and power a bit.

break out To cut a trail or road through snow at the beginning of the tapping season. Usually done with a sled drawn by a tractor or horses.

Brix A standard scale used to measure sugar concentration in sap or syrup. Developed by Austrian Adolf Brix and commonly used in winemaking. (Reading represents percent of sugar by weight in the solution.)

bucket cover Galvanized-iron top designed to keep rain, snow and debris out of sap bucket while it hangs on tree. Also shades the sap.

bucket washer Wash tub designed to facilitate the cleaning of sap buckets at the end of the season.

buddy Popular term for an objectionable bitter flavor of syrup produced at the end of the sugaring season when the trees begin to bud out.

bud run Last run of sap, occurring as the tree buds begin to expand. Considered unfit for good syrup production; used by some to make maple vinegar.

cambium Thin layer of tree cells near the outer perimeter of the trunk of a maple tree where growth occurs. (The cambial layer is between the outer phloem and the inner xylem.)

carotenes Pigments responsible, along with xanthophylls, for yellow coloration in maple leaves in autumn. (Present throughout growing season but masked by chlorophyll until fall.)

cassé Watertight rectangular birch-bark vessel used by native peoples and early Canadian settlers to catch maple sap and to store crystallized maple sugar. (Also called casso.)

chlorophyll The green pigment in maple leaves that traps sunlight to produce sugar from carbon dioxide and water and that gives the foliage its characteristic color during the growing season.

cream down To add a drop of fresh cream to hot, foaming sap in the evaporator to prevent it from boiling over. See **defoamer**.

crown The branched, leafy top portion of the tree. Sugar maples with large crowns are typically the best sap producers.

Forest tree: small crown   *Open-grown tree: large crown*

crude sap Unboiled sap as it is gathered from the tree, prior to budding in the spring.

cupola The raised section of roof that, when opened, allows steam to escape from a sugarhouse.

decline, maple Late-twentieth-century term for ill-health and premature death among sugar maples, characterized by dead or dying branches high in the tree, small, sparse leaves and defoliation. Cause and seriousness of the malaise still unknown at this writing. (Also called maple dieback.)

defoamer Oil or fat used in minuscule quantities to quell a mass of sugar bubbles or foam before it can overflow an evaporator pan or boiling container. Agent used to break the surface tension of foam. May be vegetable oil, butter, cream or animal fat, although dairy and animal fats are falling into disfavor. See **cream down**.

defoliation Loss of leaves during the growing season, especially as caused by insect pests, disease or drought. Primary indicator of stressed trees.

Dominion & Grimm Common brand name on sugaring equipment. Evaporator and sugaring equipment manufacturer, headquartered in Montreal, Quebec.

drawing syrup Syrup ready to be removed or drawn from the evaporator, having reached its correct boiling point and sugar density.

drawing tub A sap-gathering tank.

drawoff The outlet through which finished syrup is removed from an evaporating pan.

dried out Taphole condition in which sap has ceased to flow. Rather than dryness, the cause is most commonly the clogging action of microorganisms that feed on maple sap.

drop flue A type of evaporator in which the flue pan is set deep in the arch (or dropped), so that the heat-transferring flues are directly in the path of flames and heat from the fire.

dumping place Location where sap-gathering tank is drained into the storage tank at the sugarhouse.

elaborated sap Maple sap after the tree has budded.

English tin Once considered a premium material for the construction of evaporators.

érable (French) Maple tree (of any species).

érable à sucre (French) The sugar maple.

érabliere (French) A sugarbush or sugarhouse.

evaporator A stationary unit designed to heat sap to the boiling point and cause large amounts of water to be driven off as steam, leaving syrup. Consists of a long firebox for a wood fire or an oil burner, usually with two partitioned pans above the heat. Typically, cold sap enters the rear of the unit at one corner and moves in a continuous zigzag flow through the flue pan and then the finishing pan, with the thickness, or sugar density, of the fluid steadily increasing as the

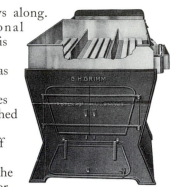

sap flows along. Additional cold sap is fed into the unit as water evaporates and finished syrup is drawn off near the front of the evaporator.

Fancy grade An official Vermont designation for the highest-quality syrup, corresponding roughly to the USDA grade Light Amber. Must be light in color with a delicate, sweet maple flavor.

fast wood Dry, quick-burning wood used to accelerate heating in a wood-burning evaporator arch. Examples include softwood slabs, construction scraps, old barn boards and fence posts.

feed pipe Pipe carrying cold sap from the sugarhouse storage tank into the evaporator.

feeder line Smaller-diameter sap-carrying hose leading from tapped trees to the tubing-system mainline. (Also called lateral line or sap line.) See **tubing**.

felt Filtering material used to remove impurities and sugar-sand, or nitre, from hot syrup.

feu d'enfer (French) Habitant (French-Canadian settler) term for roaring wood fire kept burning under sap kettles day and night in sugaring season. (Also called hellfire.)

filter(ing) tank Container to receive hot syrup as it comes from the evaporator and drains through filters, traditionally made of felt. The primary purpose is to remove nitre, or sugar-sand, from the syrup.

finishing rig Smaller-scale evaporator used by some sugarmakers for bringing syrup to the proper sugar density with better temperature control than found in wood-fired arches. Commonly heated by gas or oil burners. (Also called sugaring-off rig.)

fire To start and maintain the fire in an evaporator arch to boil sap.

first run The start of the sugaring season or the first flow of sap, usually initiated by a sudden thaw that triggers the sap flow mechanism in the maples.

float A closed metal or synthetic box or bulb attached to a valve to allow fresh sap to flow into the evaporator or to cause hot sap from the flue pan to move into the finishing pan. Floats are set to maintain a desired level of fluid in the evaporator pans to minimize the possibility of burning.

flue A metal channel in the bottom of an evaporator pan designed to conduct heat from below to sap passing through the flue above.

flue brush Specialized tool to whisk soot from the bottom of the flue pan in the arch.

flue drawoff Cleaning port for drawing sediment out of the flue pan.

flue pan Usually the rear pan in a standard two-pan evaporator, designed to remove large amounts of water from sap before it moves forward to the finishing pan. The bottom of the flue pan has deep channels or flues, maximizing the transfer of heat from the fire below to the sap in the pan.

frog run Folk designation for the last sap run of the season. So called because frogs begin to be heard at night during the warm finale to the sugaring season.

gagoose Simple cone of birch bark used to hold maple candy in colonial Canada.

galvanized Iron or steel coated with zinc; corrosion-resistant metal used in various sugaring tools and devices.

gathering pail Stainless-steel, galvanized iron or plastic bucket with a carrying handle used to collect sap from buckets. Often has a 4-to-5-gallon capacity.

gathering sled Platform or cart on runners for hauling gathered sap from the woods to the sugarhouse. (Also called a bobsled.)

gathering tank Usually a metal or wooden tank on a sled, used to receive and transport sap from the sugarbush. Such tanks often have a strainer and internal baffles to prevent sloshing of the sap as it is moved. Some gathering tanks are also stationary, used to receive sap from buckets, after which it is pumped or allowed to flow to the sugarhouse.

gathering tub Old-style gathering tank made with wooden barrel-type staves.

good day A day with a strong, steady flow of sap. Usually characterized by warm weather after a cold night, with a sharp jump in temperature of about 15 degrees F or more.

Grade A The best grade of syrup in most grading systems at this writing, except in Vermont, where the top grade is called "Fancy." Divided into Light Amber, Medium Amber and Dark Amber in the USDA grading system.

Grade B A dark, strongly flavored syrup with good maple flavor and clear overtones of caramel; generally used for cooking or manufacturing.

Grade C Commercial-grade syrup that is very dark and not generally available to consumers. Used in commercial cooking and manufacturing. The syrup found in most inexpensive table-syrup blends.

grade Official quality designation of a quantity of syrup, usually based on color and flavor. Not uniform in all states and provinces.

grading kit Government-approved color samples (usually tinted glycerin in small clear glass bottles) used in the standardized grading of syrup by degree of darkness.

grate The iron framework in a wood-fired arch. Allows ash to drop down out of the fire and feeds air to the burning logs.

Grimm Common brand name on sugaring equipment. Evaporator and sugaring equipment manufacturer, headquartered in Rutland, Vermont.

hard maple sugar Very dense, caked sugar made by heating maple syrup to 248 degrees F, stirring while hot, then pouring into a mold or storage container. See **tub sugar**.

hard maples North American term for the sugar maple and black maple, considered by some to be the same species.

heavy Syrup with a sugar density above the recommended limit. All properly packed syrup is by definition the same weight: 11 pounds per gallon. Heavier syrup forms sugar crystals during storage.

hole plugger Old term for spile or sap spout (uncommon).

hook spout Spout or spile with a built-in or attached hook for hanging the sap bucket.

hookless spout Simplified spile or sap spout, most commonly used with vinyl sap-collecting bags that some sugarmakers use in place of buckets. In the past, used when placing an extra tap above a two-tap bucket. (This practice is no longer recommended.)

hot-pack The only recommended method of packaging syrup into containers for resale. Syrup must be packed at a temperature between 180 and 200 degrees F to prevent spoilage.

hydrotherm Combination hydrometer and thermometer favored by some sugarmakers to determine standard density of syrup.

Indian sugar Granulated maple sugar; made by heating maple syrup to about 260 degrees F, at which point the molten sugar is taken from the heat and stirred continuously until large, light-brown granules form.

jack wax Settler term for sugar-on-snow. See **sugar-on-snow**.

Jones's Rule Method of determining the amount of maple sap needed to produce a gallon of syrup. Specifically, divide the constant 86 by the sugar density (in percent) of the sap to obtain the answer. Also called the Rule of 86. (In Canada, it becomes the Rule of 105 when working with Imperial gallons.)

keelers Nineteenth-century wooden sap buckets, larger at the bottom than at the top, meant to be rested on the ground beneath sap spouts. Popular in Pennsylvania.

key The winged fruit of the maple, also known as a samara. Grows in pairs, as shown.

King One of the oldest evaporator model names still in use; with a drop flue; built by Leader.

kokh Eastern Woodland Indian term for clay pottery vessel.

la secheresse (French) "The dryness"—symptom of dying maples in Quebec in the 1970s.

la tire (French) "The pull"—maple candy stretched into strands as it hardens.

Lamb Popular brand-name sap tubing, bearing the name of inventor Robert Lamb.

lateral line See **feeder line**.

Leader Common brand name on sugaring equipment. Evaporator and equipment manufacturer, headquartered in St. Albans, Vermont.

Light Amber USDA grade designation for the lightest, highest-quality syrup, as in Grade A Light Amber.

Lovibond Professional "viewmaster"-type syrup-grading device, approved by both Agriculture Canada and the USDA.

mainline Larger-diameter, flexible polyethylene piping used to collect sap from smaller feeder lines or laterals and to carry a substantial flow of collected sap from the sugarbush to the storage tank. Ranges in diameter from ½ inch to 2 inches.

Manitoba maple See **boxelder**.

maple butter See **maple cream**.

maple candy Made by heating finished maple syrup to a temperature of 237 degrees F, then cooling to 155 degrees, stirring and pouring into molds to harden.

maple cream A pure maple spread made by bringing maple syrup to a temperature of 234 degrees F, then cooling to about 70 degrees and stirring to whip air into the thickened mass. (Also called maple butter.)

maple orchard A group of sugar maples. (Also called sugarbush, sugar woods, sugar grove, maple bush.)

maple sap The watery cell fluid of a maple, usually with a sugar content of 2–3 percent, although trees with up to 10 percent sugar have been identified. Sap is mostly water but also contains amino acids, phenols, organic acids and traces of vitamins and minerals.

maple syrup Condensed maple sap with a boiling point 7 degrees above the Fahrenheit boiling point of water (approximately 219 degrees).

metabolism Taste description for an objectionable bitter flavor of syrup produced during warm conditions or near the end of the sugaring season when the trees begin to bud out. Pre-

cedes appearance of stronger "buddy" flavor. (Off flavor caused by metabolites in sap.)

michtan Native American term for the maple tree.

mokuk Native American basket or container formed of birchbark with a large base and narrow top opening used for hard or granulated maple sugar. (Also called makak, mocock.)

Moqua Legendary Indian woman of the Eastern Woodlands who substituted sap for water in her cooking pot and thus discovered maple syrup. The first sugarmaker. See **Woksis**.

NAMP The North American Maple Project. A joint investigation into the health and possible decline of the sugar maple, conducted by Canadian and U.S. researchers (1987–present).

nitre A fine, gritty precipitate that commonly forms as syrup is being made or in containers of unfiltered syrup. Considered objectionable by the maple trade, it is harmless but has reputed laxative effects. Also called nitty gritty, sugar sand or (improperly) silica, its proper chemical label is malate of lime.

nitty gritty See **nitre**.

Number 1 Canadian syrup grade, designated as Extra Light, Light or Medium. Roughly equivalent to U.S. Grade A Light Amber, Medium Amber and Dark Amber.

Number 2 Canadian syrup grade, designated as Amber. Roughly equivalent to Vermont Grade B.

Number 3 Canadian utility syrup grade. Roughly equivalent to Vermont Commercial Grade.

overtapped A tree or sugarbush that has been subjected to abusive tapping or in excess of tapping guidelines.

paraformaldehyde See **PFA**.

PFA Paraformaldehyde tablet, or "The Pill." Pesticide in tablet form promoted for use in tapholes in the late 1980s to prolong the sap flow. Banned in most states and in Canada at this writing. Now known to cause serious damage to trees.

phloem Thin layer of tree cells just under the bark of the maple that carries the products of photosynthesis down from the leaves to the body and roots of the tree.

Piggy-Back Energy-saving unit invented in the mid 1980s and used to increase the efficiency of evaporators. Causes rapid evaporation without boiling by injecting air into sap heated to a temperature of 180 degrees F. Fits (or piggy-backs) on top-rear of traditional evaporators.

pipeline See **tubing**.

Plessisville World's largest maple processing center, near Quebec City, province of Quebec.

power tapper Gasoline or battery-powered drill for placing tapholes at the beginning of the season. Used in larger-scale operations.

preheater One of many energy-saving devices designed to warm cold sap, usually taking advantage of waste steam and heat from the evaporator before it enters the flue pan.

Proctor The University of Vermont's Maple Research Center, near Underhill, Vermont. Named for Vermont Governor Mortimer R. Proctor, who personally donated funds to purchase the land in 1946.

ream out To withdraw sap spouts and freshen the inner walls of a taphole to improve the flow of sap. Usually done with a ½-inch drill bit at the midpoint or toward the end of the season. Uncommon in commercial practice.

red maple *Acer rubrum* Medium-sized soft maple tapped by some sugarmakers to augment the sap harvest. Sugar content of sap is lower than that of sugar maple. Scarlet foliage in autumn. (Also called swamp maple.)

refractometer Sophisticated device for measuring light transmission through sap or syrup to indicate the sugar content. Results measured in degrees Brix.

release The point at which a maple sapling emerges from a heavily shaded environment to one with significantly more solar energy, as after a sugarbush is thinned. The point at which tree growth accelerates.

reverse osmosis See **RO**.

RO Reverse osmosis, or the separation of water from water-soluble solids, such as the sugar in sap or the salt in seawater. Introduced in the last quarter of the twentieth century as a method of removing water from sap before starting the boiling process.

rock maple See **sugar maple**.

run A flow of sap, usually during the daylight hours of one day—occasionally longer.

salt pork Folk defoaming agent; usually a piece of fat or bacon rind tied to a string suspended over an evaporator pan. Used to prevent hot syrup from boiling over. Not recommended. See **defoamer**.

samara See **key**.

sap The watery solution obtained by tapping trees. See **maple sap**.

sap bag Heavy-duty plastic pouch designed to replace buckets for catching sap.

sap beer Home-brewed fermented beverage made with yeast and maple sap or maple sugar and water, occasionally flavored with hops or ginger. Popular in colonial era. (Also called small beer.)

sap bucket
A specialized pail of galvanized iron or aluminum (uncommonly plastic or tin), used to catch sap as it drips from a spile or spout. Capacity normally 12–16  quarts (3–4 gallons), although regional variances occur.

sap hydrometer Simple floating device used to measure the sugar content of cold sap, which ranges from about 1 percent to more than 10 percent. Used to cull poor sap producers and select the "sweet trees."

sap ice Solidified water found in sap buckets. Contains small amounts of sugar and is either discarded or melted at the discretion of the sugarmaker.

sap spout Tubular device inserted into a maple taphole to transport sap into a bucket or pipeline. Spouts used with buckets are made of galvanized iron or aluminum; those used in tubing systems are molded plastic. See **hook spout** and **hookless spout**.

scoop A boxy stainless-steel ladle used by the evaporator operator to move, skim and test syrup for doneness—as in the traditional "aproning" test. See **aproning**.

scum Waste foam that naturally rises when sap is boiled. Constantly skimmed away by the sugarmaker.

settling tank
Metal container used to receive hot syrup for filtering before storage. In outmoded practice, used to allow sugar sand, or nitre, to settle out as the syrup cooled.

Sheesheegummawis Ojibway for sugar maple tree ("sap flows fast").

silver maple *Acer saccharinum* Large soft maple tapped by some sugarmakers to augment the sap harvest.

Sinzibukwud Algonkian/Algonquin term for maple sugar.

sirop d'érable (French) Maple syrup.

Sisibaskwat Cree for maple sugar.

skimmer A boxy ladle usually made of stainless steel; has a metal mesh bottom to allow the removal of scum from boiling sap.

Small Brothers Common brand

name on sugaring equipment. Evaporator and sugaring-equipment manufacturer, headquartered in Swanton, Vermont. Canadian headquarters: Granby, Quebec.

soft maples North American grouping of trees with less-dense wood than the sugar and black maples. Includes silver, red, bigleaf, striped and Manitoba maple or boxelder.

spile See **sap spout**. Possible variation of early-settler term "spills," or carved wooden sap pipes.

stack burn Deterioration of quality of hot-packed syrup, in which just-filled containers are stacked or loaded closely together. The prolonged heat retention of the mass of containers causes the syrup to darken and drop in the grading scale.

steam hood Structure or device suspended over the evaporator to catch rising steam and funnel it up and out the roof of the sugarhouse.

steam vent Opening in the roof or cupola of a sugarhouse to allow steam to escape. Closed when evaporator is not in use. (Also called ventilator.)

storage tank Large container for receiving gathered sap or sap from pipelines; typically located in a cool, shaded spot near the sugarhouse.

strainer Simple filtering device used to strain debris (bark, twigs, insects) from sap at the gathering tank and/or the storage tank.

sucre d'érable (French) Maple sugar.

sucrerie (French) Sugarbush or sugarhouse.

sucrose The natural sugar of the maple tree and the primary sugar found in maple syrup.

sugar [verb] To make maple syrup or sugar. (Note: Despite the shift from making maple sugar to making syrup, the use of "syrup" as a verb is widely considered incorrect.)

sugarbush Grove of sugar maple trees. (Also called sugar grove, sugar orchard and sugar woods.)

sugar camp Traditionally, a maple-sugaring site used for the tapping and boiling season by native sugarmakers and early settlers. Working maple-sugar camps still exist in remote areas.

sugar can Archaic term for tinned container used to store maple sugar. Various sizes were used, from 1 to 5 or more pounds in weight.

sugar devil Auger-like pantry tool used to dig into hard, caked maple sugar to loosen it for use.

sugared-off Finished; general term used as "when it's all sugared-off" in place of "when all is said and done."

sugarhouse Simple building that shelters boiling operations for a sugarbush. Usually uninsulated, with a steam vent in the roof, a concrete floor and space for the evaporator, fuel and sap storage. Often located at the base of a hillside and accessible by road.

sugaring season The annual period, usually occurring over a span of two to six weeks, when sap flows from maple trees and syrup and sugar are made. February, March and April are the primary months for this flow in the tapping range of the sugar maple.

sugaring-off rig See **finishing rig**.

sugar loaf Hardened maple sugar molded into a cake or cone.

sugarmaker One who makes maple syrup and/or sugar.

sugar maple *Acer saccharum* A deciduous hardwood tree found in eastern North America; noted for its fine-quality wood and sweet sap. (Also called hard maple or rock maple.)

sugar mold A wood, metal or rubber form into which molten maple sugar is poured to be formed into geometric or decorative shapes.

sugar moon Native American designation for the sugaring season, the month of freezing nights and warm days usually coinciding with March. (Also called maple moon.)

sugar off To make sugar; to boil syrup to the point at which it will harden into sugar when cooled.

sugar-on-snow Freshly made maple syrup taken at about 234 degrees and poured while hot over clean snow or shaved ice. (Also called "jack wax" for the chewy texture of the confection.)

sugar pail Clean bucket to receive hot syrup as it comes from the evaporator. Typically 4 gallons in capacity.

sugar place A maple sugarbush and/or a sugarhouse.

sugar sand See **nitre**.

sugar weather Freezing nights and thawing days at the end of winter and beginning of spring.

sugar wood Firewood reserved for boiling sap, usually cut in 4-foot lengths for commercial evaporators.

sweet tree A maple that produces sap with a higher-than-average sugar content and sap flow. (Also called a sap cow or good runner.)

syrup down To reduce sap to syrup by removing most of its water, usually by boiling.

syrup drum Galvanized metal or plastic barrel used to store and transport bulk syrup, usually 32 gallons in capacity. (Popularly known as 30-gallon drum.)

syrup filter Specialized paper or white felt material used to remove nitre and any other sediment from hot, just-finished syrup.

syrup hydrometer Simple weighted glass instrument floated in syrup to measure sugar density in degrees Brix or Baumé.

syrup-off To remove finished syrup from the evaporator or finishing pan.

syrup thermometer Specialized thermometer for measuring hot sap, syrup and molten sugar in the range of 200 to 240 degrees F.

taphole Bored opening in a tree, usually 7/16 inch in diameter and no deeper than 2½ inches. Usually slanted up at an angle of 5 to 10 degrees. A new taphole must be bored each season, and old tapholes usually heal over in a year or two.

tapped out In sugaring, a state of readiness at the beginning of the season, after all tapholes have been drilled and spouts placed.

tapping Drilling a hole in a maple tree, inserting a spout or spile and hanging a bucket or connecting to a pipeline system.

tapping guidelines Rules suggesting the maximum number of taps that sugarmakers should place each year on trees of different diameters.

thinning Selective cutting of a sugarbush to increase the crown size of individual trees, thus boosting the sugar content and volume of sap produced.

tin Zinc-coated sheet metal. Used in syrup containers.

tub sugar Hardened sugar stored in metal or wooden containers. The most common maple product up to the end of the 1800s, when syrup became a more valuable commodity. Rarely made today, except for specialized commercial needs.

tubing Flexible, semirigid polyethylene hose, used to collect sap from tapped maple trees. Popularized in 1970s and 1980s as a labor-saving replacement for bucket-handling and gathering by hand. Usually of 5/16-inch diameter.

ultraviolet Sap-sterilization system using ultraviolet light to kill microorganisms that tend to lower syrup quality.

UV See **ultraviolet**.

vacuum Sap-pulling system used with many tubing installations to ensure rapid flow of sap into storage.

ventilator See **steam vent**.

Waterloo Common brand name on sugaring equipment. Evaporator and sugaring-equipment manufacturer, headquartered in Barton, Vermont.

Willits Lab Former USDA Maple Testing facility near Philadelphia, Pennsylvania.

Woksis Legendary Indian hunter of the Eastern Woodlands who first tasted maple syrup accidentally made by his spouse, Moqua. The first sugar eater.

woodshed Storage area attached to a sugarhouse where fuelwood is kept dry.

xanthophylls Pigments responsible, along with carotenes, for yellow coloration in maple leaves in autumn. (Present throughout growing season but masked by green of chlorophyll until fall.)

xylem The sap-storage and transport wood tissue of the maple tree. The sapwood that yields the bulk of the sap in sugaring is made up of xylem vessels.

yoke Early device of carved wood used to ease the burden of a person carrying two sap-gathering pails. Designed to fit over the shoulders of the worker, with hangers on each side for buckets.

Sources

Sugaring-Equipment Manufacturers

The following firms are North America's full-line evaporator and equipment manufacturers, serving all regions of the United States and Canada. All have informative catalogues and will supply names of local dealers upon request.

Dominion & Grimm Inc.
8250 Marconi
Ville D'Anjou
Montreal, Quebec H1J 1X5
(514) 351-3000

Dominion & Grimm USA
RR 1, Box 284-B
East Montpelier, VT 05651
(802) 229-9536

G.H. Grimm Company
P.O. Box 130
Rutland, VT 05702
(802) 775-5411

Leader Evaporator Company, Inc.
25 Stowell Street
St. Albans, VT 05478
(802) 524-4966

Small Brothers Evaporators, Inc.
P.O. Box 160
Dunham, Quebec J0E 1M0
(514) 295-2451

Small Brothers USA, Inc.
Airport Road
P.O. Box 714
Swanton, VT 05488
(802) 868-3188

Waterloo Evaporators, Inc.
201 Western
Waterloo, Quebec J0E 2N0
(514) 539-3663

Waterloo USA Inc.
HCR 63, Box 35A
Barton, VT 05822
(802) 525-3588

Waterloo USA Inc.
W1887 Robinson Drive
Merrill, WI 54452
(715) 536-7251

Sugaring-Equipment Dealers & Suppliers

Atkinson Maple Syrup Supplies
RR #1
Barrie, Ontario L4M 4Y8
(705) 722-3331

Bascom's Sugar House
RR #1, Box 138
Alstead, NH 03602
(603) 835-6361

Norval Blair & Sons
1421 Route 202
Franklin Centre, Quebec J0S 1K0
(514) 827-2347

The Branon Family
Fairfield, VT 05455
(802) 827-4440

Brenneman's Maple Syrup Equipment
Route 1, Box 303
Salisbury, PA 15558

Brodies Sugar Bush
HCR 75, Box 30
Westford, NY 13488
(607) 264-3225

Lloydrick Butler
Andes, NY 12093
(914) 676-3272

Butternut Mountain Farm
P.O. Box 381
Johnson, VT 05656
(802) 635-2403

Camp Can-Aqua Maple Syrup and Supplies
Box 70
Cardiff, Ontario K0L 1M0
(613) 339-2969

Coons Maple Supplies
P.O. Box 377
Monticello Road
Richfield Springs, NY 13439
(315) 858-2781

Countryside Hardware
1712 Albany Street
DeRuyter, NY 13052
(315) 852-3326

Curle's Maple Products & Supplies
Box 93
Campbellford, Ontario K0L 1L0
(705) 653-2519

Danforth's Sugarhouse
US Route 2
East Montpelier, VT 05651
(802) 229-9536

Donald Dodds
RR #2
Clayton, Ontario K0A 1P0
(613) 754-2049

Troy Firth
136 Mechanic Street
Spartansburg, PA 16434
(814) 654-7338

Jakeman's Maple Products
RR #1
Beachville, Ontario N0J 1A0
(519) 539-1366

Kidd's Home Hardware
Sundridge, Ontario P0A 1Z0
(705) 384-5344

Duncan MacArthur
Lancaster, Ontario K0C 1N0
(613) 347-3472

Maple Hill Farms
RD 1, Box 279
Cobbleskill, NY 12043
(800) 543-5379

Maple Syrup Supplies
P.O. Box 245
Potterville, MI 48876
(517) 645-7305

Mayotte's Maple Products
RD 2
East Fairfield, VT 05448
(802) 849-6810

Solomon Moser
Lowville, NY 13367
(315) 346-1032

Opeongo Maple Products
RR #4
Eganville, Ontario K0J 1T0
(613) 754-2049

Pauls Maple Products
RR #3
Lanark, Ontario K0G 1K0
(613) 259-5276

Stanley Reid
2294 Ridge Road
Huntingdon, Quebec J0S 1H0
(514) 264-3493

Reynolds Sugar Bush
Aniwa, WI 54408
(715) 449-2057

Paul Richards
545 Water Street
Chardon, OH 44024
(216) 286-4160

Robson-Smith Sugar Bush Supplies
King Road #18, RR #3
Schomberg, Ontario L0G 1T0
(416) 939-7950

Roger Sage
4449 Sage Road
Warsaw, NY 14569
(716) 786-5684

Sanders Maple Products
RR #1
Finch, Ontario K0C 1K0
(613) 984-2368

Schambach Maple Inc.
7288 Hayes Hollow Road
West Falls, NY 14170
(716) 652-8189

Shearer's Maple Products
RR #1
Desboro, Ontario N0H 1K0
(519) 363-3392

Sugar Bush Supplies Company
2611 Okemos Road
Mason, MI 48854
(517) 349-5185

Sugar Valley Maple Supplies
RR #1
Indian River, Ontario K0L 2B0
(705) 295-6353

Eli and Harvey Weber
Box 137
Heidelberg, Ontario N0B 1A0

John Wiggers & Son
No. Clymer, NY 14759
(716) 355-2511

Maple-Syrup Container Suppliers

Bacon Jug Company
RFD #2, Box 580
Littleton, NH 03561
(603) 444-6246
Plastic jug manufacturer.

Kress Creations, Inc.
349 Christian Street
Oxford, CT 06483
(203) 264-9898
Plastic jug manufacturer.

Maple Supplies Company
Route 302 East
P.O. Box 895
Barre, VT 05641
(802) 479-1827
Metal cans, cartons, shippers, labels.

New England Container Co.
75 Jonergin Drive
Swanton, VT 05488
(802) 868-3171
Metal syrup cans; "cabin-can" containers.

Richards Packaging Inc.
3115 Lenworth Drive
Mississauga, Ontario L4X 2G5
(416) 624-3391
Glass containers and caps, plastic bottles, plastic pails.

P. Stransky Equipment Inc.
Box 1
Collingwood, Ontario L9Y 3Z4
(705) 445-6871
Jugs, caps.

Sugarhill Maple Containers
Main Street
Sunderland, MA 01375
(413) 665-8102
Plastic jug manufacturer.

Specialty Equipment

Warren Allen
RD Box 254
Castorland, NY 13620
(315) 346-6706
Berliner black-nylon sap spouts and related equipment.

Forestry Suppliers, Inc.
P.O. Box 8397
Jackson, MS 39284
(800) 752-8460
Tree-diameter-measurement equipment.

Ben Meadows Company
3589 Broad Street
Atlanta, GA 30366
(800) 241-6401
Tree-diameter-measurement equipment.

Seprotech Systems Inc.
2378 Holly Lane
Ottawa, Ontario K1G 7P1
(613) 523-1641
Reverse-osmosis equipment and service.

Mail-Order Syrup & Candy

Support your local sugarmaker. To locate a sugarhouse within driving distance of your home, contact the nearest Sugarmakers' Association (page 214). The following list represents a small sampling of respected family-run sugaring operations that offer mail-order syrup, candy and other maple-food products.

Beavermeadow Farm
Herb & Brenda LaRocque
883 Ridge Road
Athelstan, Quebec J0S 1A0
(514) 264-2820

Coombs Maple Products
Arnold Coombs & Dan Purjes
HCR 13, Box 50
Jacksonville, VT 05342
(802) 368-7301

Dakin Farm
Sam Cutting, Sr., Sam Cutting, Jr. & Families
Route 7
Ferrisburgh, VT 05456
(802) 425-3971

Danforth's Sugarhouse
Nate Danforth
US Route 2
East Montpelier, VT 05651
(802) 229-9536

Harlow's Sugar House
Don & Maddy Harlow
RD #1
Putney, VT 05346
(802) 387-5852

Lamothe's Sugar House
89 Stone Road, RFD #3
Burlington, CT 06013
(203) 582-6135

Morse Sugar House
Harry Morse, Burr Morse
County Road
Montpelier, VT 05602
(802) 223-2740

Reynolds Sugar Bush
Lynn Reynolds
Aniwa, WI 54408
(715) 449-2057

Smada Farms Inc.
Route 41 North
HC 75, Box 945
Greene, NY 13778
(607) 656-4058

Vermont Maple Outlet
RD #1, Box 31C
Jeffersonville, VT 05464
(802) 644-5482

WHOLESALE MAPLE SYRUP & PRODUCTS

American Maple Products
Bluff Road
P.O. Box 685
Newport, VT 05855
(802) 334-6516
Candy manufacturer.

Maple Grove Farms of Vermont
167 Portland Street
St. Johnsbury, VT 05819
(802) 748-5141
Major maple syrup packager and
candy manufacturer.

PUBLISHERS

Cornell University
Dept. of Natural Resources
122C Fernow Hall
Ithaca, NY 14853
(607) 255-2110
"Sugarbush Management" videotape

Chapters Publishing Ltd.
2031 Shelburne Road
Shelburne, VT 05482
(802) 985-8700
Sweet Maple

The Countryman Press, Inc.
P.O. Box 175
Woodstock, VT 05091
(802) 457-1049
Backyard Sugarin'

New England Farmer
P.O. Box 4187
St. Johnsbury, VT 05819
(802) 748-1373
Publishes *The Sugarmaker* as part of
The New England Farmer. 12 issues
per year, $12.

**Natural Resources Information
Centre**
Room M1-73
Macdonald Block
900 Bay Street
Toronto, ON M7A 2C1
*Sugar Bush Management for Maple
Syrup Producers* (Single copies avail-
able by mail for $6.)

**North American Maple Syrup
Council**
Roy S. Hutchinson, Editor
P.O. Box 240
Canterbury, NH 03224
(603) 783-4468
The Maple Syrup Digest

Perceptions, Inc.
RR 1, Box 250
Charlotte, VT 05445
(802) 257-7757
The Maple Sugaring Story (video and
teaching guide)

Storey Communications, Inc.
Pownal, VT 05261
(802) 823-5811
The Maple Syrup Cookbook

**University of Vermont Extension
Service**
655A Spear Street
South Burlington, VT 05403
(802) 862-2053
Technical maple publications.

University Press of New England
Hanover, NH 03755
(603) 646-3349
Amateur Sugar Maker

Vermont Dept. of Agriculture
116 State Street, Drawer 20
Montpelier, VT 05620-2901
(802) 828-2500
Publishes *The Vermont Ag Review.*

MAPLE TIMELINE

1540 First written observation of North American maple trees, by Jacques Cartier, French explorer traveling up St. Lawrence River.

1557 First written record of maples in North America yielding a sweet sap, by French scribe André Thevet.

1606 Marc Lescarbot describes collection and "distillation" of maple sap by Micmac Indians of eastern Canada. (*Histoire de la Nouvelle France*)

1788 Quakers promote manufacture and use of maple sugar as an alternative to West Indian cane sugar produced with slave labor.

1790 "Maple Sugar Bubble" grows, with high hopes among national leaders that a homegrown alternative to slave-produced cane sugar from the British Caribbean had been found. Key advocates include Thomas Jefferson, Dr. Benjamin Rush and Judge James Fenimore Cooper.

1791 Dutch company buys 23,000 acres of Vermont land and attempts to hire local workers to make sugar to compete with cane from West Indies. Project fails; Vermonters prefer to work their own land.

1791 Thomas Jefferson and George Washington discuss plans to start "maple orchards" on their Virginia plantations. Most trees die or fail to thrive; Jefferson remains a maple booster.

1810 Augers coming into popular use to drill holes for wooden spouts or sap spiles. Crude gashing or "boxing" techniques becoming obsolete.

1818 Maple sugar selling for half the price of imported cane sugar.

1858 Early patent for evaporating pan to D.M. Cook of Ohio.

1860 Eli Mosher patents first metal sap spout.

1860 Peak maple production year for U.S.: 40 million pounds of sugar and 1.6 million gallons of syrup, from 23 states reporting to USDA.

1862 Maine Board of Agriculture report says flat-bottomed pans are better than kettles for boiling sap.

1872 Early evaporator design work described by Vermont inventor H. Allen Soule.

1875 Introduction of metal sap buckets.

1880 Cane sugar and maple sugar approximately equal in price.

1884 Early patent for sugar evaporator, G.H. Grimm, Hudson, Ohio.

1885 Price of cane sugar begins to undercut maple market.

1888 Leader Evaporator Co. founded, Enosburg Falls, Vermont. Will later popularize "drop-flue" design and become a dominant U.S. maple-equipment supplier.

1889 Small Brothers of Dunham, Quebec, begin producing evaporators with crimp-bottom pans invented by David Ingalls. Precursor design to modern Lightning evaporator.

1890 G.H. Grimm Company, major supplier of evaporators, buckets and spouts, moves from Hudson, Ohio, to Rutland, Vermont.

1891 McKinley Bill attempts to promote maple sugar manufacture by offering two-cent-per-pound bounty to producers. Bureaucrats and small farmers wrangle, and the effort fails.

1893 Vermont Maple Sugar Makers' Association formed; instrumental in setting industry-wide standards.

1904 Cary Maple Sugar Company incorporated in St. Johnsbury, Vermont. Became largest wholesale sugar company in North America.

1906 U.S. Pure Food and Drug Act makes adulteration of maple syrup with glucose illegal.

1916 Metal sap-gathering tubing invented by W.C. Brower, Mayfield, New York. Proves impractical—prone to freezing at night, leakage and vulnerable to damage by deer.

1935 Vermont institutes spring Maple Festivals; 134 towns stage events; 1,200 maple-frosted cakes are submitted for judging.

1940–1945 Maple prices frozen at $3.39 per gallon during World War II. Production suffers.

1946 First commercial power-tapping machine marketed.

1946 Proctor Maple Research Center near Underhill, Vermont, founded by University of Vermont.

1959 Plastic sap-gathering pipeline system patented by Nelson Griggs, Montpelier, Vermont.

1965 Maple leaf, a unifying symbol for both English and French Canada since about 1800, becomes central image on new national flag of Canada.

Late 1970s Reverse-osmosis technology introduced to concentrate sugar content of sap before boiling.

1982 Severe local dieback or decline of sugar maples noted in Quebec. Provincial scientists begin searching for causes.

1985 Sugarmaker Gordon Richardson's Piggy-Back unit introduced by Small Brothers Company as the first of a new-generation of evaporator attachments to enhance performance "naturally."

1988 North American Maple Project begins studying health of maple trees to determine progression, if any, of maple decline.

Sugarmakers' Associations

Connecticut Maple Producers Assn.
Jean Lamothe
89 Stone Road, RFD #3
Burlington, CT 06013

Indiana Maple Syrup Assn.
Daniel T. Garner
6776 W. Rockeast Road
Bloomington, IN 47403

Maine Maple Producers Assn.
Elaine E. Morse
RFD #1, Box 727
Readfield, ME 04355

Massachusetts Maple Producers Assn.
Jim Graves
RFD Wilson Graves Road
Shelburne Falls, MA 01370

Michigan Maple Syrup Assn.
John J. Anton
2111 Barrett Street
Lansing, MI 48912

Minnesota Maple Syrup Producers Assn.
Carmen Maschler
RR #1, Box 132
Randall, MN 56475

New Brunswick Maple Producers Co-op
Ms. Anne Meade
237 Brookside Drive, Bldg. D
Fredericton, New Brunswick
E3B 5H1

New Hampshire Maple Producers Assn.
Hank Peterson
28 Peabody Road
Londonderry, NH 03053

New York Maple Producers Assn.
Arthur E. Merle
1884 Route 98
Attica, NY 14011

Nova Scotia Maple Producers Assn.
Jean Bentley
12 Valley Road
Westchester Station, Nova Scotia
B0M 2A0

Ohio Maple Syrup Producers Assn.
Les Ober
1177 Kinsman Road, Box 20
Newbury, OH 44065

Ontario Maple Syrup Producers Assn.
Ken McGregor

RR #6
Strathroy, Ontario N7G 3H7

Pennsylvania Maple Syrup Producers Council
Jim Tice
RD 1, Box 29
Mainesburg, PA 16932

Les Producteurs de Sucre d'Erable du Quebec
Eric Lessard
2100 St. Laurent Avenue
Plessisville, Quebec G6L 2Y8

Le Regroupement pour la Commercialisation du Sirop d'Erable
Andre Morin
25 Lafayette Boulevard, Third Floor
Longueuil, Quebec G4K 5G7

Vermont Maple Sugar Makers' Assn.
Sandra Tarrier
RD #1, Box 3500
Westford, VT 05494

Wisconsin Maple Producers
Henry Grape
RR 2, Box 54
Holcombe, WI 54745

Museums & Visitor Centers

Iowa

Indian Creek Nature Center
6665 Otis Road, SE
Cedar Rapids, IA 52404
(319) 362-0664
Displays and sugaring during season.

Massachusetts

Sturbridge Village
Sturbridge, MA 01566-0200
(508) 347-3362

Costumed demonstrations of colonial sugaring using wooden spiles and hollowed-out wooden collection troughs.

New York

Adirondack Museum
Routes 28 and 30
Blue Mountain Lake, NY 12812
(518) 352-7311
Large collection of maple sugaring tools. Library with reference materials. Galleries open Memorial Day through October 15. Museum staffed year-round.

American Maple Museum
P.O. Box 81
Croghan, NY 13327
(315) 346-1107
Small, informal museum that is home of Maple Hall of Fame. (Best to call ahead if planning to visit.)

The Farmers Museum
Cooperstown, NY 13326

(607) 547-2593
Tools, buckets, yokes displayed as part of rural life of nineteenth-century settlement. Open March through December.

OHIO

Holden Arboretum
9500 Sperry Road
Mentor, OH 44060
(419) 946-4400
Museum with old tools and equipment. Sugaring season includes: interpretive outdoor trail showing development of tapping, 2,000 taps in 25-acre sugarbush, sugaring done by local Amish family with team of horses and sled. Sugarbush part of long-term research project for high-sugar-content trees.

PENNSYLVANIA

Somerset Historical Center
Route 601
Somerset, PA 15501
(814) 445-6077
Relocated circa 1850 sugar camp, interpretive tours, old tools and "sugar keelers." Open year-round, Tuesday through Sunday.

VERMONT

Billings Farm Museum
River Road
Woodstock, VT 05091
(802) 457-2355
Working farm and museum. Exhibit includes boiling methods, early tins, wooden and galvanized spiles, storage tubs, early farm inventions for sugaring, lifting crane, sap cooler. Open May 1 through October 31.

Green Mountain Audubon Nature Center
P.O. Box 18
Richmond, VT 05477
(802) 434-3068
Working sugarbush with 730 taps open to public during season.

Maple Grove Farms and Museum
167 Portland Street
St. Johnsbury, VT 05819
(802) 748-5141
World's largest and oldest manufacturer of maple candies and largest packers of maple syrup in the United States. Factory tours every day. Circa 1930 sugarhouse displays sugaring equipment. Open May through late October.

New England Maple Museum
Route 7
Pittsford, VT 05763
(802) 483-9414
History of sugaring, large collection of old tools, buckets. Working evaporator in season. Open year-round.

Shelburne Museum
Route 7
Shelburne, VT 05482
(802) 985-3344
Original nineteenth-century paintings and Currier & Ives sugarmaking prints. Historic colonial village setting, with small collection of sugarmaking tools and candy molds. Open mid-May through mid-October.

Other Vermont sugarhouses:
Vermont Department of Agriculture
116 State Street
Montpelier, VT 05602
(802) 828-2416
Publishes a brochure yearly listing Vermont sugarhouses that welcome visitors.

WISCONSIN

Lac du Flambeau Reservation Museum
P.O. Box 804
Lac du Flambeau, WI 54538
(715) 588-3333
Life-sized tableaux of Indian life in four seasons of the year. Demonstrations of Indian sugaring in March and April. Open Monday through Saturday, 10 a.m. to 4 p.m.

McKenzie Environmental Center
W7303 County Highway CS
Poynette, WI 53955
(608) 635-4498
Demonstrations of sugaring during March.

Reynolds Sugar House
Aniwa, WI 54408
(715) 449-2057
Annual Maple Syrup Festival and Pancake Day. Displays, exhibits, collection of antiques and tractors.

State Historical Society Museum
30 North Carroll, Capital Square
Madison, WI 53703
(608) 264-6400
Birch containers, cones, stirring paddles.

CANADA

Bruce's Mill
Stouffville Road
Gormley, Ontario L0H 1G0
(416) 887-5531
A working sugarbush with seasonal demonstrations of old and new sugaring methods. Festival weekend: third weekend of March.

Francis Pilote Musée
College de Ste. Anne
100 Fourth Avenue
Lapocatiere, Quebec G0R 1Z0
(518) 856-3012
Artifacts, history of sugaring in the province of Quebec.

Kortright Center
9550 Pine Valley Drive
Vaughn, Ontario L4L 1A6
(416) 832-2289
Spring demonstrations include old sugaring and modern tubing methods. Theater presents ongoing slide show of sugaring.

Maple Syrup Museum of Ontario
8 Spring Street
St. Jacobs, Ontario N0B 2N0
(519) 664-3626
Exhibits include Indian to modern methods of sugaring.

BIBLIOGRAPHY

"The older the tree, the sweeter the sap."

Bierhorst, John. *The Mythology of North America.* New York: William Morrow and Co., 1985.

Boyd, Julian P. *The Papers of Thomas Jefferson*, Vol. 20. Princeton, NJ: Princeton University Press, 1982.

Bruchac, Joseph. *The Faithful Hunter: Abenaki Stories.* New York: Greenfield Review Press, 1988.

Bruchac, Joseph and Michael J. Caduto. *Keepers of the Earth: Native American Stories and Environmental Activities for Children.* Golden, Colorado: Fulcrum, Inc., 1989.

Bryant, Margaret M. *Maple Sugar Language in Vermont.* Greensboro, North Carolina: The American Dialect Society, 1947.

Buszek, Beatrice Ross. *The Sugar Bush Connection.* Nova Scotia, Canada: Nimbus Publishing Limited, 1982.

Buzzell, George L. "Tapping Guidelines." Vermont Department of Forests, Parks and Recreation, February 1987.

Casanova, Jacques and Raymond Douville. *Daily Life in Early Canada.* New York: The Macmillan Company, 1967.

Cate, Sandal, Wilson Clark, Shirley Coombs and Douglas Sherry. "Maple Sugaring in Vermont: A Guide for Elementary Teachers." The Vermont Maple Promotion Board, 1983.

Clark, Mark F. "The Low Dynasty." *The Quarterly*, St. Lawrence County Historical Society, January 1974.

Cook, A.J. *Maple Sugar and the Sugar-Bush.* Medina, Ohio: A.I. Root, 1887.

Coons, Clarence F. "The Sugar Bush and Maple Decline in Ontario." Ontario Maple Syrup Producers' Association Information Meeting, January 1987.

Coons, Clarence F. "Sugar Bush Management—Realistic Expectations." North American Maple Syrup Council Meeting, Portsmouth, New Hampshire, October 1988.

Coons, Clarence F. *Sugar Bush Management for Maple Syrup Producers.* Ontario: Ministry of Natural Resources, 1992.

Cowles, Clarence Porter. "The Early History of Maple Sugar." *The Vermonter*, March 1902.

Crockett, Walter H. *How Vermont Maple Sugar Is Made.* Vermont Department of Agriculture, 1915.

Darrah, William C. *Textbook of Paleobotany.* New York: Appleton Century Company, 1939.

Densmore, Frances. "Uses of Plants by the Chippewa Indians." *Forty-Fourth Annual Report of the Bureau of American Ethnology to the Secretary of the Smithsonian Institution, 1926-1927.* Washington, D.C., 1928.

Department of Agriculture of Canada. "Maple Sugar and Syrup: Importance of the Industry and Manufacture of Pure Maple Sugar and Syrup." Bulletin No. 1B, January 1907.

Department of Agriculture of the Province of Quebec. "Maple Sugar and Maple Syrup Industry: Importance of this Industry in the Province." Circular No. 2, 1907.

Dillon, W.J. "Maple Syrup in Ontario: Production Costs, Returns and Management Practices." Ontario Department of Agriculture and Food, February 1972.

Doubleday, Edward Sherburne. "Highlights of the History of the Cary Maple Sugar Company." Newport, Vermont: Unpublished article, 1990.

Drimmer, Frederick. *Scalps and Tomahawks.* New York: Coward-McCann, 1961.

Duerr, William A., Dennis E. Teeguarden, Neils B. Christiansen and Sam Guttenberg. *Forest Resource Management: Decision-Making Principles and Cases.* Philadelphia: W.B. Saunders Company, 1979.

Egan, Kathryn C. and Margaret B. Holman. "Processing Maple Sap With Prehistoric Techniques." *Journal of Ethnobiology*, Spring 1985.

Eggleston, Niles. "Sweet Sugar Maple Memories." *The Conservationist*, March/April 1989.

Ellis, J.B. "Maple-Sugar Making in Olden Times." *American Agriculturist*, January 1891.

Finlay, Margaret Curtin. *Our American Maples and Some Others.* New York: The Georgian Press, 1963.

Forest Service of the United States. *Silvics of Forest Trees of the United States*, Agricultural Handbook No. 271. Washington, D.C.: U.S. Department of Agriculture and U.S. Forest Service, 1965.

Foulds, Raymond T., Jr. "Pointers on Vermont Maple Orchard Management." The University of Vermont Extension Service, Burlington, Vermont, 1968.

Foulds, Raymond T., Jr. "Retail Maple Marketing." The University of Vermont Extension Service, Burlington, Vermont, September 1952.

Gorham, R.P. "The Maple Sugar Industry in New Brunswick." *The Dalhousie Review,* Vol. 20, Issue #2, July 1940, pp. 219-226.

Grimm, William. *The Book of Trees.* New York: Hawthorn Books, Inc., 1962.

Haedrich, Ken. *The Maple Syrup Cookbook.* Pownal, Vermont: Garden Way Publishing, 1989.

Harlow, William M., Ellwood S. Harrar and Fred M. White. *Textbook of Dendrology.* New York: McGraw-Hill Book Company, 1979.

Heinrich, Bernd. "Nutcracker Sweets." *Natural History,* February 1991, pp. 4-8.

Hill, Lewis. *Fetched-Up Yankee: A New England Boyhood Remembered.* Chester, Connecticut: The Globe Pequot Press, 1990.

Hills, J.L. *The Maple Sap Flow,* Bulletin 104, Vermont Agricultural Experiment Station, 1904.

Horwood, Harold. *The Colonial Dream 1497-1760: Canada's Illustrated Heritage.* Toronto: Natural Science of Canada Limited, 1978.

Houston, David R., Douglas C. Allen, Denis Lachance. *Sugarbush Management: A Guide to Maintaining Tree Health.* Northeastern American Sugar Maple Decline Project, Radnor, Pennsylvania, 1990.

Humphreys, W.J. "Maple Sap as a Cash Crop." Ontario Ministry of Agriculture and Food, June 1972.

Jack, Annie L. *Maple Lore.* Montreal: A.T. Chapman, 1910.

Jonas, Gerald. *The Living Earth Book of North American Trees.* New York: The Readers Digest Association, Inc., 1993.

Jones, C.H., A.W. Edson and W.J. Morse. *The Maple Sap Flow,* Bulletin 103, Vermont Agricultural Experiment Station, 1903.

Kehoe, Alice B. *North American Indians: A Comprehensive Account.* Englewood Cliffs, New Jersey: Prentice Hall Inc., 1992.

Keller, Robert H. "America's Native Sweet: Chippewa Treaties and the Right to Harvest Maple Sugar." *American Indian Quarterly,* Spring 1989.

Kuhnlein, Harriet V. and Nancy J. Turner. *Traditional Plant Foods of Canadian Indigenous People: Nutrition, Botany and Use.* Philadelphia: Gordon and Breach Publishers, 1991.

La Hontan, Baron Louis de. *New Voyages to North-America (1703).* Chicago: A.C. McClurg & Co., 1905.

Langenberg, W.J. "Sugar Maple—Sticky Problems and Sweet Prospects." *Highlights of Agricultural Research in Ontario,* September 1979.

Lanken, Dane. "We're Killing Our Maples!" *Canadian Geographic,* February/March 1987.

Lanner, Ronald M. *Autumn Leaves: A Guide to the Fall Colors of the Northwoods.* Minocqua, Wisconsin: North-Word Press, Inc., 1990.

Larocque, Brenda Grant. *Maplemania: A Collection of Favorite Family Recipes.* Self-published, Beavermeadow Farm, Athelstan, Quebec, Canada.

Lescarbot, Marc. *Nova Francia: A Description of Acadia, 1606.* London: Routledge & Sons, Ltd., 1890.

Lockhart, Betty Ann C. *The Maple Sugaring Story.* Vermont Maple Promotion Board, 1990.

Mann, Rink. *Backyard Sugarin',* Third Edition. Woodstock, Vermont: The Countryman Press, 1991.

Maple Task Force Subcommittee. "The Maple Syrup Industry in the United States." Northeast Marketing Committee, Vermont Extension Service, August 1972.

Marvin, James W. "The Physiology of Maple Sap Flow," *The Physiology of Forest Trees.* New York: Ronald Press, 1958, pp. 95-124.

Mason, Carol I. "Indians, Maple Sugaring, and the Spread of Market Economies." Wisconsin: University of Wisconsin, Fox Valley, 1989.

Mason, Carol I. "Maple Sugaring Again: The Dog That Did Nothing in the Night." *Canadian Journal of Archaeology,* Vol. 121, 1987.

Meiggs, Russell. *Trees and Timber in Ancient Mediterranean World.* Oxford: The Clarendon Press, 1982.

Mieder, Wolfgang. *As Sweet as Apple Cider: Vermont Expressions.* Shelburne, Vermont: The New England Press, 1988.

Mieder, Wolfgang. *Talk Less and Say More: Vermont Proverbs.* Shelburne, Vermont: The New England Press, 1986.

Mintz, Sidney W. *Sweetness and Power: The Place of Sugar in Modern History.* New York: Penguin Books, 1985.

Morgan, Ted. *Wilderness At Dawn: The Settling of the North American Continent.* New York: Simon and Schuster, 1993.

Morselli, M.F. "Nutritional Value of Pure Maple Syrup." *National Maple Syrup Digest*, July 1945.

Morselli, M.F. *Biotechnology in Agriculture and Forestry*, Vol. 5, Trees II. Heidelberg: Springer-Verlag, 1989.

Muir, Reginald L. *The Vermont Maple Syrup Cook Book.* Woodstock, Vermont: Phoenix Publishing, 1974.

Munson, Patrick J. "Still More on the Antiquity of Maple Sugar and Syrup in Aboriginal Eastern North America." *Journal of Ethnobiology*, Vol. 9, Number 2, 1989.

Nearing, Helen and Scott. *The Maple Sugar Book.* New York: John Day Company, 1950.

Niklas, Karl J. *Paleobotany, Paleoecology, and Evolution*, Vol. II. Westport, Connecticut: Praeger Publishers, 1981.

Page, Daniel H. *Heritage of the North American Indian People.* Ottawa, Canada: Borealis Press, 1982.

Patterson, Rich and Marion. "Sugar From Your Shade Tree." *American Forests*, February 1986, pp. 34-54.

Pendergast, James F. "The Sugarbush Site: A Possible Iroquoian Maple Sugar Camp." *Ontario Archaeology*, Vol. 23, 1974.

Pendergast, James F. *The Origin of Maple Sugar.* Ottawa, Canada: National Museum of Natural Science, 1982.

Perrin, Noel. *Amateur Sugar Maker.* Hanover, New Hampshire: University Press of New England, 1986.

Perrin, Noel. *First Person Rural: Essays of a Sometimes Farmer.* New York: Penguin Books, 1978.

Perrin, Noel. *Making Maple Syrup.* Pownal, Vermont: Garden Way Publishing, 1980.

Ritchie, J.C. *Postglacial Vegetation of Canada.* New York: Cambridge University Press, 1987.

Robinson, Rowland E. "Old-Time Sugar-Making." *The Atlantic Monthly*, April 1896.

Rupp, Rebecca. *Red Oaks and Black Birches: The Science and Lore of Trees.* Pownal, Vermont: Garden Way Publishing, 1990.

Schuette, H.A., A.J. Ihde. "Maple Sugar: A Bibliography of Early Records, II." *Wisconsin Academy of Sciences, Arts and Letters Transactions*, Vol. 38, 1946, pp. 89-184.

Schuette, H.A., Sybil Schuette. "Maple Sugar: A Bibliography of Early Records." *Wisconsin Academy of Sciences, Arts and Letters Transactions*, 1935.

Siegrist, Jan. *Maple Sampler: A Collection of Maple Syrup Recipes.* Shelburne, Vermont: The New England Press, 1986.

Simpson, Ruth M. Ramsey. *Hand-Hewn in Old Vermont.* Bennington, Vermont: Ruth M. Ramsey Simpson, 1979.

Sinclair, N.B. "Maple Syrup Evaporator House." Ontario Department of Agriculture and Food, March 1971.

Smith-Kappel, Diana. "Pipeline in the Sugarbush." *Country Journal*, February 1982.

Snow, Dean R. *The Archaeology of North America.* New York: Chelsea House Publishers, 1989.

Thevet, André *Les Singularitez de la France antarctique autrement nommée Amérique, 1557.* Rare Book Room, National Library of Canada.

Tyree, Melvin. "Maple Sap Exudation: How It Happens." *Maple Syrup Journal*, 1984, pp. 10-11.

Upton, L.F.S. *Micmacs and Colonists: Indian and White Relations in the Maritimes, 1713-1863.* Vancouver: University of British Columbia Press, 1979.

Vermont Department of Agriculture. *The Official Vermont Maple Cookbook.* The Vermont Maple Promotion Board and The Vermont Department of Agriculture, 1983.

Vermont Department of Agriculture. "Vermont Maple Sugar and Syrup." Montpelier, Vermont: Vermont Development Commision and The Vermont Department of Agriculture, 1959.

Vermont Maple Sugar Makers' Association. "The Story of Maple Time in Vermont," Bulletin No. 38, 1972.

Vermont Maple Sugar Makers' Association. *A History of Vermont's Maple Sugar Industry*, December 1912.

Vidler, Virginia. *Sugarbush Antiques.* New York: A.S. Barnes and Company, 1928.

Viola, Herman J. *After Columbus: The Smithsonian Chronicle of the North American Indians.* Washington, D.C.: Smithsonian Books, 1990.

Vogel, Virgil J. "The Blackout of Native American Cultural Achievements." *American Indian Quarterly*, Winter 1987.

Wells, Wesley R. "Maple Syrup: What Consumers Ought to Know About It." *American Forests*, January 1967.

Wilbur, C. Keith. *The New England Indians.* Chester, Connecticut: The Globe Pequot Press, 1978.

Williams, Sumner. "Maple Syrup Container Study." Proctor Maple Research Center, University of Vermont, unpublished study-in-progress, 1993.

RECIPE INDEX

GENERAL INDEX

PHOTOGRAPHY & ILLUSTRATION CREDITS